Biopolitics and International Values

A Volume in the Pergamon Biology and Politics Series
Albert Somit, Editor

Pergamon Titles of Related Interest

Fitzgerald COMPARING POLITICAL THINKERS
Foreign Affairs AMERICA AND THE WORLD 1980
Khoshkish THE SOCIO-POLITICAL COMPLEX
Lebedev A NEW STAGE IN INTERNATIONAL RELATIONS

Related Journals*

CURRENT ADVANCES IN ECOLOGICAL SCIENCE
ETHICS IN SCIENCE AND MEDICINE
INTERNATIONAL JOURNAL OF INTERCULTURAL RELATIONS
PROJECT
STUDIES IN HISTORY AND PHILOSOPHY OF SCIENCE

*Free specimen copies available upon request.

PERGAMON POLICY STUDIES ON INTERNATIONAL POLITICS

Biopolitics and International Values
Investigating Liberal Norms

Ralph Pettman

Pergamon Press
NEW YORK • OXFORD • TORONTO • SYDNEY • PARIS • FRANKFURT

Pergamon Press Offices:

U.S.A.	Pergamon Press Inc., Maxwell House, Fairview Park, Elmsford, New York 10523, U.S.A.
U.K.	Pergamon Press Ltd., Headington Hill Hall, Oxford OX3 0BW, England
CANADA	Pergamon Press Canada, Ltd., Suite 104, 150 Consumers Road, Willowdale, Ontario M2J 1P9, Canada
AUSTRALIA	Pergamon Press (Aust.) Pty. Ltd., P.O. Box 544, Potts Point, NSW 2011, Australia
FRANCE	Pergamon Press SARL, 24 rue des Ecoles, 75240 Paris, Cedex 05, France
FEDERAL REPUBLIC OF GERMANY	Pergamon Press GmbH, Hammerweg 6, Postfach 1305, 6242 Kronberg/Taunus, Federal Republic of Germany

Library of Congress Cataloging in Publication Data

Pettman, Ralph
  Biopolitics and international values.

  (Pergamon policy studies on international
politics)
  1. International relations. 2. Political
science. 3. Biology. I. Title. II. Series.
JX1255.P47 1981   327.1'01   80-22926
ISBN 0-08-026329-1   AACR1
ISBN 0-08-026328-3 (pbk.)

Printed in the United States of America

Contents

I'm looking at the river
but I'm thinking of the sea
thinking of the sea

R. Newman

Preface

On August 17, 1979, I gave an address to the biopolitics panel of the 11th Congress of the International Political Science Association on the subject described by the title of this book. The highly compressed paper I tabled then has been parlayed into the first two chapters. All the rest has been written since.

I am well aware that much of what follows might seem rather remote from what goes on in the world. I have a longstanding interest, nonetheless, in the way what we *are* prevails upon what we *think* and *value,* and what we actually *do.* I seek, in other words, as profound an understanding of human behavior as possible. This means sorting out the subjective meanings we share with other people that define our cultures and the symbolic contexts that surround us all. It also means asking: what are we like when looked at as objectively as we know how?

The relationship between these two approaches—the *hermeneutic* and the *empirical*—may well turn out to be both closer and more significant than is commonly supposed. That is the premise, anyway, and, while it may be somewhat premature to take it overly far, there are claims to this effect that we are justified, I think, in examining with care. "Are passions, then, the pagans of the soul? Reason alone baptized?" Kierkegaard didn't think so, and, though no Kierkegaard, nor do I. Hence one more essay in what a skeptical colleague calls "nervous politics," and no apology there for.

I begin with a bit of a bump. Our being and our beliefs are very big subjects. Those proceeding further are urged not to skim, since they will almost certainly be disappointed if they do. The issues are important ones and in some cases are new and, without following reasonably closely what I have to say, my judgments will inevitably appear somewhat arbitrary, unsystematic, and glib. They may still seem so on closer consideration, of course, but I hope not. I have tried to treat the main lines of debate as fairly as possible, but a personal analysis like this one strikes the balance I prefer. I can only trust that where I have failed to please, I may prompt others to pry.

Chapter 1, *The Scientific Understanding of "Modern" Values,* is a discussion of the sources of order in contemporary world politics, in particular the intellectual and moral values that have come to prevail there (the European doctrines of social justice and human rights, and the underlying assumptions they make about human fraternity, equality, liberty, and felicity). Any essay on human values is predicated upon prior conceptions about human nature and, ultimately, the predisposing features of our basic biology. I begin with a review of our scientific understanding of the latter in the light of current theories of evolution, the nature/nurture dichotomy, consciousness, and will.

Chapter 2, *Fraternity: Are We Naturally Selfish or Not?*, examines the individualistic ethic of the American polity, counterposing the collectivist concerns of the Soviets. Divergent assumptions about human nature are implicit in each, and the chapter surveys the contemporary debate in sociobiology about the "genetics of altruism" (i.e., whether or not we are innately selfish in social affairs). Sociobiological research has thrown new light here on what I would consider to be one of the most important political arguments of our time.

Chapter 3, *The Relative Irrelevance of Inequality: Intelligence, Race, and Sex*, discusses the various meanings of equality and the ways in which it has historically been used in political and philosophic discourse. Ideas about natural inequalities have traditionally been employed to defend social differences or the legitimacy of established political and economic hierarchies. The most important of these are intelligence, race, and sex, and I examine each in turn and the biological evidence for regarding them as politically significant or not.

Chapter 4, *Freedom from Hunger and Freedom to Choose*, looks at various attempts by political theorists to analyze liberty, a concept that covers a very wide range of issues and ideas. It fastens upon the familiar longstanding distinction between negative freedoms and positive ones, but develops this in the light of more recent scientific evidence—in the former case, for the importance of adequate nutrition (i.e., freedom *from* biological deprivation) and, in the latter, evidence that demonstrates the extent to which we as a species are defined by our evolutionarily derived capacity to make choices (i.e., our freedom *to* construct cultures and to change them at will).

Chapter 5, *States of Happiness and States of Mind*, asks what a biological understanding of human nature makes of that most abiding and most elusive of contemporary political aspirations—human happiness, of our preference for positive futures (the "biology of hope"), and of our intermittent or abiding sense of the spiritual and the transcendent (the "physiology of faith").

Chapter 6, *Science, Society (and Can They Survive)*, reviews current biological research into such areas as genetic engineering (particularly recombinant DNA) and the possible consequences this might have for society and politics. It raises the question of whether the truth as we presently pursue it "has a future," and whether science, survival, and "conviviality" can be reconciled.

Talking of conviviality, I would like to dedicate this work to Tom and Jenny McDonnell. I hope they know why.

1

The Scientific Understanding of "Modern" Values

Three old men, so the story goes, were once discussing the relative antiquity of their respective skills. "Consider," said the surgeon, "how God made Eve of Adam's rib. Now that was a very daring operation, and, I must say, a highly original one too. I submit we recognize medicine as the world's most ancient profession." "No, no," the second interrupted. "I protest. Long before that event took place He brought the Universe itself into being. Such a marvel of construction and design! Imagine manufacturing a cosmos out of chaos! Surely you will admit that it is engineering that must take precedence." The third member of the group, a politician, waited his turn to speak with uncharacteristic humility. He spread his hands before him and gazed at his fingers. "Ah gentlemen, gentlemen," he murmured. "And who do you think created chaos?"

How the others responded is not known, though this hardly matters here since I begin with such an anecdote not to settle a frivolous debate but to point up one of the most common ideas about how people live when they are governed badly or not at all. And how readily we relate such ideas to those about ourselves.

ORDER

Thomas Hobbes, who graphically depicted chaos as the natural condition of humankind, did so in terms of people's unbridled passions and brutish uncivility: *"In the nature of man,"* he wrote [my italics], "we find three principal causes of quarrel. First competition; secondly, diffidence; thirdly, glory. The first, maketh men invade for gain; the second, for safety; the third, for reputation."[1] Behind these three there lies, he thought, the primary desire of all humankind which is the "perpetual and restless" pursuit of "power after power." A sense of secure

1

possession of whatever influence and wealth one already enjoys may only be had, he argued, by striving for more.

> Hereby it is manifest, that . . . when men live without a common power to keep them all in awe, they are in that condition which is called war; and such a war, as is of every man against every man. For WAR, consisteth not in battle only, or the act of fighting; but . . . in the known disposition thereto during all the time there is no assurance to the contrary.[2]

In domestic terms this breeds battle-lords and brigands, and it is not difficult to find historic or contemporary examples of anarchy of this kind—family feuding against family, tribe fighting tribe, plain against mountain, and mountain against plain.

On a grander scale, however, it means that

> in all times, kings, and persons of sovereign authority, because of their independency, are in continual jealousies, and in the state and posture of gladiators; having their weapons pointing, and their eyes fixed on one another; that is, their forts, garrisons, and guns upon the frontiers of their kingdoms; and continual spies upon their neighbours. . . .[3]

Such circumstances engender "continual fear" and the prospect of "violent death," and they largely preclude any progress in human industry, society, commerce, or culture. Furthermore, under conditions of this sort concepts of right and wrong, of justice and injustice, are largely irrelevant, since "where there is no common power, there is no law: where there is no law, no injustice. Force, and fraud, are . . . the two cardinal virtues." This leads Hobbes to conclude that justice and injustice "are none of the faculties neither of the body, nor mind. If they were, they might be in a man that were alone in the world, as well as his senses and passions. They are qualities, that relate to men in society. . . ."[4]

Are we really like this? Should we surrender all prospect of civilized life? The picture is not entirely hopeless, as Hobbes himself admits. Fear of death, the "desire of such things as are necessary to commodious living," the voluntaristic hope of attaining them—all prompt human beings to subscribe to "articles of peace" that can regulate their affairs. And they do so not only locally but also on a world scale. (While it is worth remembering that "order" does not denote nonviolence alone and that the governing process itself can render civic life every bit as mean and brief as more anarchic alternatives, the Hobbesian presumption, that without respect for the value of order it must prove very difficult —though not in fact impossible—to secure any other considered preference at all, does persist. This is a dangerous doctrine since it so readily allows the advent of autocracy and the rationalization of repression. In international affairs, for example, it leads to the concept of *raison d' état,* which is the recognized right of any regime to suspend particular moral codes for national advantage and the good and safety of all. Such a concept obviously lends itself to abuse and the pursuit of individual group or class interests in the name of the state. Its kernal of good sense should not be lost altogether, however, despite the fact that it is so widely perverted in practice.[5])

The mass media document the grim consequences of interstate insecurity and competitive self-concern. Strategic analysts measure and weigh those factors that go to make up the calculus of comparative international advantage, in their attempt to assess how significant the "known dispositions" of the diverse actors might be. *Old Moore's Almanac* blithely predicts "chaos in Africa" for the coming year. In reality, however, the global environment remains (with spectacular exceptions) relatively orderly, and images of unalleviated disruption are distorted ones, applicable only in part to the way in which the world works. Governments do flourish, generating authoritative decisions that articulate their various priorities. Regularity of a kind can be found in both domestic and world affairs, buttressed by laws and customs and common cultures.[6] Centers of administration are established, power balances form and reform, and class-coded patterns of exploitation permeate the whole.

THE ADVENT OF GLOBAL NORMS

The advent of order does not interest me here so much as the values that inform it. And, again, while human beings have preferred a great many things over the years, I am concerned at present not with any and every human value we can find, but in the contemporary emergence of that more or less coherent body of ethical and intellectual propositions that define what one might call the modern milieu.

Westernization

In the cultural descent of our species, we have made any statements about what we consider to be useful, right, good, beautiful, meaningful, or true. As one consequence of the Westernization of the world, however, we now have a singular body of material and moral concepts that receive universal acclaim. The scientific-industrial culture of the West is the mutual concern of the majority of national elites, and, while this cosmopolitan commitment may be rather superficial in many if not most cases and is not something shared by any particular civic populace at large, it does include a common moral culture and set of intellectual aims.

Given the wide range of emphases and interests there are *within* the Western tradition, this may stretch too far the idea of a common source. Certainly non-Western elites, in looking elsewhere, have had more than one such organizing system to choose from, including most conspicuously those of liberal capitalism or command socialism. One could argue that it is *this* we should be discussing and not the business of Westernization per se.[7] In the larger and longer-term perspective, however, I am not so sure.

It is also possible to dismiss the particular values concerned, and particularly the ethical ones, as the partial choice of powers possessing hegemonial influence and the military, economic, or cultural muscle to make their concepts prevail. What such an argument does not account for, however, is the extent to which Western moral discourse has managed to achieve something of the same objectivity that typifies its science. With Mabbott and many others, "I cannot agree that local variations in standards must involve relativity,"[8] and this need not be as ethnocentric a statement as it sounds.

Westernization has meant many appalling things. Modern imperialisms and modes of production and exchange are not pretty; they can be and have been both savage and cruel. Westernization has also meant, however, the dissemination of certain fundamental values thought through in the name of Everyman. Such values have become, like gunpowder, cotton clothes, antibiotics, and the wheel, the potential property of Everyman too. In apologizing for the dreadful harm that the West, now rather the global North, has done and continues to do, we may lose sight of the constructive humanist doctrines of its philosophic heritage and the concern these doctrines enjoin for reasonable, caring human beings wherever they live. Perhaps this part would not have enjoyed the widespread credence it does today if it had not been somehow so compatible with the destructive elements that those from outside the West, who have had to suffer the combined effects, rightly deplore. But such a part does exist, and it is now a common global possession to be developed and refined further should others choose so to do. (They may not have much of a choice, of course. The value comparisons forced upon us under contemporary circumstances have made "reluctant moral philosophers of us all"[9]).

Industrialization. If we are to understand this question of values in the modern world we must look a little closer at what Westernization means. It has, in analytic parlance, two conceptual components. The most potent of these, and the most potent influence to act through and upon humankind in the present-day world, is that of *industrialization*. More broadly, we may speak of a process of *modernization* and the spread of certain intellectual and moral predilections that those in the global North, in theory at least, have come to prefer.

There is more than a little of a materialist bias in saying this, but I think that conditions warrant it. How human beings produce what meets their human needs undoubtedly has *some* influence on the way they organize their political, legal, and administrative affairs and the values they share. Certainly the *same* productive means can have *different* effects, and similar moral, judicial, civil, and bureaucratic orders do recur in human societies despite what seem to be their divergent modes of production.[10] The quality and the degree of influence is therefore a much debated point, Marxists tending to view the relationship as a determining one, and non-Marxists as subject to the mediating effects of the human imagination. I see no conclusive case either way. I would only say that in an age like our own that has had to accommodate a most wide-ranging revolution in how we actually produce what we need, want, and use, I think we are warranted in taking historical materialism very seriously indeed. And since industrial manufacture has proved so pervasive, at the present time we find closer links than there might otherwise have been between this, the dominant means of global production, and the sort of societies that have come to exist there. Hence whatever we may make of our defining characteristics as a species, our present capacity for industry remains of paramount concern, a capacity not yet shared by all earth's people but one well on the way to being so.

Modernization. *Modernization* is a highly charged concept, as is the dichotomy of modernism versus traditionalism upon which it is based, and which has figured so largely in debates about socioeconomic and political development. Critics of these debates have made much of the value preferences implicit in them. Not surprisingly, it is argued that the central hypotheses, however analytic and abstract, serve to depict Western liberal democracies as the progressive end products of world change. They give scant credence to socialistic alternatives that emphasize the importance of the process of distributing goods and services as well as that of producing them, and they tend to ignore the extent to which the exploitation of the poor by the rich may have successfully stalled the diffusion of developmental opportunities that ought, in principle, to have meant more for all. Furthermore, the sort of typology that arranges societies in a line, from the most "primitive" to the most "advanced," tends to obscure the extent to which the failure to "develop" complements (and/or contradicts) success in other terms. In this sense, underdevelopment is just as "modern" as development. It is the systematic expression of a singular process that subsumes both effects. All that is "modern" need not as such be preferred. "Modern" does not mean merely "Western" anymore, either, and not all that is Western modern. Modernization can reinforce as well as inhibit traditional social traits, and indeed the latter will often actually further the former. Modernization may also occur only in part, leaving important societal values untouched, thus prompting a process of global differentiation that runs counter to the propensity for global elites to become more alike.

Despite this radical and now increasingly conventional attempt to recast the basic debates about global change, I still see a point in preserving the concepts of modernity and modernization. Though they have indeed been abused, and more often than not to utterly odious ideological ends, there are meanings these ideas convey that no other manages to do quite so well. A checklist of the sorts of developments modernization refers to (which is really only a description of the common properties of those societies that have extensively industrialized) would include the advent of contemporary forms of the state (centralized and demo-cratized) within an emerging world capitalist economy; increased emphasis upon national and nonlocal loyalties and styles of life; rapid rises in standards of material well-being and in societal size; contemporary modes of class formation and role function, both within states and between them, engendered more by the industrialized style of production (mechanized, capital-intensive, and specialized) than by social ascription or ethnic identity; the increased prevalence of nuclear families; and the growing importance of personalized moral claims and accountabilities that are separate from those of kith and kin. We might add some consideration of the global setting within which such processes proceed, where modernization occurs because a people is taken into that ''historically unique network of societies that arose first in Western Europe in early modern times and today encompasses enough of the globe's population for the world to be viewed for some purposes as if it consisted of a single network of societies,'' or a world society per se.[11]

I repeat: the key feature is *industry*. It seems not unfair to say that the events we define in retrospect as the Industrial Revolution have meant the most fundamental moves in human history away from previous modes of life and patterns of belief toward novel experiences that create novel combinations of old values as well as altogether new ones. The advent of this extraordinary process owed a good deal in its time to the peculiar temper of the educated European mind and the extent to which those who were most active in shaping events had come to subscribe to a self-consciously secular, individualistic, rationalistic, and materialistic understanding of our physical and social domains. The physical dimensions of what they wrought—the revolution in the scale and sophistication of manufacture by machines; the vastly expanded use of nonhuman sources of power; the discovery in due course of new and more efficient such sources; the enormous increases in agricultural productivity, in per capita income, and in population itself; the demand for a literature and often highly trained labor force physically located close by, for resources, for consumers, for radically more effective and extensive systems of transport and communications—these things are not in dispute. The less tangible factors are no less important, however, though they are more difficult to define in hard and fast terms. Have the great cities, thrown up all over the world to serve industrial processes, reinforced similar sorts of human values, ones less conducive to a sense of social intimacy or community and rather more to the rational calculation of self-interest? Does the division of labor appropriate to industrial production—the highly detailed distribution, that is, of different parts of the manufacturing process among different workers—serve to atomize society, thus sustaining value systems that fasten upon the individual more than the group? Does this allow a system of divide and rule, that places inordinate power in the hands of those whose task it is to coordinate and control factory output as a whole? If this is so, does it disadvantage collectivist ideologies like socialism which appeal to values that industrial enterprise tends to deny? Then again, if the denial flies in the face of other preferences that can be authoritatively established as better in some way, can we expect significant reactions against industrial production, and the part or complete rejection of its value premises too?

Taking the last question first, we can say that this has not been the global experience so far, despite various attempts to stem the tide either in the name of religion or of environmental conservation or some other social or spiritual good. Growing numbers of individuals want the products that industry can provide (however contrived that wanting may be), and to get them they are willing to espouse the values (of the desirablity of personal achievement, for example, or of social mobility) with which such systems are imbued. Will every new society fall prey to what Kumar calls the "massing" of citizens into centralized nation-states under populist auspices and ideologies?[12] Will we see the inexorable erosion of social diversity as industrializing peoples make over their cultural environments into places as standardized and as predictable as the products of their newly acquired machines? Can we expect the relegation of organized religion to the status of a "marginal and minority preoccupation, like a hobby,"[13] and the further diversion of conventional faith into such secular channels as nationalism and materialism? These are large questions but the short answer seems to suggest that this is what is happening in fact. Despite the considerable inertia of traditional forms, even the resurgence in places of threatened belief systems like Islam, for example, one has the distinct sense of their pushing uphill against pointed sticks. Modern industry provides a most potent creed that tends to displace its rivals altogether rather than accommodate them. Indeed, it does not seem too extreme to assert "that industrialism has undermined and vanquished every social order which it has encountered" (a process prosecuted both by force of arms and force of example); and that "it is this unprecented phenomenon of total victory," as one commentator tells it, "which makes the rise of secularism [for example] different in kind from the rise of other religions, and which makes it perverse to deny the real break in continuity of beliefs entailed by industrialization."[14]

The pursuit of the sort of material advancement that an industrial culture can bring has served then to disseminate and endorse the outlooks on which it is built. There is, of course, a countercase. We do well to acknowledge, as Moore reminds us, that "there is no evidence that the mass of the population anywhere has wanted an industrial society, and plenty of evidence that they did not. At bottom all forms of industrialization so far have been revolutions from above, the work of a ruthless minority."[15] I think he is wrong but the argument is there. Furthermore, one ought not underestimate the importance of those orders that have sought and continue to seek to defend their world views, and in many direct and indirect ways to minimize the influx of "modern" Western ideas. Nor would I suggest these orders have no worth. To take the example already used, the spiritual force of Islam in its diverse socioeconomic and civic forms has been employed not only to defend entrenched traditional interests and autocratic regimes but may also serve to mobilize third and fourth world movements in the fight to win freedom of maneuver in a world supervised by industrialized states. Many would count this progressive, since it might help maximize the life chances of the peoples involved.

The European rationalists who witnessed the dawn of industrialization tended to view any spiritual impetus as a surrogate for science, to be totally transcended once the latter had revealed the "truth." Religious traditionalists have argued ever since that their faith addresses puzzles no less important that those that scientists attempt to explain and which science as such does not and perhaps cannot solve. And enough would seem to remain outside the rationalist's domain to lend such claims popular cogency at least.

The final argument against the sort of Westernization I have described comes from those who characterize the contemporary mode of cognition and its ethos of objectivity as ultimately inhumane. A sufficient number of values are denied in the process of becoming industrial to seriously disturb those concerned to secure not only our material welfare, but our sense of aesthetic and spiritual well-being as well. What price the individual who has lost not only his (or her) animistic sense of nature as actually alive, but also

> his Ptolemaic astronomy that assured his position in the centre of the universe; his faith in a hereafter that endowed him with eternal life; his belief in the supreme and infinite worth of his person that assured him a position of isolate dignity in an otherwise meaningless and impersonal world; and even perhaps his faith in a God whose attributes, under the impact of man's rationalistic scrutiny . . . [have become] ever more abstract until He [himself has] vanished in the metaphysical concept of the Whole?[16]

And yet, that is the mentality modern life portends. Most people manage in one way or another not to live under such rigorous conditions. They prefer to keep a hold of such traditional comforts as a sense of a transcendental deity, for example, or cosmic self-importance, or a belief in personal persistence after death. The deep premises of contemporary thought, however, go against them.

Rationalism

The reference above to "rationalistic scrutiny" is particularly important since in many ways, as Weber recognized, it is this, the unbridled advance of *rationalism*, that so profoundly pervades the modern milieu. This is the key value that informs all the rest. In strict terms, I refer here to the use of reason as an arbiter and as basis for discovering truth: the belief, that is, that, in the search for knowledge, ". . . there are no mysterious incalculable forces that come into play,"[17] and that "human reason can understand the relationship of various behaviors to one another and, as a result of this understanding, manipulate events to insure desired outcomes."[18] The concept has also come to mean much more that this however; namely, "the embodiment of the method and substance of science in the institutions, practices, and beliefs of . . . society."[19] Such embodiment, once in train, has an influence over all civil and individual life, shaping politics, economics, and systems of adjudication and administration in characteristic ways. The efficient pursuit of explicit objectives, arrived at by a process of detached evaluation, becomes the prime criterion of political and economic performance, of bureaucracy, and of social behavior too. This leads on the one hand to the worship of technique and the assumption that where one observes the proven means, the substance of efficiency will surely follow. (To secure a minor administrative service, for example, one is asked to fill out specific forms—in quintuplicate—which are promptly forgotten, along, of course, with the request they were meant to make. This sort of bureaucratic practice, while it serves additional functions like holding at bay an importunate public who ask too many things of too few resources, also betrays a fixation with the *appearance* of rational management that operates at the expense of whatever the end of the exercise might be.) On the other hand, rationalism can influence the very aim of the exercise itself, leaking through to color, if not craft, the ultimate objectives. Existence itself takes on the qualities of calculation cited above, losing as a result something of that freedom that Western political philosophers in particular tend to prize.

Rational calculation has always figured as an aspect of behavior and as an organizing principle in human society. One might well expect as much of thinking creatures like ourselves. The critical point here, however, is the way such a rational process as industrialization, like some mechanistic Midas, turns anything it touches to a tool. This occurs to the detriment of nonmaterial values, and in capitalistic society in particular at cost to the noncommercial quality of life. One can, "in principle, master all things by calculation," or so the assumption goes.[20] This is a voluntaristic ethos of a very practical kind, highly conducive to innovation and change, but also highly disruptive of cultures not geared in this way—geared being the operative metaphor indeed.

Let us reflect on what has been said so far. There is nothing new in the phenomenon of cultural confrontation between the West and the rest of the world, nor in the revision of traditional beliefs and values that this has brought about. It is only the global scale that is unique. The concept of culture denotes the transmission of preferred behaviors and meanings from one generation to the next. Cultures consist of "complex sets of alternatives which having been chosen at some time in the past, have become fixed and repetitive in their form."[21] When they are handed down without thinking, we witness a kind of millennial mime, peoples doing what their ancestors have done because nothing else intervenes. Taught deliberately and consciously, however, culture can be used to defend what has prevailed in the past; to endorse in a conservative fashion those habits and sentiments that have become customs or conventions, that include social conceptions of what is most commonly condemned or held in high regard. The teaching process need not be a gentle one: to "maintain and transmit a value system, human beings are punched, bullied, sent to jail, thrown into concentration camps, cajoled, bribed, made into heroes, encouraged to read newspapers, stood up against a wall and shot, and even taught sociology."[22] Nowadays, however, many peoples, including those ostensibly already modern, are called upon to *un*choose their values, to revise their expectations and their standards and the ways they have been used to ranking them so as to justify different kinds of conduct that are more appropriate to the seeming imperatives of industrial life. And this is not easy. The sort of revision necessary is never a simple concern, since the values under attack are usually closely bound up with quite profound feelings, affecting quite personal emotions—like that of self-esteem, for example, or the complex of emotions associated with one's diverse "needs." Any real change in values is likely to signal profound shifts in important aspects of individual personality as well as social status and place. Values are

the cognitive representation not only of individual needs but also of societal and institutional demands. They are the joint results of sociological as well as psychological forces . . . sociological because society and its institutions socialise the individual for the common good to internalise shared conceptions of the desirable; psychological because individual motivations require cognitive expression, justification, and indeed exhortation in socially desirable terms.[23]

Westernization can cut very deep indeed.

Values are fundamental sources of human behavior and have the widest ramifications, so we do not on the whole shift our personal or social perceptions of what is worthwhile in a cavalier way. The agent of change may be mature reflection. Or it may be plain curiosity, prompting individuals to think again about what is socially despised or esteemed. More important in historical terms, however, has been the process of diffusion and borrowing that has accompanied transcultural contact for centuries, contact evident even for those periods when humankind occupied the most widely dispersed of ecological niches and shared only the most intermittent and tenuous of social or commercial or martial contacts. It is epidemic today. The fact that societies are not the same, and have enjoyed in the past different patterns of development, means that they are likely to respond to the same transcultural influence in divergent ways. I think it remains sensible to say, however, that the most significant stimuli of all—the geographic expansion of European power, the growth of a world economy, and the self-evident success of industrial production in transforming material standards of life—have been homogenizing ones. Where the touch of this extraordinary sequence, this historical Midas has not yet been fully felt; where the consequences of it have been more exploitative than beneficial; there is still the *promise* of largesse, and the old, gold-making King's insistent ministers grow ever more difficult to elude. I say again: the effects of global industrialism have not been visited equally upon all persons in the world, nor is the application of that process complete. The most significant outcome so far has been the emergence of a world society of bourgeois modernizers who share, despite their obvious differences, an urban culture of minority mien. They are the world leaders, however; their values shape those of the rest; and these values derive from the West. These include the cognitive embrace of a scientific frame of reference (often coexisting quite happily with traditional ideas of a seemingly incompatible kind), *plus* the specific adoption of and support for moral concepts that were originally European but are now the legacy of all. I would cite in particular here the doctrine of *social justice* and the values related to *human rights*, and it is these values I want to look at below. Whatever we make of the problems and puzzles that rights talk poses; whatever we decide about the specific definition of what is actually just in any one context or another; however stifling we find the air of artificiality inherent in asserting values like these, that prove in practice so difficult to enforce; the fact remains that standards of this sort have received close attention within an emerging world society, and declarations of them attract both regular and near-universal support.

How one demonstrates this conclusively is as problematic as demonstrating the advent of a world culture in general. It is not difficult to mount an effective disclaimer to assert the fact of a progressively more plural world made possible by the very ethos that I have described above as having such solidarist consequences (for those at the top of the global social hierarchy at least). However, if we consider the debates that take place in a global forum like the United Nations and other such international institutions and conferences; if we read their various declarations; if we consider the number of pertinent treaties, conventions, and national constitutions that exist—even the phenomenon of constitutionalism itself—then I think we have sufficient evidence to sustain the point I have in mind about the universality of Western moral discourse.

We do have a further problem, however. Any one value can be given highly divergent, even contradictory, interpretations in practice, leading to the legitimation of quite different, even contradictory, social and political orders. What is just for some, like the maintenance of private property, for example, may seem unjust for others who will recommend its abolition. This difference reflects the different frameworks within which specific judgments are made. Thus *good* and *bad* do not stand alone but relate to particular ethical programs with their own shared premises and value prescriptions. As a result the same value categories can mean quite different things depending upon the contexts in which they are applied. That they do command nominal global agreement is an aspect of world affairs open to inspection, and one that is, I would argue, confirmed by it. Despite the diverse interpretation of the value concepts that abound in world affairs, transcultural traffic has already become sufficiently heavy to insure at least some common ground for debating what we mean by specific ideas. For example, it is now very widely accepted by cosmopolitan elites, in principle at least, that social justice does not denote (as it used to do) a natural social hierarchy, but refers rather to some sort of equal status—for women *and* men. Counterexamples are instructive if only because they seem now so exposed. Cosmopolitan sensibilities revolt likewise against the use of the word *freedom* to characterize what is patently repression, or *equality* to describe what is widely accepted as exploitation. Words are notably elastic, of course, a point to which I shall return, but they do have limits or they cease to have any social utility at all. And though those with competing political interests will be selective in their arguments about what a given value involves, and whether it is being realized or not in any particular situation, empirical referents do exist, as bodies like Amnesty International or the Minority Rights Group heroically affirm.

Part of the inspiration and support for social justice and human rights can be attributed to the existence of very general and widely dispersed agreement on concepts of individual entitlement, and on what "rightly" obtains in the way an individual should relate to the group. Evidence does exist of a widely shared human commitment to the idea, for example, that political power should be legitimate and that revolt is justified when such legitimacy is somehow lost and government becomes arbitrary; that judicial procedures be impartial; that there be the civil freedom to travel and to work in other places and to make criticisms of authority; and that freedom be buttressed by material security and economic well-being.[24] While consensus of this transcultural sort cannot account for the range and subtlety of what any one of us might experience as members of particular life-worlds,[25] general common ground *can* be found between the disparate value systems we subject to comparative study, and this ground can be quite specific too. There is further support for such universalistic arguments in contemporary evidence for a set series of innate stages, common to individuals of all cultures and all socioeconomic groupings, that define the acquisition and development of a sense of moral judgment.[26] The final phase of this process, or so it is claimed, prompts the principled and conscientious pursuit of what is most just.

On the whole, however, when we talk nowadays about the advent of global norms we are talking not about the parallel but largely unrelated correlation of certain sorts of moral conduct, nor the preprogrammed capacities of the maturing human unit, but about cultural imperialism. We are talking about the emergence in Europe of a system of nation-states and of industrial capitalism; about the communist revolutions within and against it; about the imposition of these systems upon the nonindustrial peoples of Latin America, Asia, Africa, and the Pacific and the advent of intermediary elites who proved quite capable of turning the moral premises of their overlords back upon the metropolitan powers themselves, and who came, once nominal independence for their subject peoples had been secured, to service a world economy dominated by those who had got in on the ground floor. This gives no more than the crudest outline of what was, and is, a very complex process, involving a host of separate and different confrontations[27] but which does indicate the location of their very vigorous source and helps to explain why certain conceptions of intellectual and moral discourse are now so widely propounded, if not preferred. Once the stream of events and opinions that had been coursing through post-Reformation Europe for centuries had "fused" into an "intrinsic whole,"[28] nothing seemed able to prevail against it. The doctrinal focus upon liberty, equality, fraternity, and felicity as fundamental categories in global normative debates became well-nigh irresistible.

Motives are always mixed, and disagreements can be acute. The original French Declaration of the Rights of Man and Citizen, for example, was a defense of the bourgeois interests of its formulators (which were quite different from proletariat or peasant ones) as well as the authentic expression of more universalist beliefs (which were not).[29] Recent codifications have been similarly compromised. Despite the prevalence of self, group, or class interests, however, a like language persists. And the moral antagonists who confront each other today on the global platform, and increasingly those we find at local levels too, can be assumed to be talking about the same issue areas despite the depth of their differences about what to adopt in practice.

THE AIM OF THIS STUDY

It is this universalized relevance that prompts me to consider such categories more closely here, while looking at the same time at what is known about the sort of beings we are and trying to decide whether there is any cause to revise our traditional understanding of the range of issues involved. All debates about human values, and particularly ones about which values we ought to prefer, turn upon basic ideas about human nature. The pessimistic perspective of a Thomas Hobbes, for example, diverges sharply from the optimism of Karl Marx, and their respective ideas about politics and economics and society reflect their preconceptions of "man" (if the preconceptions were not in fact built to fit their respective philosophies in the first place). The link between what we know about people and what they accept as having value or choose to believe (or more important even, what we think they *ought* to accept and believe) is very close.

It is useful here to distinguish *beliefs*, which are the cognitive assumptions we make about what does or does not exist and what seems to be more or less true or false (influencing what we do without really involving our sentiments), from *attitudes*, which are the positive or negative feelings we have toward particular beliefs, and *values* as such, being the criteria we use in deciding what to desire or resist or to denote as worthy or good. Values defined like this involve reason as well as emotion, thoughts as well as feelings, and the mix is a very "human" one in this regard.[30]

There is a large overlap between the psychological processes these three concepts describe, since not only is what we believe clearly shaped by our attitudes and by what we value, but our values reflect our feelings and what we take to be fact, and our attitudes depend upon what we think is worthwhile and true, or worthless and false. This blurs the distinction between them, though it does not invalidate it. Nor do such concepts tell us everything we might want to know about behavior, since we also need the notion somewhere of volition or *will*. What we think and feel is not necessarily what we actually do. Particular beliefs, for example, have never prevented social engineers from acting in ways that spite their understanding of what we "be": "We want the socialist revolution," Lenin said, "with people as they are now, with people who cannot dispense with subordination, control and 'foremen and accountants.' "[31] Nor do such beliefs tell us much about the specific institutions we might construct to realize one particular interpretation of a value as against another. Most important, perhaps, they do not tell us much about our deepest predispositions and how these prompt our choices in matters of this sort—and for good reason. "We cannot pass," Plamenatz argues,

> from such statements as 'unless men had biological needs peculiar to their kind, there would be no families' or 'unless men cooperated to produce and exchange goods and services, there would be no communities larger than families' to conclusions like 'how men satisfy their biological needs determines moral relations inside the family' or 'how men cooperate to produce and exchange goods and services determines social relations inside the community.' We cannot do it because how men satisfy their needs and how they cooperate cannot be adequately defined without bringing these relations into the definition.[32]

Extending one of Durkheim's dicta, we get a similar conclusion: innate factors that are too opaque to predetermine one of the social forms of a value rather than another, cannot explain *any* of them; a property so protean, so abstract, so vague as human nature tells us everything in general and nothing in detail, generating either grand trivialities or transparent untruths.[33]

Values and Human Nature

Beliefs about our human being are used nonetheless to justify value assertions. Hence, it would seem worthwhile discussing just what we make these days of what we "be," and that is the central task I have set myself here. Perhaps the task is pointless, however. Just how important is this influence? Perhaps it exists as I have described, but is largely irrelevant? If our human nature should prove so plastic, so far removed from any fixed or developmental effects as to preclude any very useful statement about species-specific characteristics and their social and political and economic implications, then the attempt to describe and define natural human attributes will really not contribute much to a discussion about values and how these might be realized or ranked. Anthropologists like Clifford Geertz argue that we find humankind suspended in "webs of significance" that we spin ourselves. The analysis of a culture, which is the stuff of this web, prompts "not an experimental science in search of law but an interpretive one in search of meaning." In his view the concept of an invariant human nature somehow outside particular human experience is illusory, since what "man" is happens to be so involved with "where he is, who he is, and what he believes"[34] that an uncontaminated concept of the human essence simply does not exist. Any distinction we make between the "natural, universal and constant" and the "conventional, local and variable"[35] will positively confuse and confound. On the other hand, the truth is not to be found in relativism either ("man" dissolved "without residue, into his time and place, a child and a perfect captive of his age").[36] Nor does it reside in any unilinear cultural evolution that would engulf us all in its "terrible determinism." Rather, he feels, we must research those patterns that are themselves "the defining elements of a human existence which, although not constant in expression, are yet distinctive in character."[37]

Consequently, Geertz also criticizes the stratigraphic separation of biological, psychological, social, and cultural perspectives and the hierarchy in which they are usually arranged.[38] And he specifically resists the tactic employed very briefly above of seeking what seems common to all cultures, or of accounting for commonalities in terms of insights drawn from other underlying disciplines. What is shared is too broad and general, he says, adequately to account for the cultural milieu of any single individual.

It is interesting, however, that despite all these admonitions he still maintains that in the end generalizations *can* be made about humankind that are more significant than mere remarks about our diversity and variety. Which prompts one to ask: What are they, then, and where do we look for them? And to add something Geertz does not, i.e., that any comprehensive answer must now include: (1) the contemporary scientific understanding of human evolution and, in particular, those findings that throw light on the concomitant emergence of our physiological structures and mental skills; and (2) contemporary scientific discussions of the qualities of the human brain and the character of those most curious and extraordinary of the talents that we inherit—"consciousness" and "will."

The Scientific Understanding of Human Nature

What is it that I am claiming here, when I appeal to findings and discussions like those above? It is the *scientific* standing of such knowledge that is so important. And this not because science in aspiring to statements that are objective and amenable to disproof, is the only way we can know things (nonscientific ideas are not wrong, simply because of their nonscientific status. It might be that such ideas are just not amenable to scientific concepts and analysis, at least, not yet—though any conclusions about them will not currently be able to claim what one publicly attested and *scientific* ostensibly can, that "the evidence of our senses makes it irrational not to accept it"[39] The counter to this last point calls attention to the fact that our senses, and the perceptions upon which scientific judgment ultimately rests, remain fallible, regardless of how widely they are shared). Nor are scientific theories always up-to-date since they are apt to persist even when empirical evidence contradicts them. Since they are usually part of a reigning paradigm and someone using such frameworks may well resist experimental novelties, preferring, until his or her problems become acute, the certainty of what is presumed known,[40] we must account for those occasions when a theorist is not convinced of an error in his or her ways. Contradictory facts may be pertinent, but they are not usually as persuasive as we like to think. Disproof usually requires at least some consensus on what has been disproved, and those concerned to defend their theories will tend to that defense first. In this sense objectivity is always relative, since facts are only comprehensible in the context of some more general theoretical construction that is placed upon them. All theories embody human values, and their acceptance will depend at least in part on who is winning the competition for influence and power in the socioeconomic and political environment at large.[41]

While we acknowledge these weaknesses, we should not exaggerate them. Scientific findings appeal above all to human objectivity, and objectivity is still the most profound feature of the post-Ionic world view, despite our growing appreciation of the importance of viewer participation. And in terms of the development of human knowledge, it has had signal consequences. Just because it cannot be achieved absolutely does not mean that we can deny its impact outright.[42] The "primitive" sense (still prevalent in all parts of the contemporary world) of humankind as continuous with the physical universe, as a profoundly *subjective* enterprise, leads to the attempt to ground all values and morality in natural laws: "the whole universe . . . harnessed to men's attempts to force one another into good citizenship."[43] Objectivity gives us the opportunity to assess, or attempt to assess, just what physical laws are relevant to what we believe and what we value, and just what the constraining and the predisposing factors might be that limit (if limits are found to exist at all) what we choose to do, or what we think we ought to do. Objectivity is in itself a value, and always contentious because ultimately unattainable. I cannot hope to establish in one paragraph here what I would consider the worth of choosing it, though I shall return to some of the problems associated with such a choice in a moment. Suffice to say that under objectivist auspices "is" and "ought" can be taken apart the better to put them back together again, as aspects of the human reality they constitute and help define. Human understanding, we may safely assume, is not perfect, and many of the things we have done as a result of what we now know are pernicious in the extreme. But there have been benefits, too, and in terms of our comprehension these should not be ignored. "The only consistent way" indeed "to deny the reality of . . . objective standards, which necessarily implies that meaningful discourse is impossible, is that of Cratylus. When he became convinced of the Heraclitean doctrine that everything was constantly changing, he concluded that, as nothing true could be said, he would never again speak and thereafter he only wagged his finger."[44]

Let us look at the two areas I numbered earlier as particularly pertinent to our task—first, *human evolution*.

Human Nature as a Product of Evolutionary Adaptation

From the biological point of view, human nature is fundamentally a product of *evolutionary adaptation,* and, as the results of biological research have become better known, they have been brought to bear upon the image we hold of ourselves. Darwin's synthesis emphasized the evolutionary *means* as the basic mechanism of biological development and change, not any seeming *end*, and this has had all sorts of disturbing consequences for our sense of where humanity is going. It puts, in effect, "reasons for survival in place of reasons for having been born . . . causes in place of purpose . . . [and] an all-determining past in place of an all-important future."[45] The universe is characterized as a place of "blind chances and harsh necessities":[46] *chancy* in the sense that no general propositions, however precise, will ever explain the biological universe in terms that can be deduced from first principles; and *necessitous* in the way chance developments are monitored by the biological and environmental systems in which they occur for the contribution they make to the capacity of the bearer to survive. The contingent is discarded or captured as the case may be in a fashion wholly random but eminently reasonable in its results. "A totally blind process" as Monod points out, "can by definition lead to anything; it can even lead to vision itself."[47] Hence the emergence of entities such as ourselves, capable of the sort of awareness that was once and still might be called soul.[48]

A concept so antagonistic on the whole to that of divine intervention has drawn closely argued critiques. It is said, for example, that reason and objectivity are ultimately contingent upon intuition and imagination, and that these latter capacities allow of human access to transcendental truth, and, more particularly, the sense of a Being to whom we can attribute that Universal Order that includes humankind. For those imbued with such a vision, who are unable to conceive of a cosmos that is both finite and unbounded or eternal *and* contingent (and not a Creation, or purposive in some way), anything other than a spiritual appreciation of life seems a reductionist and a materialistic one—the deluded conceit, that is, of an analytic mode of thinking that presumes to apprehend the whole of which it is but a part, but which it fails to grasp because it is not that Whole. Having defined as real only what is acknowledged as objective, scientific analysis decrees (a transcendentalist would charge) all else as of no account, which is to lose sight of the ways in which subjectivity and objectivity can be combined. Counterposing chance (mutation plus sexual recombination) and antichance (natural selection) in this way is to obscure, they argue, the novel and opportunistic ways in which these come together. While such processes may well be accidental and unpredictable, they have had truly progressive[49] results—namely, us, and anyway, without a sense of purpose, life is too bleak to bear. The denial of ultimate meaning is simply not demonstrable and therefore is not true.[50]

This debate takes us far beyond what can be reasonably affirmed empirically, into a realm where our questions have fewer and fewer material referents. Traversing this terrain, we tend to make up answers to stock it with. Whether we are persuaded by what we thus come to know depends largely upon how readily convinced we are that the answers we make up are real ones. Either God, though put at a distance, is considered imminent regardless, or He (she, it, them) is an anthropomorphic illusion to be done without. One possible ploy is to defer any decision until the two realms *can* be finally reconciled: ". . . where science and religion conflict we do give superior allegiance to science, but to a more complete science of the future, and not by a dogmatic adherence to every temporary scientific assertion."[51] So far, however, one makes a personal choice or accepts what particular cultures decree.

The theory of evolution has been used in a more general way to reflect upon human behavior from the point of view of adaptation, selection, and survival.[52] The principal problem here, however, as Darwin himself posed it, resides in our sense of humankind as a "frontier instance . . .";[53] in the capacities for reflection and imagination that infuse our every act. Because cultural patterns are so important in determining behavior, and because of their comparatively rapid rate of change, it seems difficult to say whether or not we are ever adapted. Certainly, how we behave determines in large part whether we persist, and in that sense we have to secure our survival if we are to do anything else at all. Equally important, however, is the fact that what we attempt over and above survival can bear back directly upon this fundamental process.

Can we really believe, as Waddington does, for example,[54] that the direction evolution takes can be made clear and can then be used as the ultimate value against which to judge all other ethical beliefs? A capacity for ethical behavior, for moral concepts and a conscience, does appear to be a part of our biological endowment—an adaptation, that is, that has helped us survive. The content of that capacity can vary widely, however, and one may well take issue with those who argue for a naturalistic ethic defined in terms of evolutionary purpose alone. Physical survival is basic. Agreed. But we can survive more or less successfully or happily, more or less free, and more or less the recipients of equality of opportunity. Furthermore, how one actually judges freedom or equality, for example, will depend to a large extent upon the frame of reference used. The same phenomenon, as I have mentioned above, can be invested with quite contradictory moral and political properties depending upon one's point of view. So long as we physically persist, evolution as such is oblivious to qualities like these. Human beings, however (beyond the most wretched of them), are not.[55] What is evolutionarily adaptive may *not* necessarily be ethically good, and there is definitely more than one way to survive.

Take the two questions: "How does a particular social phenomenon help (or hinder) the human animal in satisfying his [sic] survival needs? And how does it affect the survival and reproductive efficacy of his society as a collective?"[56] Not only can we not predict, except in the extreme case, what helps or hinders or otherwise affects the prospect that we will persist; not only does short-term adaptation prove as often as not maladaptive in the long run (and vice versa); but if these needs include self-actualization, as the usual list suggests (and people can die of a lack of meaning and purpose as well as a lack of shelter or food), we will be hard-pressed, given the range of human potential and biological capacities, to nominate any specific indices that we can say will secure the sense of individual well-being and hence survival.[57] Such potentials contribute little to our understanding of the process of selection and how it now occurs. Our biological advantage *is* this very indeterminancy. Even if human beings do have an essence, it is not easy to deduce from that fact alone any particular ethical principles. "That there are purposes *in* life does not at all show or even suggest that there is a purpose *to* life or a purpose *of* life or that man was made *for* a certain purpose. But it is this last sort of purpose that we need in order to show that there are natural moral laws."[58]

In the realm of competing nation-states, the concept of adaptive social evolution proves even more inappropriate since there are only a few great powers, and they are so influential in determining the values of the global society that selection is likely to be rapid and radical, rather than ordered and sure. The fact that we fight wars in ways learned earlier will contradict this to some extent, and group adaptation to what has gone before can readily prove pernicious, particularly so under contemporary strategic circumstances. (It is usually some such idea that lies behind the argument that nuclear weapons have rendered nationalism a maladaptive emotion and a distinct threat to the survival of us all.)[59] In domestic terms, a large number of sociopolitical systems are potentially compatible with survival as such and choosing between them requires more than an evolutionary perspective can provide. Survival is a perennial, if for many a second-order, problem, but however basic it might be it confers only limited philosophic advantage on those who build the social systems for humankind. Values presuppose the capacity for evolving them, a capacity transmitted genetically from generation to generation; values also help shape the process of human evolution. Yet between the two is a gap that the doctrine of naturalism has still to close.

Brain Research

The second area I argued we should consider is that of what might very loosely be called *brain research*. This opens up some fundamental scientific debates about the nature/nurture dichotomy, about free will versus determinism, and about the nature of human consciousness. I shall be returning to these debates at several points in all that follows, but shall pause briefly to survey their basic parameters now.

Nature/nurture. As far as the nature/nurture dichotomy is concerned, the most popular contemporary view of the combination of forces involved is an *interactionist* and *developmentalist* one. The reciprocal effects of both genetic and environmental factors are a fundamental feature of how we arrive and grow. There are adaptable aspects, therefore, to nearly all complex behavior, "however stereotyped it may appear,"[60] and in humankind this sort of adaptability is very great indeed—some would say well-nigh total. Thus behavior determined intrinsically does not in fact denote something automatic, unalterable, or fixed. Indeed the quality of human competence renders the concept of determination in human beings so marginal, it is argued, as to appear almost irrelevant. It is the *almost*, however, that is important here.

In evolutionary terms, the genetic capacity and cultural behavior of human beings are seen to have developed together in such a symbiotic fashion that to place the propensity we inherit for symbolic interaction prior in time to its actual employ is to misconstrue the extent to which culture has been "ingredient," as Geertz would say, and not just an "accessory" after the fact.[61] (The human endowment is so open-ended, he argues, as to allow no necessary connection between the nature of "man" and any specific way of life at all. "Human," from this point of view, is "consummately social: social in its origins, social in its functions, social in its forms, [and] social in its applications."[62] And indeed our biophysiological substructures *do* seem so inadequate to the task of producing a proper human being as to suggest that it is culture rather than any purely intrinsic qualities that shape most decisively what we think, feel, and do. And yet, can we write biological factors off altogether? Is this a counsel for biopolitical despair?

Free will and determinism. I would argue not. The neurosciences, for example, have made many new discoveries about how to conceptualize mind and brain, and about how the latter works; and since we do on the whole assume it is possible at least to attempt to comprehend the physical universe in scientific terms, there is no reason to suppose that our consciousness itself (including the unconscious) cannot be included in the scientific attempt to make of mind a legitimate object of inquiry. Biofeedback research, for example, has confirmed claims from diverse esoteric disciplines that human volition alone can be used to monitor and control autonomic bodily mechanisms like blood pressure and pulse rate; that the mind can lead the body in a very direct way. It is now possible, furthermore, to give quite precise physical referents for at least some mental events; for a specific thought, for example, or memory, or mood, or even for the mental exercise of one's will. These are at least the beginnings of a neurophysiology of consciousness and mind.

I would remain cautious nonetheless. However close the correspondence may be between the physical and mental domains, an "inescapable distinction" does seem to persist. The "phenomenal" experiences we have on "acquaintance," and the "discursive knowledge of the nonmental domain" that we get "by 'description' . . . which transcends that experience"[63] do still seem to diverge. Perhaps this distinction is an illusion and, as Weimer suggests, the brain possesses some more fundamental property that generates what gives meaning to *both* sets of events; that could then be used to explain them, if we could only find and formulate it, in a singular way. *How* we know could then account for the dualistic nature of *what* we know (by both reflection *and* acquaintance) and also, perhaps, account for the very sense of self.[64] Perhaps our contemporary scientific capacities are simply not equal yet to the task of formulating the deepest paradoxes in ways that would allow us to resolve them. Certainly reductionism in all forms is out of favor,[65] and materialist arguments, even the most common one for some kind of identity between mental and neural events, continue to founder on our innate apprehension of "something else" beyond cells, molecules, atoms, quarks, and the void.

Consciousness. Perhaps it is the capacity for what has been termed the holonomic coding and decoding of information, and hence for language and communication, that best explains the nature of how we think?[66] Perhaps it is a revamped version of *emergence*, suitably modest, that will prove most fruitful?[67] Roger Sperry has argued that "mental events are . . . not merely *correlates* of brain activity, but also *causes*. . . ." Conscious mental experience he conceives to be a "holistic emergent of brain activity, different from and more than the neural events of which it is composed,"[68] with a "working role in brain function and a pragmatic reason for being and having been evolved." Subjective states of mind become, in his view, a legitimate, indeed a basic, datum in neurophysiological research. And the way the neural system operates as a whole *is* the property of consciousness (as well as other things). This is not to deny the influence of structural specializations that reflect our evolutionary history—the brainstem that automatically regulates the heart, blood, and respiration; the ritualistic archeocortex; the emotive meso-cortex (limbic system); and the reasoning neo-cortex or new brain.[69] It is simply to say that in terms of the properties of the brain as a whole and the emergent dynamics of its neural networks, there is a configuration that is more than a *mere* sum of the parts and a whole that can act back to varying effect upon these parts should it (one) choose so to do.

Such a concept requires a very general understanding of evolutionary hierarchies and the way what happens at subordinate levels—specific components performing in and of themselves—cannot pre-empt superordinate activities occurring at the level of the whole.[70] If we imagine that the "principles governing the isolated particulars of a lower level" actually leave "indeterminate conditions to be controlled by a higher principle,"[71] then we have a case for "emergence" as Sperry imagines it. Consciousness then occurs as "nothing but" the outcome of a material process, but "nothing but" in a particular, and, Sperry would say, nonreductionist sense.

It remains true, however, that in our thinking we can also mentally move outside both ourselves and our societies in ways that suggest something transcendent. Whether this transcendence is real, or whether it is a luminous delusion, we can probably never really tell. As Darwin pointed out, in discussing consciousness no one could ever actually discover if he or she "had not it."[72]

Some analysts have extended the concept of emergence to society too: "Just as human and octopus eyes have a functional wisdom that none of the participating cells or genes have ever had self-conscious awareness of, so in social evolution we can contemplate a process where adaptive belief systems could be accumulated which none of the innovators, transmitters, or participants properly understood, a tradition wiser than any of the persons transmitting it."[73] What they neglect, of course, is the fact that persons may contemplate their eyes and their belief systems in ways cells and genes cannot. This is an important difference.

Not all of the emergent properties of the brain are to do with being conscious, and it remains to be seen if further research will be able to establish whether the overall outcome of functional cerebral circuit activity can truly account for its mental as well as its physical properties.[74] Sperry himself specifically states that he is not dealing with such forms of awareness as *self*-consciousness, nor with consciousness of "other selves . . . external objects, situations and events,"[75] though he does express the hope that an understanding of what is more simple will come to elucidate such things, which are much more complex.

If we decide, as people like Sperry do, to talk in terms of the emergence of consciousness, and to allow for subjective values as objective factors at work on the brain, we are still left with a decision to make about comparative potency. How important, that is, in causal terms, are conscious experiences compared to nonconscious ones? Could there not be cases where the conscious and nonconscious conflict? What exactly is the difference between the concept of emergent *un*conscious properties and the more familiar idea of biologically induced needs? If we accept the autonomy of our value predispositions, and hence the idea of free will, and reject the idea of biological determinance as a necessary (in the strong sense of a *sufficient*) force, we are still left with the weaker concept of unconscious *limits*, the idea of *predispositions* and *constraints*. These may not allow of prediction in a cause-and-effect way because they are tempered by our will, but they might well be at work anyway, modulating how we survive, learn, organize social hierarchies, separate the sexes, outlaw incest, defend territory, and aggress. When we look at it closely, we see that Sperry has not in fact managed to detach values from the conditioning effect of other influences, and his model of the mind as an autonomous monitor is incomplete. To the extent that *unconscious* determinants of human behavior prevail on a species-specific basis, we are less than free (though in knowing that we might also be able to account for them "consciously").

Determinism and Human Needs

The most common way to resolve this whole problem—of how driven we might be—is to smuggle back a "stratigraphic" concept of human needs.[76] Thus "the basic structure of every human society," it is argued, ". . . is 'determined' in a general way by a number of ongoing and species-specific biological needs (subject to some individual and geographical variation) that must continually be satisfied if the species, and the individuals who compose it, are to survive in the long run."[77] The list of such attributes usually includes the urges that pertain to basic physical welfare, to reproduction, to family nurture, and the like, but it is often expanded to cover significantly more than this. Abraham Maslow, for example, has distinguished a hierarchy of five groups of them, namely, those of physical well-being, security and safety, society and affection (a sense of belonging), self-esteem, and self-actualization (or self-development).[78] And he has argued that once our more fundamental requirements have been met it becomes possible to satisfy those further up the scale.

Need statements make both empirical and normative demands. Hence, to seek a naturalistic basis for human norms in this way usually means that we end up asserting the very phenomena we seek to explain. This becomes immediately evident as we move away from the more fundamental of them toward what seems essential to realize the human as opposed to the merely physical ones. The link between needs and what makes for biological survival becomes progressively more tenuous, and the capacity for biological *adaptation*, whether purposive or inadvertent, dramatically expands. This would suggest that the concept of limits is irrelevant, and indeed, those who attempt to order needs into a hierarchy of some kind usually seem to lose a good deal of their historical perspective on how human beings fare in the societies in which they live,[79] and how it is that *governments* can define what human nature means. Not unsurprisingly, Maslow's hierarchy has an escape clause. Given the range of possible ways in which "self-realization" might be reached, the concept becomes so open that it provides a blank sheet for one to prefer as a "need" well-nigh anything at all. This leaves us with no measure of what *bad* or *good* fulfillment might mean in evolutionary or any other terms, and we are back with the familiar questions about what we value and how we view the good life.[80]

The naturalism implicit in this whole approach is inevitably deterministic, fatalistic, and reified.[81] Needs-talk has revolutionary implications; it has reactionary ones too. In attempting to define what we "naturally" require, do we define the conditions under which we "best" behave? Radicals reply that in the extreme, and perhaps not so extreme, case, "when the participants in social debates turn to ethology, to genetics or to psychology or evolutionary theory for guidance, what they hear is, to a considerable extent, the echoes of their own debate, mediated and mystified in the form of science."[82] (How considerable this mystification might be is a point of some dispute. Between the concept of science as essentially apolitical, and the argument that it serves as the handmaiden of those who would defend a particular socioeconomic *status quo,* there is much scope for disagreement.[83] Following my earlier discussion of objectivity, while according science its due, we should also recognize that though not "merely ideology," it *is* "ideology as well," and remain alert at least to the fact that any scientific definition has political implications. "We must recover," radicals continue, "our right to define our own nature through our struggles to overcome our limitations," which does not preclude, of course, a better understanding of what those limitations might be.)

On the one hand then we have the assertion that science cannot tell us what we should want; it can only tell us what *is*. In this view the value we attach to what is, and the interest we show in it, are separate activities. (Note the astronomer, Sandage, who pursues an "ultimate truth . . . out there": "It doesn't matter what anyone says. The ultimate judge is nature. The majesty and excitement of the thing is just that; that is independent of man" and yet can still speak to him.)[84] Scientific observation can provide causal explanations but not assessments of worth, of good or bad; these must come from somewhere else. On the other hand, we have science as the questing edge of a materialistic ideology that is very far from value-free and seeks something to say on ethical judgments of every other kind. The sociobiologist, Wilson, argues that "innate censors and motivators exist in the brain that deeply and unconsciously affect our ethical premises; from these roots, morality evolved as instinct. . . ." This permits him to say that "science may soon be in a position to investigate the very origin and meaning of human values, from which all ethical pronouncements and much of political practice flow." And in what is probably one of the strongest statements of the case to date, he concludes that "for our own physical well-being if nothing else, ethical philosophy must not be left in the hands of the merely wise. Although human progress can be achieved by intuition and force of will, only hard-won empirical knowledge of our biological nature will allow us to make optimum choices among the competing criteria of progress."[85]

All those who follow a positivistic path into the social realm seek similar truths "out there." The fact is that their subject matter, however much this might be defined in terms of things external, actually comes from "in here." Reality is placed outside the thinking and feeling mind. We objectify the mind itself and for our investigative purposes invest it with particular qualities that seem extrinsic to us. There remain, however, intrinsic attributes too. Even Wilson admits that the duality is deceptive: "The search for values," he says, "will . . . go beyond the utilitarian calculus of genetic fitness. Although natural selection has been the prime mover, it works through a cascade of decisions based on secondary values that have historically served as enabling mechanisms for survival and reproductive success.[86]

The main critique of the positivist position rejects its objectivist aspirations outright and decrees an ultimately irreducible gulf between science and the humanities, between truth and meaning. This gulf cannot be bridged, it is claimed, despite all endeavor to do so, because human behavior cannot be explained in terms of any of its more fundamental components, however compelling such explanations seem. Human behavior is comprehensible only because of what it actually *means* to those who do the behaving and to those who do the analyzing. The context of shared symbols and assumptions that drapes any act that is not patently insane in a rich cloak of social significance is an essential part of every explanation of any human event.

What does all this imply for a scientific understanding of human values? There is an important distinction here between an intuitive appreciation of values that locates them outside of nature, of the sort Plato had, for example, and one that grounds them in biosocial needs and the "fulfillment of natural tendencies," as Aristotle did. The latter appeals to *science;* the former *philosophy*. However, the distinction is ultimately not important and once made can only be useful if the line between the two is fudged again, and truth and meaning recombined. To accept the dichotomy as it is, we must assume too objectivist, too positivist a concept of science and of scientists, and too personalist and subjectivist a concept of philosophy and of philosophers (who, even as they seek comparative judgments of worth, still respect the right use of argument and empirical evidence and examples that bring their abstract debates down to earth).[87] Speculation that is unsupported by insights from less discursive disciplines tends to waft aloft on the warm talk of its devotees with nothing more substantial than human conviction to keep it attached to the world.

What can we conclude? Whether we are a ''frontier instance,'' or whether we are located somewhat deeper within the biological domain, the territory is at least contiguous. Our human characteristics do derive, at least in some part, from what has most enhanced our capacities to reproduce.

On reflection, there is something almost anachronistic about the attempt to define human values in the light of naturalistic accounts of human nature. Eighteenth-century proclamations of social justice and human rights did so and have been roundly assailed ever since for having dressed up value preferences, however justified these might have appeared to be, in an objectivist garb that simply did not fit.

Much has changed since the eighteenth century, not the least of which is our knowledge of the natural universe and that bit of it that is ''man.'' Wilson writes of genes holding culture on a leash. The leash, he says, is a long one, but how long? Is it a leash in fact, or does the metaphor radically mislead? Perhaps we should talk not of *constraint* but of *opportunity*; not of biopolitical *predisposition* but of *potential*. ''It is an old notion,'' as may be apparent by now,

> that a belief in the universal reign of physical laws implies that all explanations must be in the vocabulary of the natural sciences. To be sure, if the necessary physical conditions were not present, human beings would not have the plans, projects, ideas, or emotions that they do. These are, in this sense, physical events, and proper objects of study for the natural sciences. Yet this does not imply that they cannot also be studied quite independently of the natural sciences, or that nothing of significance will be revealed by such independent study.[88]

Nor does it imply, a sociobiologist would say, that we cannot extend scientific analysis to the content of such plans, projects, ideas, and emotions themselves. And here I am with the sociobiologists, at least some of the way.

The suspicion lurks, then, despite the best attempts to dispatch it, that material conditions are not only *present* but to a significant degree (and the order of significance is the key question) *presumptive*. The idea is not popular. Its ''open mention,'' it has been said, ''like . . . [that] of sex in polite Victorian circles, can only incite wicked thoughts,''[89] and certainly there is every good reason to fear the bad effects of biopolitical ideas. The products of our genius do not make for the social good simply as a matter of course. But then knowledge is also instrumental in negating exploitation. If we understand ourselves better, we may well evolve values that are better too, not in the sense that they are higher somehow, but simply more comprehensive, and more conducive to human felicity.[90] When individuals or societies are denied such knowledge, whether wittingly or unwittingly, and they are unable therefore to realize the values that would liberate them, then we may say that they *are* exploited and in a quite important sense. We need possess no more fundamental understanding of what is *good* as opposed to *bad*; we need merely moot fundamental psychological and social facts about what *is*, and, therefore, what might possibly be. Of course, having been given such knowledge, people do not necessarily choose to use it to improve themselves or to serve others. But if we can establish, to paraphrase Plamenatz, that, by standards anyone would accept if they understood human nature better than they actually do, they were being badly treated, then we have a powerful argument for condemning such treatment and for advocating changes that would probably, under the circumstances, be an improvement. Is it philosophic sleight-of-mind to talk of standards "anyone would accept"? Not if we admit the species-specific relevance of a scientific point of view.

Modern social thinking has made much of the distance between the classical predilection for universalizing human attributes and contemporary doctrines of cultural and value relativism. Berlin argues that it is Machiavelli who first forced this into the open. In counterposing public and private morality, Machiavelli implied the existence of more than one ethical system and the absence of any common ground for choosing rationally between them.[91] Dispense with traditional notions of natural law, however, and the deep identity between human values and what ought "naturally" to obtain disappears. We then get the attempt to explain one realm entirely in terms of the other or to push them so far apart that they are no longer within even hailing distance.

This does not mean we need leave it at that. Having opened such a gap, though, how do we close it again? "The real issue," one author argues,

is whether one can extricate the ancient insight into the unity of human nature from the ancient illusion that humanity is unchanging through history. The task is to develop a doctrine that recognises the unity of human nature in a more than trivial fashion while affirming that this nature changes in history and that it is reinvented and transformed by each new form of social life. . . .[92]

Even this careful statement may allow too much. The most extreme of naturalists would say that values are only a gloss on basic *interests* (or some such word) and that science will eventually be able to account for all such phenomena in biophysiological terms. The less dogmatic talk of *translation*, of finding material referents for human beliefs, and leaving it there. The most modest speak of *consistency* and of value language having to come to terms with known facts about the natural sources of human behavior.[93]

Perhaps Hume, who made the dichotomy most clear, had the answer already. His treatise on human nature was, we might recall, a deliberate attempt to apply "experimental reasoning" to ethical affairs. "He argued," we are also reminded,

> that judgements both of fact and of value can have metaphysical certification, that both are justifiable only as they serve human purposes. We are able to discuss matters of fact because we have similar organs of perception, similar data-integrating intellects, and similar interests . . . we are able to discuss values, can found a science of morality, because we have [to a more significant degree than cultural relativists allow] similar feelings and similar techniques for integrating these feelings. Fact and value come together in our human nature. . . . The parallel structures of fact and value, of perception and intelligence and of feeling, and their common basis in our nature imply that if we may assert that certain systematically investigated factual statements deserve belief, we may also justify action. . . .[94]

If we give reasons for our values, in other words, some of which are matters of fact, we have already reduced the distance between what is an extra- and what is an intrascientific affair. Can this distance be made so small as for all useful purposes to be irrelevant? Or does fact approach value like an asymptote, coming closer and closer but never crossing the line? First we must see what science has to say.

We no longer believe so readily these days that our reasoning will arrive at what is true, and that what is true is somehow good too. One can do different things with the one truth anyway—try and ignore it, for example, or use it to a "good" or "bad" purpose defined by other, less rational means. But what *is* cannot be ignored, or pursued in "unnatural" ways, with impunity.[95] Hence the perennial Aristotelian concern about how values express in thought, word, and deed our inherent human needs. The concern seems to me well placed, if only because the "question of interest is no longer whether human social behaviour is genetically determined; it is to what extent."[96] That exact extent will remain ambiguous, particularly for a subject like ours, since learning what "is" requires evaluation at every point, and the stench of our presence, however hard we try by methodological devices to minimize it, remains all-pervasive. The valued options that "is" portends will also diverge. All our ideals rarely prove compatible, and so we seek ". . . better ways of stating [them] . . ."; we seek "less misleading symbols for [them] . . ."; we argue. And this in turn is necessary if we are ultimately to change, as I believe we should, those institutions that make human lives "gratuitously harder. . . ."[97]

NOTES

1. T. Hobbes, *Leviathan* (London: Fontana, 1962), pp. 142–3. The introductory anecdote, by the way, comes in this particular form from Isaac Asimov.

2. Ibid., p. 143.

3. Ibid., p. 144.

4. Ibid., p. 145.

5. Locke put against Hobbes a concept of human nature as basically sociable. "The only way," J. Mabbott says,

> to convince a Golden Age theorist of Locke's type is to ask him to conduct a business in a state where the legal system is corrupt, to take a journey through mountains where there are brigands, to go and live in a city or country where authority has disappeared. . . . No doubt every man is not naturally and constantly a would-be murderer or thief, but Locke forgot that the bad men do not go about labelled. [*The State and the Citizen* (London: Arrow Books, 1958). pp. 21-2].

R. McShea, in "Human Nature Theory and Philosophy," *American Journal of Political Science*: 22, no. 3 (August 1978): p. 675, states: ". . . not every society is equally a felicitous arrangement. There are some which are, in relation to their opportunities, so poorly constructed to contribute to the happiness of their members that they are not worth breaking a treaty to preserve, whose diplomats, sent abroad to lie for their country, would do well to defect."

6. H. Bull, *The Anarchical Society* (London: Macmillan, 1977), Ch. 2, "Does Order Exist in World Politics?"; A. D. Lindsay, *The Modern Democratic State* (New York: Oxford University Press, 1962), pp. 93–99, "International Politics and Ethics." Also, pp. 96–97:

> Law lets morality grow, and as it grows the standard of law is pulled up, and morality helped further. . . . The influence of the one on the other is reciprocal. It is significant of the close connection we ordinarily suppose to exist between law and morality that we most of us assume that anarchy . . . is a state of continual violence and conflict. The contrary belief . . . that anarchy is a state of blessedness and harmony is an exaggeration of the truth that morality is not created by law.

7. Bull, *Anarchical Society*, p. 317.

8. Mabbott, *The State and the Citizen*, p. 7. Also L. Kohlberg, "From Is to Ought: How to Commit the Naturalistic Fallacy and Get Away with It in the Study of Moral Development," in T. Mischel, ed., *Cognitive Development and Epistemology* (N.Y.: Academic Press, 1971), p. 156: ". . . the value-relativity position often rests on logical confusion between matters of fact (there are no standards accepted by all men), and matters of value (there are no standards which all men ought to accept) that is, it represents the 'naturalistic fallacy.' "

9. P. Berger, "Are Human Rights Universal?" *Commentary 64, no. 3 (September 1977): 61.*

10. Hence the distinction J. Plamenatz makes between *requiring* and *determining:* "one thing *requires* another, when, given any form of the one, there is a need for some form of the other, and one thing *determines* another, when, given a particular form of the one, there arises a particular form of the other." See his *Man and Society*, vol. II (London: Longmans, 1963), p. 278. The Marxist propensity, for example, to subsume the relations of production under modes of production and then to say that they are determined thereby is, as Plamenatz points out, an important weakness in this approach. On the other hand, Plamenatz misses the particularly pervasive character of the modern (industrial) milieu.

11. T. Hopkins and I. Wallerstein, "The Comparative Study of National Societies," *Social Science Information* 6, no. 5 (October 1967): 39.

12. K. Kumar, *Prophecy and Progress:* The Sociology of Industrial and Post-industrial Society (Harmondsworth: Penguin, 1978), p. 90.

13. Ibid., p. 97.

14. Ibid., p. 101.

15. B. Moore, *Social Origins of Dictatorship and Democracy* (Harmondsworth: Penguin, 1966), p. 506.

16. R. Seidenberg, *Posthistoric Man* (Boston: Beacon Press, 1957), p. 238.

17. H. Gerth and C. Mills, *Max Weber: Essays in Sociology* (London: Routledge and Kegan Paul, 1961), p. 139.
18. D. Brown and M. Harrison, *A Sociology of Industrialisation* (London: Macmillan, 1978), p. 89.
19. K. Kumar, *Prophecy and Progress*, p. 103. See also my chapter 6.
20. Gerth and Mills, *Max Weber*, p. 139.
21. J. Freeman, "Choices, Values and the Solution of Human Problems," unpublished.
22. Moore, *Social Origins*, p. 486.
23. M. Rokeach, *The Nature of Human Values* (New York: The Free Press, 1973), p. 20.
24. J. Hersch, "Is the declaration of human rights a Western concept?" in H. Kiefer and M. Munitz, eds., *Ethics and Social Justice* (Albany: State University of New York Press, 1968); cf. C. Geertz, *The Interpretation of Cultures* (London: Hutchinson, 1975), pp. 37–43.
25. C. Geertz, "The Impact of the Concept of Culture on the Concept of Man", in his *Interpretation of Cultures*.
26. See L. Kohlberg, "Education, Moral Development and Faith," *Journal of Moral Education*: 4, no. 1 (1974): 5–16; also the critique by J. Gibbs, "Kohlberg's Stages of Moral Development," *Harvard Education Review* 47, no. 1 (February 1977): 43–61 where he makes the key distinction between the *naturalistic* and the *existential* dimensions of Kohlberg's sequence.
27. T. Hopkins, "Third World Modernisation in Transnational Perspective," *The Annals of the American Academy of Political and Social Science* 386 (November 1969): 134.
28. Kumar, *Prophecy and Progress*, p. 88.
29. G. Rudé, *Revolutionary Europe 1783-1815* (London: Fontana, 964), p. 107. The evolving interpretation of the American Constitution is another obvious case in point.
30. A. Elms, *Attitudes* (Milton Keynes: The Open University Press, 1976), Part One: "Beliefs, Values and Attitudes."
31. V. I. Lenin, "The State and Revolution," *Collected Works*, vol. 25 (June–September 1917) (London: Lawrence and Wishart, 1964), p. 425.
32. Plamenatz, *Man and Society*, vol. II, p. 285.
33. E. Durkheim, *The Rules of Sociological Method* (Chicago: University of Chicago Press, 1938), p. 108.
34. C. Geertz, *Interpretation of Cultures,* p. 35; p. 34: "Whitehead once offered to the natural sciences the maxim 'Seek simplicity and distrust it'; to the social sciences he might well have offered 'Seek complexity and order it.' "
35. Ibid., p. 36.
36. Ibid., p. 37.
37. Ibid., p. 37.
38. For a typical example of this stratigraphy, see M. Polanyi, "Life's Irreducible Structure," *Science*: 160 (1968): 1308–12. Geertz summarizes the argument thus:

    As one analyses man, one peels off layer after layer, each such layer being complete and irreducible in itself, revealing another, quite different sort of layer underneath. Strip off the motley forms of culture and one finds the structural and functional regularities of social organisation. Peel off these in turn and one finds the underlying psychological factors—"basic needs" or what-have-you—that support and make them possible. Peel off psychological factors and one is left with the biological foundations—anatomical, physiological, neurological—of the whole edifice of human life. [*The Interpretation of Cultures*, p. 37].

39. Geertz, *Interpretation of Cultures*, p. 18.
40. T. Kuhn, *The Structure of Scientific Revolutions* (Chicago: University of Chicago, 1970), p. 64. "In science . . . novelty emerges only with difficulty, manifested by resistance, against a

background provided by expectation." Indeed, "no process yet disclosed by the historical study of scientific development at all resembles the methodological stereotype of falsification by direct comparison with nature . . . the act of judgement that leads scientists to reject a previously accepted theory is always based upon more than a comparison with nature . . ." (p. 77). This intolerance has its productive side, contributing in no small measure to the capacity of science to come up with cumulative knowledge, and to its capacity for generating truly radical advances in explanatory and predictive power.

41. R. Young, "Evolutionary Biology and Ideology: Then and Now," *Science Studies*: 1 (1971): 177–206, and the extensive footnotes thereto.

42. Note how we normally cope:

If I had to choose to regard my subjective reality as purely private and you regard yours in a like manner, we have a choice. We can either retreat to our own cosmos and deny the world, or, like oscillating wheels shuttle our private experience between us through communication. In order to keep such communications open—infinite—we "invent," construct a real world which includes the distinction between the "other" and the "self." [K. Pribram, "Problems Concerning the Structure of Consciousness," in G. Globus et al., *Consciousness and the Brain:* A Scientific and Philosophical Enquiry (N.Y.: Plenum Press, 1976) p. 310].

43. M. Douglas, *Purity and Danger* (London: Routledge and Kegan Paul, 1966), p. 3.

44. S. Letwin, "Nature, History and Morality," R. Peters, ed., *Nature and Conduct* (London: Macmillan, 1975), pp. 239–40.

45. S. Luria, *Life: The Unfinished Experiment* (London: Souvenir Press, 1966), p. 3.

46. Ibid., p. 120. Also J. Monod, *Choice and Necessity* (N.Y.: A. Knopf, 1971).

47. J. Monod, *Choice and Necessity*, p. 98.

48. "What doubt," Monod declares,

can there be of the presence of the spirit within us? To give up the illusion that sees in it an immaterial "substance" is not to deny the existence of the soul, but on the contrary, to begin to recognise the complexity, the richness, the unfathomable profundity of the genetic and cultural heritage and of the personal experience, conscious or otherwise, which together constitute this being of ours: the unique and irrefutable witness to itself. [Ibid., p. 159]

49. "There is no concept of progress which is 'best' in the abstract. . . . Different criteria of progress may be preferable in different contexts" (F. Ayala and T. Dobzhansky, *Studies in the Philosophy of Biology*, [London: Macmillan, 1974], p. xvi). While we may suggest such indices as increasing complexity or the development of self-awareness, these denote no necessary evolutionary end point. On the other hand, there has certainly been progress in the sense of a movement *away* from physico-chemical determinancy. See also J. Passmore, *The Perfectibility of Man* (London: Duckworth, 1970).

50. T. Dobzhansky, "Two Contrasting World Views," in J. Lewis, ed., *Beyond Chance and Necessity* (London: Garnstone Press, 1974); J. Chiari, *The Necessity of Being* (London: Paul Elek, 1973); W. Thorpe, *Purpose in a World of Chance* (Oxford: Oxford University Press, 1978).

51. D. Campbell, " 'Downward Causation' in Hierarchically Organised Biological Systems," in Ayala and Dobzhansky, *Studies,* p. 183.

52. E.g., R. Alexander, "The Search for a General Theory of Behavior," *Behavioral Science*: 20 (1975): 77–100 and "The Search for an Evolutionary Philosophy of Man," *Proceedings of the Royal Society of Victoria*, vol. 84, (1969); P. Corning, op. cit.; E. O. Wilson, *op. cit.*

53. H. Gruber and P. Barrett, eds., *Darwin on Man* (N.Y.: E. P. Dutton, 1974).

54. C. H. Waddington, *The Ethical Animal* (London: George, Allen and Unwin, 1960).

55. C. Turnbull, "Human Nature and Primal Man," *Social Research* 4, no. 3 (Autumn 1973): 530.

56. P. Corning, "Human Nature Redivivus," in J. Pennock and J. Chapman, eds., *Human Nature in Politics* (N.Y.: New York University Press, 1977), p. 36.
57. Cf. S. Pepper, "Survival Value," *Zygon* 4, no. 1 (March 1969): 4–11; F. Cloak, "Is a Cultural Ethology Possible?" *Human Ecology* 3, no. 3 (1975): 161–82; J. Harrison, *Our Knowledge of Right and Wrong* (London: George, Allen and Unwin, 1971), Ch. XI, "Evolution and Ethics", particularly p. 248. For more on (1) survival of the individual, (2) survival of his or her society as a collective, and (3) survival of our species, see the next chapter.
58. K. Nielsen, "The Myth of Natural Law," in S. Hook, ed., *Law and Philosophy* (New York: New York University Press, 1964), p. 13.
59. D. Campbell, "On the Conflicts between Biological and Social Evolution and between Psychology and Moral Tradition," *American Psychologist* 30 (1975):1106.
60. S. Barnett, *"Instinct" and "Intelligence": The Behaviour of Animals and Man* (Harmondsworth: Penguin, 1970), p. 260.
61. Geertz, *Interpretation of Cultures*, p. 83.

> As culture . . . accumulated and developed a selective advantage was given to those individuals in the population most able to take advantage of it—the effective hunter, the persistent gatherer, the adept toolmaker, the resourceful leader—until what had been a small-brained, proto-human . . . became the large-brained fully human. . . . By submitting himself to governance by symbolically mediated programs for producing artifacts, man determined, if unwittingly, the culminating stages of his own biological destiny. Quite literally, though quite inadvertently, he created himself. [Ibid., p. 118]

Cf. P. Corning, "The Biological Bases of Behavior and Some Implications for Political Science," *World Politics* 23, no. 3 (April 1971): 336.
62. Geertz, *Interpretation of Cultures*, p. 360.
63. Globus et al., *Consciousness and the Brain,* pp. 1, 8.
64. W. Weimer, "Manifestations of Mind: Some Conceptual and Empirical Issues," in ibid.
65. F. Ayala distinguishes three sorts: ontological, methodological, and epistemological. *Ontological* reductionists assert "that the laws of physics and chemistry fully apply to all biological processes at the level of atoms and molecules. Vitalism is now practically a dead issue . . ."; *methodological* reductionists argue that "the only biological explanations worth seeking are those obtained by investigating the underlying physicochemical process" (an *anti*reductionist would tend to exclude such explanations altogether); *epistemological* reductionists seek ever more comprehensive principles such that "the theories and experimental laws formulated in one field of science can be shown to be special cases of theories and laws formulated in some other. . . ." (Ayala and Dobzhansky, eds., *Studies,* pp. viii, ix. See also S. Rose, *The Conscious Brain* (London: Weidenfeld and Nicolson, 1973), Ch. 13, pp. 16–35.
66. Pribra, "Problems."
67. C. Broad, *The Mind and its Place in Nature* (London: Kegan Paul et al., 1937), Ch. XIV; cf. B. Rensch, *Biophilosophy* (New York: Columbia University Press, 1971); S. Rose, *(Conscious Brain)* argues that only nonpredictive explanations will be possible since: "at any given hierarchical level", "it is possible only to make probabilistic statements about either the present or future brain state of the individual. . . . In view of this uncertainty, which is built into the core of the preoccupations of neurobiology itself, the concern . . . with the 'free-will paradox' seems a little redundant" (p. 292).
68. "In Search of Psyche," in F. Worden et al., eds., *The Neurosciences* (Cambridge: MIT Press, 1975), p. 43. Also J. Eccles, "Cerebral Activity and Consciousness," in Ayala and Dobzhansky, *Studies*.
69. P. Maclean, *A Triune Concept of Brain and Behaviour* (Toronto: University of Toronto Press, 1973); also the critique of this thesis in N. Calder, *The Mind of Man* (London: BBC, 1970), pp.

176–278. For light relief, see the satirical interview with "Sir Clarence Lovejoy" on the Australian Broadcasting Commission's Science *Insight* program no. 500, "Dissecting the Mind" (September 15, 1974).

70. Campbell, in Ayala and Dobzhansky, *Studies*.

71.   Voice production leaves largely open the combination of sounds into words, which is controlled by a vocabulary. Next, a vocabulary leaves largely open the combination by words to form sentences, which is controlled by grammar, and so on. Consequently the operations of a higher level cannot be accounted for by the laws governing its particulars on the next lower level. You cannot derive a vocabulary from phonetics; you cannot derive grammar from vocabulary; a correct use of grammar does not account for good style; and a good style does not supply the content of a piece of prose. [Polanyi, "Life's Irreducible Structure," p. 1311]

72. Gruber and Barrett, eds., *Darwin on Man*.

73. Campbell, "On the Conflicts," p. 1107. See also V. Potter, *Bioethics* (New Jersey: Prentice Hall, 1971), p. 10.

74. R. Sperry, "Mental Phenomena as Causal Determinants in Brain Function"; and W. Winsatt, "Reductionism, Levels of Organisation and the Mind-Body Problem," in Globus et al., *Consciousness and the Brain*.

75. Sperry, "Mental Phenomena," pp. 163–4.

76. C. Fay, "Ethical Naturalism and Biocultural Evolution," *Zygon* 4. no. 1 (March 1969): 24–32. See P. J. Taylor, " 'Need' Statements," *Analysis*, vol. 19 (1959), who argues that what human beings need and ought to receive is not necessarily all to their "good"; a question that must be answered on grounds other than those of "need" alone. K. Nielsen, "On Human Needs and Moral Appraisals," *Enquiry*, vol. 6 (1963), argues that the fact that someone needs something contributes at least the "standing presumption" that he or she should have it.

77. P. Corning, "The Biological Bases of Behavior," p. 339; also E. Ryle, "Genetic and Cultural Pools: Some Suggestions for a Unified Theory of Biological Evolution," *Human Ecology* 1, no. 3 (1973): 201–15.

78. A. Maslow, "A Theory of Human Motivation," *Psychological Review* 50 (1943): 370–96. See the related continua in J. Knutson, *The Human Basis of the Polity* (New York: Aldine, 1972), p. 253. Also J. Davies, *Human Nature in Politics* (New York: John Wiley, 1963) and his article, "The Priority of Human Needs and the Stages of Political Development," in Pennock and Chapman eds., *Human Nature*. Davies has subdivided the list into *substantive* needs (physical, social-affectional, self-esteem, and self-actualization) and instrumental ones (security, knowledge, and power). Corning would add the need for stimulation and goal-directed activity ("Human Nature Redivivus" in Pennock and Chapman, *Human Nature*, p. 49); Marx would have defined self-actualization more specifically as the need to work in a creative, unalienated way, where labor is not just a means to live but is in itself the "first necessity" of being. See his *Critique of the Gotha Programme* (Moscow: Foreign Languages Pub. House, 1947). Also R. Lane, *Political Thinking and Consciousness*: The Private Life of the Political Mind (Chicago: Markham, 1969), Ch. 2, "Human Needs, the Emerging Sources of Political Thought."

79. C. B. Macpherson, "Needs and Wants: An Ontological or Historical Problem," in R. Fitzgerald, ed., *Human Needs and Politics* (Elmsford, N.Y.: Pergamon Press, 1977). Note also K. Boulding, *Ecodynamics* (Beverly Hills: Sage, 1978), p. 21, "We learn not to learn much more than we are limited by biogentically induced barriers in the brain."

80. R. Fitzgerald, "Abraham Maslow's Hierarchy of Needs," in *Human Needs*, p. 50.

81. R. Young, "The Human Limits of Nature," in J. Benthall, ed., *The Limits of Human Nature* (London: Allen Lane, 1973).

82. Ibid., p. 241.

83. Ibid., p. 263.

84. T. Ferris, *The Red Limit* (London: Corgi, 1977), p. 142.

85. E. O. Wilson, *On Human Nature* (Cambridge: Harvard University Press, 1978), pp. 5, 167, 177. In the same vein (pp. 6–7):

> The challenge to science is to measure the tightness of the constraints caused by the programming, to find their source in the brain, and to decode their significance through the reconstruction of the evolutionary history of the mind. . . . Can the cultural evolution of higher ethical values gain a direction and momentum of its own and completely replace genetic evolution? I think not. The genes hold culture on a leash. The leash is very long, but inevitably values will be constrained in accordance with their effects on the human gene pool. The brain is a product of evolution. Human behaviour—like the deepest capacities for emotional response which drive and guide it—is the circuitous technique by which human genetic material has been and will be kept intact. Morality has no other demonstrable ultimate function.

86. Ibid., p. 199. See also R. Sperry, "In Search of Psyche," in F. G. Worden et al., eds., *The Neurosciences* (Cambridge: MIT Press, 1975), p. 430: "Science" he sees as "man's most important means for determining ultimate value and meaning . . . ," as the "source and arbiter of values and belief systems at the highest level . . . the final determinant of what is right and true, and the best authority available to the human brain for finding ultimate axioms and guideline beliefs to live by. . . ."

87. B. Parekh, "The Philosopher and the Polis in the Thought of Hannah Arendt" (Paper presented to the 11th World Congress of the International Political Science Association, August 1979).

88. C. Frankel, "Sociobiology and its Critics," *Commentary* 68, no. 1 (July 1979): 44.

89. Ibid., p. 46.

90. Plamenatz, *Man and Society,* vol. II, pp. 321–2.

91. I. Berlin, "The Originality of Machiavelli" in *Against the Current* (New York: The Viking Press, 1980).

92. R. Unger, *Law in Modern Society*: Toward a Criticism of Social Theory (N.Y.: Free Press, 1976), p. 42.

93. See A. Caplan, "In What Ways are Recent Developments in Biology and Sociobiology Relevant to Ethics?" *Perspectives in Biology and Medicine*, Summer 1978, p. 528.

94. R. McShea, "Biology and Ethics," *Ethics* 88 (1978): 149, and "Human Nature Theory and Political Philosophy," *American Journal of Political Science* 22, no. 3 (August 1978): 657–677.

95. J. Burrow, *Evolution and Society*: A Study in Victorian Social Theory (Cambridge: Cambridge University Press, 1966); M. Midgley, *Beast and Man*: The Roots of Human Nature (N.Y.: Cornell University Press, 1978), pp. 25–6, Ch. 9.

96. Wilson, *On Human Nature,* p. 19.

97. Midgley, *Beast and Man,* pp. 188–9.

2

Fraternity: Are We Naturally Selfish or Not?

"In prose," Orwell once said,

> the worst thing one can do with words is to surrender to them. When you think of a concrete object, you think wordlessly, and then, if you want to describe the thing you have been visualizing you probably hunt about till you find the exact words that seem to fit. When you think of something abstract you are more inclined to use words from the start, and unless you make a conscious effort to prevent it, the existing dialect will come rushing in and do the job for you, at the expense of blurring or even changing your meaning.[1]

THE SEMANTICS OF FRATERNITY

What might we make of *fraternity*? A "company of common interests," perhaps, which is the way one dictionary puts it? Or "any group whose members enjoy close and brotherly relations"? These are "words," but they are words that give us—depending of course upon our personal experience and associations—some rudimentary feeling for the concept at work. We can imagine a group of like-minded people who strive toward a goal they all share. We can imagine the sense of support that each gives the other in doing so. And we can think of examples of organizations and of people who have behaved like this, and we can contrast them with other cases where they have not. What we refer to is still difficult to visualize as a "thing," which is unsatisfactory since it suggests we will have to hide behind half-meanings and fuzzy formulations as Orwell says. We put up with this, however, if only because abstract concepts are necessary and useful; if only because our actual experience of what they try to describe is more compelling than the failure to find unambiguous references for them in the real world.

The problem of language will always remain, as will its capacity to both mislead and inform. When we choose words that help defend the indefensible; when our euphemisms and cant phrases are used to suck the sting out of what we have to say, then confusion follows and the truth becomes that much more obscure. Which is not to say that lies cannot serve a constructive purpose, and that is the paradox. As Steiner points out:

> The genius of language for planned counterfactuality is . . . overwhelmingly positive and creative. . . . Man's sensibility endures and transcends the brevity, the haphazard ravages, the physiological programming of individual life because the semantically coded responses of the mind are constantly broader, freer, more inventive than the demands and stimulus of the material fact. . . . Metaphysics, religion, ethics, knowledge—all derive from man's will to art, to lies, from his flight before truth. . . . At every level, from brute camouflage to poetic vision, the linguistic capacity to conceal, misinform, leave ambiguous, hypothesize, invent is indispensable to the equilibrium of human consciousness and the development of man in society.[2]

With this prologue, let us proceed. When we use the word fraternity, we signify human relationships analogous to the nurturing ones we find within the family, to all the sharing and caring and filial affection that kin loyalty is supposed to involve. Fraternity implies a feeling of affinity. It emphasizes those qualities we *share* with other people rather than those we do not. When we call something by this name, we are trying to give some sense of what is felt to be a natural human propensity for society and for dependence on others; a preference for intimacy, that is, rather than isolation. It is an appeal to the communitarian impulse at large. As such, true fraternity may only be possible in small groups, though we still find claims for an attenuated form of it in bigger human aggregates like the nation, and in its application to humankind as a whole (the so-called "brotherhood of man").

Fraternity is a description, then, of particular emotions that attend particular sorts of human interaction. The range and intensity of those emotions is not just intuitive; they are also taught. Human societies display wide differences not only in the number of people fraternal bodies include but also in the sort of rights, roles, and duties they confer and in the intensity of members' feelings about their entitlements and obligations. These differences are culturally acquired. The "natural" inclination to feel like this (plus the particular propensity, Tiger argues, for males to bond in fraternal association)[3] is not. It is inherited, and many would say that it is therefore very valuable and would recommend more of it for every form of society. By inculcating greater respect for fraternal feelings, it is claimed, other human values like liberty, equality, and happiness will be enhanced, too, and the impoverishing effects of modern individualism reduced. Description becomes prescription, as those who see the worth of the requisite emotions strive to keep them alive.

FRATERNITY AND MODERN SOCIETY

The massed character of industrial society makes fraternal feelings particularly difficult to sustain, however. The remoteness of modernist governments tends to alienate client populations rather than consolidate them. "Even if philosophers were kings, they might know 'man' but they would not know *me*,"[4] a fact that affects every other value contemporary polities espouse. *Justice* becomes ever more impersonal and procedural; rights become the progressively more remote application (or evasion) of written codes. And yet, "the highest justice demands the greatest sharing of value and the deepest mutual knowledge; it demands fraternity."[5] *Human* rights require no less too.

The formal liberal reflex is to opt in the first instance for ordered consensus, for that self-regulating system of pluralistic politics that the liberal hopes will do least harm. To the extent that this rather mechanical notion overlooks the amount of fraternity that does in fact exist in the world, particularly in this instance among the groups of those who rule, it radically misleads. The sort of bourgeois class cohesion Marxists talk about when they describe what goes on both within states and between them has much of the same sense of shared origins and interests and outlooks that fraternity talk involves. For the majority in modern states who must be sold (sometimes quite literally) upon surrogates like nationalism to compensate for their lack of communitarian supports, we find the signal failure, however, to provide for what seems to be a fundamental human need.

I argued in chapter 1 that the scientific-industrial culture that arose first in Europe has now become an important concern of practically all the world's elites. The value preferences of this culture are both intellectual and moral, the latter being fixed primarily upon the doctrines of social justice and human rights. When we look at the documents drawn up in eighteenth-century Europe and America to defend commercial elites against domestic and imperial monarchs, we find a direct challenge to the latter's right to absolute rule. Bourgeois opposition focused on the defense of freedom and property as well as the right to life. Though the protagonists commonly appealed to a sense of fraternity in holding their side together, they cast their defense in terms of the individual entitlements that no secular authority (or religious one, for that matter) was supposed to be able morally to deny. In place of a sense of society as a community, as an organic whole, they put the case for personal responsibility and the importance of individual initiative and the protection of private possessions.

It was notions of this kind, among others, that the administrators of the European empires carried around the world. One of the key aspects of the sort of consciousness thus encouraged was the belief in human autonomy and the concept of society thus favored was one that implied a prevalent sense of mutual enmity, of a people held together by no more than reciprocal need, an aggregate, that is, of discrete selves, not more than their mere sum, and sustained only by the interests and the will of its clientele. We belong to such a society, they thought, because we get things that way we otherwise could not, and it is we, rather than the group as such, that is somehow the more basic and the more "real"phenomenon. All of which stood in stark contrast to the collectivist concepts of many of the traditional peoples they encountered, for whom the group *did* have a kind of life of its own (at least, it *felt* like that), with values (usually embodied in elaborate myths) that were independent of those of any individual member.[6] This did not prevent colonial dissidents buying the European package and selling it back again, since the deal was one way of pointing up the hypocrisy involved on the part of those who ruled them and who enforced their subject status.

Where the populace in the metropolitan powers won a degree of political freedom and some limited capacity to hold their leaders accountable, they began, however tenuously, to argue for public welfare policies that would improve their standards of living. The distinction between a civil and a social domain became more confused. Socialists sought to obliterate it altogether. The emphasis in the ranking of rights began to shift from the liberal guarantee of self-defense (the individual as protected against the rulers of the state and their power to use the people to their own ends) to that of the common good and of socioeconomic development (the individual as entitled, where resources might permit, some minimal measure of life's supports and opportunities). Initially espoused as a moral shield behind which an expanding bourgeoisie could advance its claims for a greater share of political power and enhanced personal competence, the doctrine was revised to accommodate rights that required not just civil restraint but ever broader governmental intervention in the name of the general good. Every time we dichotomize rights as *individual* versus *social*, we tell this kind of historical tale.

INDIVIDUALISM AND COLLECTIVISM

The analytic distinction is actually more subtle again, since individual rights only make sense in social terms. Personal self-actualization, for example, which many regard as the most profound of the human freedoms, is usually realized in a social setting. Meditating monks may find deep meanings in a mountain cave, but can they be seen as exercising a *right* except in terms of their withdrawal from the world? Burns is surely wrong to go so far as to argue that "the concept of right against society, or a right which is not intrinsically connected with the social structure which creates and protects it, is self-contradictory."[7] This is true only of Robinson Crusoe rights, that lie *outside* society. If there are such things, it is worth remembering that even the most individual rights have a specific social reference, which leads to the larger argument that we are only truly ourselves when we engage the interest of other people. Individualism and collectivism are *both* aspects of our humanity: each contains part of the other and is a component of the whole. The dichotomy is not a dichotomy at all, but a continuum, allowing differing emphases but no distinction of absolute degree.

Differing emphases remain important nonetheless. An ostensibly pluralist regime like that of the United States, for example, defends the precedence placed upon personal integrity, freedom of speech, thought, and movement, and equality before laws that are fairly and impartially applied: the civil and political rights so called. The Soviets, on the other hand, give priority to such principles as those of full employment, the right to work, to be housed, and to be healed and educated.[8] This is in line with their general assertion that to make civil and political rights possible we must see tangible progress, both qualitative and quantitative, in social and economic development first. And their assertion is a convincing one, as many a starving voter might testify. (It remains true that if we reverse the traditional liberal preference and place social and economic rights prior to political and civil ones, we then depend on the good faith of governing groups to use their power in the public interest. Without the sanctions civil freedoms allow, those who rule all too easily come to abuse the privilege. They invariably come to claim not *privilege* but a governing *right*, and, without public protection of the capacity for private censure, autocratic repression is the rule. A totalitarian order can nominate foreign foes to distract from domestic distress: "Either totalitarian states march inexorably toward war or they change into simple tyrannies and bureaucratic oligarchies. They have no answer to the privatizing logic of modernity."[9] But, then, neither do the class-ridden polities of the liberal capitalist West.)

The Soviet argument for social and economic rights over and above civil and political ones is also an argument for *social justice*. It is an argument for the moral benefits that come from treating equally those we find in comparable circumstances and calling for good reasons for treating people differently where the differences seem to us arbitrary in terms of human need, merit, desert, capacity, or prior contract. Concepts of social justice imply explicit definitions of the good society, which are predicated in turn upon prior ideas about human nature. Thus we find the relative emphasis the Soviets accord a collectivist approach buttressed by an appropriate image of the sort of creatures we happen to be:

While the demand for comradely mutual assistance may bring to mind the Christian imperative to love one's neighbor . . . Marxist-Leninist commentators claim . . . [it] as a distinctive socialist trait and oppose the slogan "one for all and all for one" . . . to the slogan which for them typifies the egoistic, individualistic human relations in the capitalist world: "man is a wolf to man."[10]

Unfair to wolves, in fact, but the American ethic of human competition certainly has something of a predatory quality, built as it is upon an exaggerated reverence for personal achievement and self-help.

The dichotomy is crude, and neither regime fits the extreme. American society, for example, has marked fraternal as well as atomistic characteristics. Alexis de Tocqueville, reflecting upon his experience in the United States, declared: "The most natural privilege of man next to the right of acting for himself is that of combining his exertions with those of his fellow creatures and of acting in common with them. . . . In no country in the world has the principle of association been more successfully used or applied to a greater multitude of objects. . . ."[11] The results have been mixed, and it is commonly argued that the sustained growth of a military-commercial-administrative conclave at the heart of the American state has successfully emasculated any opportunity there may once have been to secure interests other than those serving capitalist enterprise and a ruling class. Be that as it may, the ideology of personal competence persists and, in theory at least, an individualistic ethic is a pluralistic one in the sense that it does not defend any one definition of the human condition. The American sense of association depends in turn upon one of (white, male) equality, which suggests a concept of (human) nature as self-aggrandizing, acquisitive, selfish, and asocial—and this despite much domestic practice to the contrary, and despite many manifest examples of American charity and good works.

The Soviet view, by contrast, endorses Marx's concept of the "human essence" as "not an abstraction inherent in each particular individual . . . [but] the totality of social relations."[12] The right relation of each to each, its theorists argue, is one of "union, harmony, brotherhood, common sharing, [and] mutual help."[13] Marx considered human nature to be creatively conscious and active, qualities that are realized only in society. In his earlier work in particular he saw this as presupposing an innate empathy for others; hence, perhaps, the human capacity for altruism (though as Marx was well aware a social *relationship* does not as such imply social *benevolence*). Though he felt that patterns of economic production define the sort of awareness possible at any particular point in time, plus the specific range of human needs, Marx believed that historical progress would ultimately liberate humankind from all such constraints and allow the material consolidation of communism and hence of every individual, as truly free. Humanity's potential for cooperation and communality would finally be able to take effect. Liberated from the malevolent influence of bourgeois competitiveness, each would give what he or she could afford, taking in turn only necessities.

The moral assessments the Soviets make of the human enterprise depend upon this vision and the extent to which action promotes or hinders the process of realizing it. The Communist Party and its policies are seen to be the political means of attaining communism, but it remains much debated (rather more outside the country than within it) whether this is in fact what is being achieved, or whether totalitarian rule, however well-intended, has not subverted socialist intent and the ideal of socioeconomic and political transcendence as Marxists typically espouse it. In reality, hierarchy prevails in Soviet society, too, and critics have argued that the advent of a bureaucratic party-class, plus increasing opportunities for individual aggrandizement, will probably preclude further progress toward the sort of collective utopia Marx envisaged where unfettered human beings fulfill their diverse capacities under conditions of socioeconomic plenty and peace. Again, however, it is the ethos I am interested in, and though I have drawn these pictures in broad strokes, caricature helps to make more vivid their basic points of view and the differences that lie between them. It is the differences that are important here since so much follows from them in terms of what is seen to be valuable, what gets taught, the sort of politics and economics that is practiced, and how social life proceeds in each place.[15]

Though I have used a contemporary example, the individualist/collectivist distinction is not a novel one. In the Western tradition, at least, the question of where to locate the individual with respect to the larger society of which he or she is a part recurs throughout. As a male member of the ancient polis, for example, the slave-owning Greek was on highly personal terms with civic authority. The difference between Sparta and Athens was marked—in the former, like so many traditional societies, they "believed that fraternity can be taught,"[16] while those in the latter relied more on the educative capacity of participation itself. The sense of a collective ethos was ostensibly very strong in both, however, and the line between a public and a private realm was difficult to discern.

The perspective of a corresponding member of the Roman Empire, as one might expect, was much more expansive, the closer horizons of the city-state giving way to the cosmopolitan vistas of those with a world to run. This led to a more general sense of human commonality and at the same time to a more particular emphasis upon personal rights, dues, and enjoyments. The passing of this empire left the majority of Europeans subject to a mixed jurisdiction, which included that of the Catholic Church and of whatever combination of secular rulers could win local predominance. Authority was dispersed between overlapping religious, feudal, and municipal domains, and ties of "varying strength, and none clearly political, attached a man to his guild, city, abbey, manor, baron, king and pope."[17] This highly diverse system was simplified somewhat after the Reformation by the bid for enhanced command on the part of royal elites. When challenged, the overarching claims of the Church were not sustained, and, as the growth of a European commercial culture began to displace the feudal nobles and the municipal corporations, it became possible to envisage centralized regimes wielding sovereign power. Carried to its philosophical conclusion by Thomas Hobbes, we find the idea of citizens contracting a single civic personality (either a monarch or an assembly—Hobbes allowed for either) sufficiently powerful to curb competition and secure order and peace. This required a highly individualistic conception of human motives. (In measuring the Church by what it could deliver to each believing soul, critical religious thinkers also articulated the general sense that a society had to be built; it did not just happen. There were, moreover, those who sought to defend the primacy of the spiritual domain from the inroads of skepticism and secularism and who promoted a right to rebel. This defense quickly moved beyond the original terms of the debate to underpin personalized claims for moral autonomy.)

Across the hall from the cartoon of human nature that Hobbes had drawn, Locke put his picture of people as inherently fraternal. Yet, the doctrine of natural rights that he espoused only reinforced the abiding doctrine of individualism. The desire of eighteenth- and nineteenth-century utilitarians like Bentham to secure the greatest happiness for the greatest number worked the same way, though their felicific principle could also be used, as it was, in fact, to argue the case for collective measures against the appalling working and living conditions that newly proletarianized populations had to endure as bourgeois entrepreneurs built up their industries and towns. The logical end point of *this* sort of ethic was the Hegelian belief in the state as something divine, and the will of any individual as finding its fullest expression only in that of the group. This was the Greek ideal of civic fraternity with a difference, and under the mass conditions of the modern day it proved to be pernicious in the extreme.

As we watch these two doctrines weaving in and out of the historical narrative, there are common positions that recur. Aristocrats, for example, almost always believe "that the distribution of ability and morality is steeply pyramidal and tends to perpetuate itself by heredity." As a result, they tend to argue that fraternal feelings cannot be relied upon to check our self-seeking tendencies, ". . . [while] a relatively small and intelligent part of the whole . . . can. . . ."[18] Those not impressed by aristocratic capacities for sustained public service, however well-intentioned the aristocrats themselves might be, look to ways of securing a civil right to dissent.

HUMAN NATURE: SELFISH OR SOCIAL?

The question then occurs: given what seems to be an irreducible contrast between such basic human qualities, how selfish or how social *are* we? What empirical evidence is there that might suggest one conception or the other as the more significant cause of how we behave? And if both attributes are characteristic ones, as common sense suggests, then how are they combined? In other words, are we fundamentally egoistic or altruistic? Do we serve ourselves first, or do we prefer to promote the good of others even if it means some personal sacrifice along the way? And if both together, then when and in what proportions and under what circumstances and to what effect?

The possible conclusions can be quite bizarre: "A hydrogen bomb," as Bigelow reminds us, "is an example of mankind's enormous capacity for friendly cooperation." And so it is, which gives some idea of the complexity of the phenomena with which we have to deal. Such puzzles only reflect the original dichotomy, however. At the heart of the ethic of individualism and the concept of competition upon which it is based lies the assumption that primarily we are egoists and hence *ought* to be so; while at the heart of the ethic of collectivism and the concomitant concept of mutual aid lies the assumption that primarily we are and hence *ought* to be altruistic.

The interesting point for our present purpose is that the central theoretical problem (as a leading exponent puts it) of the emerging scientific discipline of *sociobiology* (being the "systematic study of the biological basis of all social behavior") bears directly upon this debate. "How can altruism", Wilson asks, "which by definition reduces personal fitness, possibly evolve by natural selection?"[20] How can a pattern of behavior, genetically orchestrated not to serve the self, be inherited? Should it not have disappeared by now? If natural selection works in the way Darwin and those who have refined his theory describe, then would not the ruthless, the malicious, the egoistic come to prevail, and ought not such predilections spread through the breeding population as each generation produces progeny progressively less altruistic and more selfish than its own? And yet, as has long been recognized, evidence of altruism, both "natural" and self-consciously motivated, abounds. (As Midgely argues: "A consistently egoistic species would be either solitary or extinct. . . ."[21]) How indeed could a species possibly have evolved "which did what Hobbes supposed, and became calculating before becoming social?"[22] Hence Kropotkin's conviction that society is based upon an instinct for human solidarity, for the sense that the happiness of each flows from the happiness of all, and that the rights of Anyman are equal to one's own.

The *sociobiological* answer to the question is "kinship: if the genes causing the altruism are shared by two organisms because of common descent, and if the altruistic act by one organism increases the joint contribution of these genes to the next generation, the propensity for altruism will spread through the gene pool."[23] If a parent dies defending two or more children who then survive, the predisposition to self-sacrifice of this sort, which is presumed part of the genetic endowment (and it ought, by rights, to be demonstrated in each case that particular sorts of behavior actually *do* have a specifiable genetic basis) will persist; while any predispositions passed on by a cowardly parent, whose children consequently do not survive, will not. (The more remote the genetic connection between the one making the sacrifice and those who continue to live, the more of the latter will need to be held from harm if the altruistic genes are to be carried down.)

THE GENETICS OF ALTRUISM

Let us look at this apparent paradox in more detail. To begin with, it seems generally agreed among sociobiologists that, while the principal unit of *survival* and of evolutionary change is the breeding *population*, the principal unit of *selection* is the *individual*. While *group* selection (where adaptive pressure operates on several individuals as a unit) does seem possible, its significance is held to be controversial at best, and the conditions under which it might naturally occur are considered to be very limited indeed.[24] The advantages of extended altruism for the individual human being (in terms of reproductive advantage) seem so limited to many sociobiologists that they think it not unreasonable to expect everyone to behave as if free to do "not whatever does not interfere with the freedom of others, but whatever will indeed interfere with the freedom of others without interfering with his [sic] own—whatever, in other words, has a better than average chance of bringing net gain, or whatever will bring the largest net gain to himself, his mate and his offspring—especially his offspring."[25] Action, they argue, that benefits the society at reproductive cost to the individual who belongs to that society is only likely to persist and develop under rather special circumstances. Because of the *disadvantages* of altruism, those who behave in this way tend to lose out to those who do not. Thus individual opportunism is the order of the day, and cultural creeds promoting human solidarity fly in the face of immediate pressures to breed and the sort of competition this promotes.

How can we reconcile such a conclusion with the human record of living in groups and societies, of extensive communal cooperation? What advantages do individuals perceive in the group as a way of sustaining self, particularly where the interests of the individual can be shown to conflict with those of his or her confreres?

In the case of human beings, most environmentally derived factors, like the greater efficiency of group defense against predators or of group-based food-gathering procedures, are not relevant. They have long been transcended by our capacity for socialization, for learning symbolic identities that reach beyond kith, kin, local culture, and [which is the key] by a "new predator," that is, the "groups and coalitions within . . . [our] own species."[26] This latter development, it is claimed, may have had much more to do than is generally supposed with the human evolution of sociality, intelligence, and culture, as well as accounting for the extermination of the closest relatives of man and even, perhaps, for the social structures of the great apes that still survive.

When we come to human beings, in other words, who war so much among themselves and who tend, as a direct result, to prize cooperation and allegiance, loyalty, and conformity, we find a great susceptibility to group effects. Thus Bigelow argues the case of "cooperation-for-conflict"—the thesis that "the ability to learn cooperation was actually favored by the selective force of warfare." Hence the argument that the " 'highest' human qualities . . . [have been] demanded by the 'lowest' . . .", and the "powerful *biological* reason," it is said, "for having neighbors: [since] this was the most effective defense against the *hatred* of foreigners."[27] And the suggestion Wilson makes that indoctrinability exists partly perhaps because the self-denying willingness to die in battle favors *group* survival, even though the consequences are lethal for the individuals who carry the genes (which is the "extreme possibility" where the group *is* the unit of selection. He does add *self*-interest as a cause for conformity, and particularly so when the benefits that accrue from such behavior outweigh the disadvantages of competition. This is an individual level hypothesis. There is of course the possibility that the two also reinforce each other[28] or that the whole case is misconceived, and the conceptual distance between the "differential reproduction of genes" and how we understand Wall Street,[29] for example, or the proceedings of the Praesidium of the Supreme Soviet, is greater than biologically inclined theorists of human behavior like to allow. The very term *altruism* is somewhat "unfortunate, both because it implies a cognitive process that may well be uniquely human and because any of the [posited] evolutionary mechanisms [group selection, kin selection, reciprocity, and parental manipulation] involve benefits to the altruist genes that necessarily exceed the cost; accordingly, they are all selfish in the long run."[30] To use the same term to describe "instinctive" behavior in animals and that of human beings who are aware, however dimly, of the nature of death and what they are doing would seem to stretch the meaning of this one concept rather too far.)

From an *interactionist* point of view, if group living evolved because it was advantageous in some way in terms of an individual's capacity to reproduce, but could only be made to work by the choice of norms and values that served in part at least to circumscribe (reproductive) competition in favor of mutual aid, then it is the *relationship* between the individual and the group that is important rather than the attempt to establish the preponderance of the one over the other. While particular cultural habits may cause the selection of specific genetic predispositions, it is the accidental incidence (or absence) of specific genetic predispositions that may have prompted divers societies to adopt whatever their distinctive customs are in the first place! The process can work both ways at once. In this view the sociobiological view of altruism appears to be a reductionist one, eliminating, as Wilson himself points out, most of any sense of good will by depicting it as merely another mechanism for replicating DNA. "Spirituality" becomes "just one more Darwinian enabling device"[31]

This does not trump the argument though. In organizing ourselves socially we can actively *teach* altruism, plus enough of a sense of reciprocity to mitigate our selfishness and our capacity for malice and spite. We can if we choose use our belief systems to do so, and we can consciously detach these teachings from what sociobiologists see as our more basic drives. The human capacity for this sort of thing is large, and whatever limits genetic competition sets upon our propensity for self-sacrifice, or for social cooperation and organization, can seem as a consequence so subtle and imprecise as to be almost imperceptible.

Human beings are preoccupied, what is more, with many other activities than that of reproducing themselves, and surviving in order to reproduce, which is all that an evolutionary viewpoint strictly allows. We can see this when we examine animal behavior which is more clearly the product of biological urges. The actions of individual members of animal societies can be construed much more readily in terms of the maximization of inclusive fitness—each member doing as best it can on its own behalf. (When we talk about people in this way, the idea of selfishness becomes slightly absurd: "If someone said . . . 'he thinks of nothing but how many descendants he will have in five centuries time,' we could hardly fail to reply, 'But why do you call that *selfish*? You surely mean that he is either (1) clannish or (2) crazy.' "[32])

And yet, who except the most throughgoing Lockean or existentialist or behaviorist perhaps would claim that natural inclinations do not exist for humankind—so refractory and so repressible in turn? That there are things we "like" doing and feeling such as eating and sleeping, making love, and receiving esteem that have distinct evolutionary advantages and suggest a naturally selected source. As such these things are manifest in the progressive development of the growing child and the organizing principles of language and moral conduct. They denote innate influential behavioral sequences in all of us. And if altruism does have a genetic basis, however incomplete, then should we not find it more among immediate family than those further removed? This does not exclude other, nongenetic determinants. It means only that we must work out in each particular case what seems the more important motivating force.

In other words, the sociobiological sense lingers that we *have* been selected to behave in altruistic ways toward close relatives; that we *will* tend to risk less and less for those more remote from us in the pattern of sociogenetic life; and that, given our likely evolutionary history as hunters and gatherers, living in small bands, such an outcome is hardly a surprise. *Reciprocal* altruism[33]—I help you now (not necessarily at risk to life or limb) if you can say you will help me later—is said to be effective at greater social distances, but as such it is also a system more open to abuse. (As Hardin argues, *coupled egoism* may often be the better term.)[34] Those who do not reciprocate and who cheat or dissimulate (accepting help now but *not* giving it later) might be expected to win an advantage in the long run and hence to prevail (a phenomenon that works between *groups* as well as between *individuals*), however, evolution may be assumed to have taken place in the capacity to recognize such behavior too, and in the capacity to resist it. Friendship, moralistic aggression (indignation), guilt, and sympathy can be construed as a result of adaptive behavior patterns that control and moderate mutual altruism. Each allows in turn for the false representation of the real thing, which has led to adaptive detection devices like the capacity for suspicion and for assessing the motives of those we confront, their trustworthiness and their potential for hypocrisy. With the possibility for further false representation, we sink into a cognitive morass, which may indeed have been one source, it is said, of the selective pressure that so rapidly enhanced the mental skills of early man.

The analyst referred to here does admit that there is "no direct evidence regarding the degree of reciprocal altruism practical during human evolution nor its genetic basis today. . . ." Given the "universal and nearly daily practice of genetic altruism among humans," however, he argues that it is "reasonable to assume that it has been an important factor in recent human evolution and that the underlying emotional dispositions affecting altruistic behavior have important genetic components."[35] Others remain agnostic, concluding that "the fact that man acts altruistically does not mean that he is altruistic."[36] And as has already been indicated, even the most altruistic act can usually be given a selfish construction of some sort. The kamikaze pilot gratifies his selfish urge for self-actualization, though in terms of the biological consequences he has in fact been altruistic (by denying himself the chance to breed). Hebb says that truly empathetic altruism *has* been observed in animals, and this casts doubt on the assumption that unlearned motives in humankind are biologically self-regarding and that altruism (and generosity) have to be taught.[37] Krebs, however, points out the problems involved in excluding reinforcement as a causal factor (like the rewards offered for helping and the punishment given for not) and in discriminating between *cooperation* (where the benefits are mutual) and *altruism* (where, at least in the short run, there are none).

The question of discriminating between various sorts of altruism is indeed a vexed one. It is possible to depict *all* human motives, including altruism, as selfish and the consequence of individual calculation. And if we relax the definitions far enough, then of course they are. Thus "if you say 'I obey only egoistic impulses,' I cannot prove you wrong. . . ."[38] Certainly some amount of egoism is a necessary defense against those who would deceive us, but to depict altruism as *nothing but* a calculated response

not only deprives us of our actual virtues; it credits us with others we do not have, at least in the necessary degree: a steady, unfailing prudence, . . . a stern intellectual honesty and consistency, a brisk readiness to act on extremely remote probabilities, such as we never

actually see. (Since these really are important virtues, of which we are partly capable, the
appeal of Egoism lies partly in celebrating them, as well as in attacking hypocrisy).[39]

A world of only egoists would be a non-society of the vicious and the morally
depraved, as studies of concentration camps and severely impoverished cultural
environments have shown. Altruistic motives are often abused by others to their
own advantage; selfish people do exploit those more generous than themselves,
but such abuse would not be possible if the real thing did not exist. We are ever
learning ways to distinguish the two, and the process of "growing up" is in part
a process of "gradually becoming aware of the quid pro quos of the world—the
obvious ones first, the less obvious ones later. Different people grow up at
different speeds. Some seem hardly to mature at all; some of the cleverest of
these write books on ethics."[40]

Altruism would appear to be a real human *motive* then, a fact that is clear when
we contrast ourselves with species that act seemingly unself-consciously in this
way, as well as those that do not. Yet the sort of concern that makes altruism
possible, regardless of the particular shape it takes or its actual strength, must
have come from somewhere and the fact that it conferred a selective advantage
on human populations in the past is as likely an explanation as any. Genetic
mediators, Wilson argues, "drive and guide" our sense of what is good and bad,
right and wrong.[41] He remains firmly convinced that kin selection *counts* and that
the "most elaborate forms of social organization, despite their outward appearance, serve ultimately as the vehicles of individual welfare."[42] Can we ever
assume genetic *preponderance,* however, when "genes are not little men . . .
[they] do not make decisions, so they cannot take advice. . . . For the same
reason, they can no more have a morality than they can play the trombone.
. . ."[43] Perhaps we should look more closely at the concept of "kin selection"
and at what the anthropologists have to say.

Sahlins asserts that human society is much more complex than Wilson
suggests. Taking the argument about familial defense, he points out that blood
ties, for example, are *not* the only way in which people reckon kin. This being
so, the sociobiological endorsement of kin selection and of individualism looks
much less convincing. The ethnographic record offers "no system of human
kinship relations" in fact, ". . . in accord with the genetic coefficients of
relationship as known to sociobiologists,"[44] and since it is typically "the
culturally constituted kinship relations" that "govern the real processes of
cooperation in production, property, mutual aid, and marital exchange, the
human systems ordering reproductive success have an entirely different calculus
than that predicted by kin selection and, sequitur est, by an egotistically
conceived natural selection." Indeed, one can say, and Sahlins would, that
sociobiologists have it the wrong way around: "Human reproduction is engaged
as the means for the persistence of cooperative social orders," he argues, "not

the social order the means by which individuals facilitate their own reproduction."[45] Where do the sociobiologists go wrong? Their distortions and errors are predictable enough, Sahlins concludes, when we consider that the whole project is actually a mirror trick, assuming one particular concept of human nature, imposing it upon the biology of behavior, and then reimposing it back upon "man." Sociobiology contributes in this way to the "final translation of natural selection into social exploitation";[46] the emphasis on individual selection having led to the concept of egoism and thence to competition, to self-maximization, and, finally, to the use and abuse of others for selfish ends. The imagery that sociobiologists use is steeped in the language of utilitarian economics and the "possessive individualism" of market capitalism. Thus, he says, the arguments for *reciprocal* altruism project a sentiment like moral aggression onto the human species as a whole despite ethnographic evidence that patterns of behavior like this depend upon cultural milieu. In doing so sociobiology reflects the "economics of petty commercial exchange,"[47] reducing selection to a simple calculus of profit and loss, and reducing the reproduction of people to the reproduction of commodities. It construes society as the outcome of rational actors striving to meet their needs, an approach ultimately based upon assumptions about our brutish origins and the persistence of the savage within. "What is inscribed in the theory of sociobiology," Sahlins concludes, "is the entrenched ideology of Western society: the assurance of its naturalness, and the claim of its inevitability."[48]

Sociobiologists remain largely oblivious to this sort of critique. Their own general rules, they say, are as fair and objective an analysis of what holds in human society as it is possible to make, and their endorsement of human individualism and of our preference for pursuing enlightened self-interest remains prime. Trivers, for example, argues that "no concept of group advantage is necessary to explain the function of human altruistic behavior, and though by aiding the group the individual may aid self, sociobiologically at least the impulse is more likely to be a particular rather than a general one."[49] All of which is *consistent* with the findings of behavior genetics, but is it *sufficient* to explain human values and human action?

What Trivers and the rest cannot fully account for are culturally mediated expressions of empathy used to override their general rules. Altruistic behavior can be socioculturally advantageous for group survival, with no *innate* component to it except a *permissive* one. Nepotism (and the like) may assert itself with tireless frequency, as sociobiologists affirm. Hence the Ten Commandments, the various codifications of human rights, the imperatives of socialist reciprocity, and moral preoccupations with temptation and sin—all attempts to contain and civilize our primeval antisocial impulses.[50] The effort of imagination required to feel altruistic may well be greater the more remote the human relationship between the people involved. As circumstances grow more extreme, our altruistic range may well restrict itself to kin, and ultimately familial defense. None of these effects are incontrovertible, however, and humankind has powerful facilities for their contravention. Sociobiologists close the argument (to their own advantage) when it is said that evolution may have produced in people the propensity to suppress their sense of selfishness the better to further it; that selection has consistently favored the human capacity for ignorance in this respect.[51] When we meet circular logic of this sort, then we do well to look to the fundamental premises. In other words, is "selection" sufficient to explain the sort of behavior involved? As I have argued earlier, it is not.

THE SIGNIFICANCE OF CULTURE

What then may we conclude? For *innate* altruism to spread throughout a human group, rather particular conditions must obtain. We cannot *exclude* the concept of individuals preoccupied with self, and culture and moral systems as the mitigating influences that allow the intricate interdependencies that sustain society to persist. Nor can we ignore the idea of *innate* sociality of a more general sort that involves cooperation and loyalty and the prevalence of human genes of a group-functional kind. We must treat with caution the more extreme statements of either view, however, simply because humankind actively *creates* so much of the ecological niche within which we so far survive and to which we adapt, and the meanings we make of it, including those of "survival" and "adaptation" themselves.

This leads us back, in the end, to the qualities of our species that are seemingly unique. Animals may have cultures of their kind, and human beings may display biologically based behavioral traits, but differences remain which means that in terms of human survival the ethical distance between individualism and collectivism is an arena for political accommodation; it is not something we can legislate scientifically either way. Perhaps there are grooves in the mind down which particular patterns of behavior more readily run. Perhaps, as Wilson argues, ethical pluralism *is* innate. Perhaps Machiavelli was right—that there really is no rational way of deciding between competing value systems like Christianity and real-politik. I rather suspect, however, that this understates our capacity to choose, and our power to imagine and reflect. "Biology, while it is an absolutely necessary condition for culture," remains "equally and absolutely insufficient" and "completely unable to specify the cultural properties of human behavior or their variations from one group to another."[52] Since the "same human motives appear in the same forms, and fixed correspondence being lacking between the character of society and the human character, there can be no biological determinism."[53]

What, however, of the weaker link, that of biological *constraints* or *predispositions*? Even if we allow something of this sort, we must still account for the open character of the human endowment and the need to give reasons for what we do, and to engage in endless (but not pointless) arguments about consequence and result, means and ends. The principle of emergent properties applies at the level of human society, too, and while "biology is physics and chemistry plus natural selection," culture is "biology plus the symbolic faculty"[54]—and the last cannot be sociobiologized away. The argument that social evolution cannot transgress general laws of biological evolution[55] is simply wrong. They cannot be transgressed with *impunity*, but humankind is quite capable of choosing suicide in a self-referential way; indeed, our social interactions may yet render us extinct in exactly this fashion.

Recognition of the human commands of symbols[56] leads away from a view of values as an expression of innate properties (environmentally *conditioned* but not *determined*—human nature must include after all the *capacity* for a sense of good and bad and right and wrong), toward the concept of customs and conventions established by design. The attempt to naturalize ethics, to establish basic species-specific injunctions or an objective biological yardstick that lies beyond them, stumbles still over the human possession of an *extra*natural imagination. Thus, while biopolitics has wonderfully invigorated the debates between individualists and collectivists, it has no where near resolved them. And what in principle the most judicious combination of the two might be remains a highly contentious affair. Between the scientific ethics of the Soviet academies and the liberal relativists and existentialists of the West lies a large domain of mutual mis-construction and a real difference in understanding and emphasis. That is not a domain that an evolutionary perspective has yet dispelled.

A *command socialist* perspective is a group survivalist one. It places considerable emphasis upon material needs and the collective necessity to articulate and defend them. It is also more than this, since the Marxist vision of the truly "free" human being is also individualistic. The powerful expression it provides of what fulfillment might mean in humane, nonexploitative, nonalienated terms, where self-actualization occurs because individuals work in harmony with each other to the benefit not of some but of all, has a personal component as well as a communist one. A *liberal capitalist* approach, in emphasizing the authority and autonomy of the self, is a survivalist one in *individual* terms. Again, however, the social welfare legislation common in the West is an explicit acknowledgment of a communal duty to protect human well-being, on the utilitarian ground that right action secures to the greatest number the greatest good. This is sustained by an abiding sense that personal freedom may be optimized (rather than just maximized) in a solidarist as well as a particularist way.

Even in these more sophisticated forms, neither frame of reference alone is adequate to the moral tasks facing the present-day world, if only because humankind espouses more values than are encompassed within each one. And yet, if human values are to be consolidated on a global scale, there must be some accommodation between the two that is more than the nominal endorsement of social justice and bills of rights. "Marxists-Leninists reduce morality to social conformity, personal life to social life, and spiritual values to social values" in such a way as to "sacrifice . . . the present individual in the name of the moral superiority of future masses."[57] Liberal capitalists erect the bourgeois preference for freedom into a social ethic that successfully prevents a large mass of men and women from bettering themselves. It is the human hope that there is something superior to both; and it is the biopolitical conclusion that betterment is a possible, though not an inevitable, outcome. (It is useful to remember that while there has been "no single line of development with liberty, equality and fraternity on one side, and tyranny and oppression on the other. . . ." And though it is true that the idea of "a liberty, an equality and a brotherhood which would include every class, colour, and nation has been only the rare dream of isolated individuals, yet the universal element has persisted and grown in spite of partial interpretations and frequent betrayals.")[58]

Human nature is a varied and heterogeneous phenomenon. Bearing the "indelible stamp" of our "lowly" origins,[59] we include among these marks our propensities for both self-interest *and* for sharing our lives with others. "Looking at Man," Darwin said, "as a Naturalist would at any other Mammiferous animal, it may be concluded that he has parental, conjugal and social instincts. . . . These instincts consist of a feeling of love [and sympathy] or benevolence . . ."[60] though we must add malice, hate, and selfish indifference too. No one really expects in the name of some higher global good, rich peoples to aid the poor in altruistic ways that would require meaningful self-sacrifice (particularly so when we consider the extent to which the rich, whether capitalist or socialist, actually engineer poor-state dependence for their own exploitative ends). And yet, as organisms we are also sufficiently aware of the problem to allow of collective debate about ethical purpose, and about the renewal of socioeconomic and political means. We make *philosophy,* and we make it *together,* which is the point I would like to stress here. "It is not alone," Loren Eiseley said, "that I can reach out and receive within my head a hands-breadth replica of the far fields of the universe,"[61] a replica that brings to life, by the light of our understanding and awareness, an otherwise pointless expanse of inorganic, and hence insignificant, functions and forms.[62] Camus (whom Wilson also cites) celebrates in similar vein the "higher fidelity that negates the gods and raises rocks."[63]

The human mind, in attempting to comprehend the whole, renders it visible and meaningful; and this fact would seem to place a singular burden upon the value of creativity itself, serving the sense that as a cosmic faculty, perhaps unique, it ought to persist in its own right. Is persistence enough, however? Certainly not, and given the barest of essentials, that creative faculty alone will invariably ask for more. Nothing is guaranteed. To survive we must try to survive; we have to intend it. But what *of* our intentions; how good or bad might they be? They are never neutral, and that is the heart of the matter since leaders can build more than one mansion with the human material at their command.

Sociobiologists search for species-specific blueprints and beyond. They have a disconcerting habit of coming up with the obvious, declaring, for example, that "both . . . cultural integration and cultural differentiation . . . may be expected to be present in man's genetic make-up." And that "both compete with an even older and more deeply rooted genetic predisposition: toward non-conformity and innovation."[64] Ultimately, it is what we make of the project ourselves that counts. Through our studies in biopolitics, we come to appreciate just how true it is that the quality of our trying determines the quality of our lives.[65]

Why try, though? We still need a purpose, and preferably one, as Polanyi put it, that "bears on eternity." Perhaps that is where science and philosophy, truth and meaning, ultimately converge, since, as he says, truth itself does that, and so do our ideals, "and this might be enough. . . ."[66]

NOTES

1. G. Orwell, "Politics and the English Language," in M. Stein et al., *Identity and Anxiety* (Glencoe, Ill.: Free Press, 1960), p. 318.
2. G. Steiner, *After Babel* (Oxford: Oxford University Press, 1975), pp. 226–8.
3. L. Tiger, *Men in Groups* (London: Nelson, 1969), p. 60: "Male bonding I see as the spinal column of a community, in this sense: from a hierarchical linkage of significant males, communities derive their intra-dependence, their structure, their social coherence, and in good part their continuity. . . ."
4. W. McWilliams, *The Idea of Fraternity in America* (Berkeley: University of California Press, 1973), pp. 18, 73.
5. Ibid.
6. R. Unger, *Knowledge and Politics* (New York: Free Press, 1975), pp. 81–3.
7. J. Burns, "The Rights of Man Since the Reformation: An Historical Survey," in F. Vallant, ed., *An Introduction to the Study of Human Rights* (London: Europa Publications, 1970), p. 28.
8. For clear examples of a contemporary kind, see the Department of State *Bulletin*, vol. 74, no. 1978 (May 1977)—the speeches by Secretary of State Cyrus Vance and President Carter; the contrasting order is obvious from the section on "The State and the Individual" in the Soviet Constitution of 1977. See also E. Lazlo, ed., *Goals for Mankind* (London: Hutchinson, 1977), Ch. 18.
9. McWilliams, *Idea of Fraternity*, p. 68.
10. R. T. De George, *Soviet Ethics and Morality* (Ann Arbor: University of Michigan Press, 1969), p. 93. Also V. Kubálková, "Moral Precepts of Contemporary Soviet Politics," in R. Pettman, ed., *Moral Claims in World Affairs* (London: Croom Helm, 1979).

54   Biopolitics and International Values

11. A. de Tocqueville, *Democracy in America* (New York: Alfred Knopf, 1953), Vol. 1, pp. 191, 195–6.
12. This is the much quoted Sixth Thesis on Feuerbach, e.g., K. Marx (ed. by T. Bottomore), *Selected Writings in Sociology and Social Philosophy* (Harmondsworth: Penguin, 1963), p. 83.
13. De George, *Soviet Ethics*, p. 142.
14. J. McMurtry, *The Structure of Marx's World-View* (New Jersey: Princeton University Press, 1978), p. 28. See also, S. Avineri, *The Social and Political Thought of Karl Marx* (Cambridge: Cambridge University Press, 1968), pp. 86–95 on "social man"; E. Fromm, *Marx's Concept of Man* (New York: F. Ungar, 1961); T. Bottomore, "Is There a Totalitarian View of Human Nature?" *Social Research*, 40 (1973): 429–42; I. Fetscher, "Karl Marx on Human Nature," ibid., pp. 443–67.
15. See L. Stevenson, *Seven Theories of Human Nature* (Oxford: Clarendon Press, 1974).
16. McWilliams, *Idea of Fraternity*, p. 28.
17. J. Mabbott, *The State and the Citizen* (London: Arrow Books, 1958), p. 11.
18. J. Pennock and J. Chapman, eds., *Human Nature in Politics* (New York: New York University Press, 1977), p. 5. A salutary reminder of the richness of non-Western traditions of thought can be found, for example, in D. Munro, *The Concept of Man in Early China* (Stanford, Calif.: Stanford University Press, 1969).
19. R. Bigelow, *The Dawn Warriors* (London: Hutchinson, 1969), p. 3.
20. E. Wilson, *Sociobiology* (Cambridge: Harvard University Press, 1975), p. 11.
21. M. Midgley, *Beast and Man*: The Roots of Human Nature (Ithaca, N.Y.: Cornell University Press, 1978), p. 94.
22. Ibid., p. 167. Cf. P. Kropotkin, *Mutual Aid: A Factor of Evolution* (London: Heinemann, 1910), and *Ethics: Origin and Development* (New York: Tudor, 1924); A. Caplan, ed., *The Sociobiology Debate*, (N.Y.: Harper and Row, 1978).
23. Wilson, *Sociobiology*, pp. 3–4.
24. D. Barash, "Evolution as a Paradigm for Behavior," in M. Gregory et al., *Sociobiology and Human Nature* (San Francisco: Jossey-Bass, 1978), pp. 16–17.
25. R. Alexander, "The Search for an Evolutionary Philosophy of Man," *Proceedings of the Royal Society of Victoria* 84 (1969): 109.
26. R. Alexander, "The Evolution of Social Behavior," *Annual Review of Ecology and Systematics* 5 (1974): 335.
27. Bigelow, *Dawn Warriors*, pp. 19, 20.
28. Wilson, *Sociobiology*, Ch. 5, "Group Selection and Altruism," p. 562. Also G. Williams, *Adaptation and Natural Selection* (New Jersey: Princeton University Press, 1960), the most influential modern exponent of individual selection; and the powerful attack on the "individualist" hypothesis in M. Sahlins, *The Use and Abuse of Biology* (London: Tavistock, 1976), Ch. 2, "Critique of the Scientific Sociobiology: Kin Selection."
29. R. Alexander, "The Search for a General Theory of Behavior," *Behavioral Science* 20 (1975): 90.
30. D. Barash, *Sociobiology and Behavior* (Amsterdam, Elsevier, 1977), p. 97.
31. Wilson, *Sociobiology*, p. 120.
32. Midgley, *Beast and Man*, p. 129.
33. R. Trivers, "The Evolution of Reciprocal Altruism," *The Quarterly Review of Biology* 46, no. 1 (March 1971): 46.
34. G. Hardin, *The Limits of Altruism* (Bloomington: Indiana University Press, 1977), p. 14. Note his Table 1: "Effect of Intraspecific Actions on Reproductive Success" and his attempt to derive an exclusively descriptive term for altruism that implies nothing about motives, i.e., his "protagonist-loss, antagonist-gain" or "PLAG" behavior.
35. Trivers, "Evolution of Reciprocal Altruism," p. 40. See also G. Tullock, "Altruism, Malice

and Public Goods", *Journal of Social and Biological Structures* 1, no. 1 (1978): 3–9; the reply by H. Frech, "Altruism, Malice and Public Goods: Does Altruism Pay?" in the next issue (pp. 181–185), and Tullock's counter (pp. 187–89).

36. D. Krebs, "Altruism—An Examination of the Concept and a Review of the Literature," *Psychological Bulletin* 73, no. 4 (1970): 298. See also D. Wright, *The Psychology of Moral Behaviour* (Harmondsworth: Penguin, 1971), Ch. 6.

37. D. Hebb in his reply to Krebs (fn. 36), *Psychological Bulletin*, Vol. 76, No. 6 (1971), pp. 409–44.

38. Hardin, *Limits of Altruism*, p. 1. Also R. Milo, ed., *Egoism and Altruism* (Belmont: Wadsworth, 1973) and N. Rescher, *Unselfishness*: The Role of the Vicarious Affects in Moral Philosophy and Social Theory (Pittsburgh: University of Pittsburgh Press, 1975), for a discussion of the range of philosophical concepts at issue here.

39. Midgley, *Beast and Man*, p. 128.

40. Hardin, *Limits of Altruism*, p. 24.

41. E. Wilson, *On Human Nature* (Cambridge: Harvard University Press, 1978), Ch. 7, "Altruism." See also the lucid critique by Stuart Hampshire, "The Illusion of Sociobiology," *The New York Review of Books* 25, no. 15 (Oct. 12, 1978).

42. Ibid., p. 159.

43. Midgley, *Beast and Man*, p. 93.

44. Sahlins, *Use and Abuse*, p. 57.

45. Ibid., p. 60.

46. Ibid., p. 73.

47. Ibid., p. 88.

48. Ibid., p. 101.

49. Trivers, "Evolution of Reciprocal Altruism," p. 40.

50. D. Campbell, "On the Conflicts between Biological and Social Evolution and between Psychology and Moral Tradition," *American Psychologist*, vol. 30 (1975); "On the Genetics of Altruism and the Counter-Hedonic Components in Human Culture," *Journal of Social Issues* 28, no. 3 (1972): 21–37.

51. Alexander, "Evolution of Social Behavior," p. 377.

52. Sahlins, *Use and Abuse*, p. xi.

53. Ibid., p. 11.

54. Ibid., p. 65.

55. R. Gerard, "The Rights of Man: A Biological Approach," UNESCO *Human Rights* (London: Alan Wingate, 1949), p. 208.

56. G. Kinget, *On Being Human*: A Systematic View, (New York: Harcourt, Brace, Jovanovich, 1975); J. Ellul, "Symbolic Functions, Technology and Society," *Journal of Social and Biological Structures* 1, no. 3 (1978): 207–218.

57. De George, *Soviet Ethics*, pp. 140–1.

58. K. Martin, *The Rise of French Liberal Thought* (New York: New York University Press, 1954), pp. 10, 11.

59. H. Gruber and P. Barrett, eds., *Darwin on Man* (N.Y.: E. P. Dutton, 1974), p. 242.

60. Ibid., p. 398.

61. L. Eiseley, *The Firmament of Time* (N.Y.: Atheneum, 1962), p. 165.

62. L. Mumford, *The Myth of the Machine*, vol. 1 (New York: Harcourt, Brace and World, 1976), pp. 30–37.

63. A. Camus, *The Myth of Sisyphus* (London: Hamilton, 1955), p. 99.

64. D. Layzer, "Altruism and Natural Selection," *Journal of Social and Biological Structures* 1, no. 3 (1978): 303.

65. J. Shotter, *Images of Man in Psychological Research* (London: Methuen, 1976), p. 89.

66. M. Polanyi, *The Tacit Dimension* (London: Routledge and Kegan Paul, 1967), p. 92.

3

The Relative Irrelevance of Inequality: Intelligence, Race and Sex

If we are equal, then in some way or other we are the same.[1] This may seem self-evident, but it is also ambiguous and, in support of any *principle,* is particularly unclear unless we can say what we actually mean and what the consequences of holding to such a belief might be; how, that is, we actually propose to compensate for the individual and social *in*equalities that so obviously obtain between us all. And yet it is not and never has been either odd or irrelevant to assert that equality exists and that it can work as a political doctrine. It is a particularly insidious idea in fact, and, followed through in any thoroughgoing fashion, its implications are radical ones indeed. As a

> matter of historical fact *unequal* access to the means of personal well-being and prestige has been taken for granted in most societies, by both those who have benefited from the inequality, and those who have been deprived by it. . . . Inequality was simply in the order of things. . . . It is not that the impoverished masses bore no animus toward those whose access to the means of well-being and prestige far surpassed theirs. It is simply that until recently in most societies there existed few cultural justifications for questioning the persistence of inequalities in individual life circumstances—for widely held rationales emphasizing equalitarianism in any manifestation. . . .[2]

And now there *are* some. "Most human societies have been beautifully organized to keep good men down" (and good women too). They have placed strict limits on the "realization of individual promise." They have "not set out consciously to achieve that goal. It is just that full realization of individual promise is not possible on a wide scale in societies of hereditary privilege—and most human societies have had precisely that characteristic."[3] (Hence the idea that those most likely to advocate equality are those who have a modicum of it already. They are the exceptions to an age-old social rule, and as such they help now define an important set of global expectations).

EQUALITY AND INDIVIDUALITY

It is no accident that liberty gained currency in the world at the same time as the concept of equality. Both defend a sense of the self—an idea of the individual—at odds with the historic norm. That sense—let us be clear—does not ignore the importance of the community as such; the group, in a social species like our own, always precedes the person. It rather brings society to a focus in every one of us, investing each with the significance of all in such a way as to affirm both the collective and the individual at the same time. "In effect, if the whole of humanity is deemed present in each man [sic], then each man should be free and all men are equal. This is the foundation of the two great ideals of the modern age."[4] Hence ". . . humanity is made up of men, and each man is conceived as presenting, in spite of and over and above his particularity, the essence of humanity."[5] This sounds rather abstract, but it is actually quite concrete. Each individual is the more or less autonomous "point of emergence" of a collective, of a particular society (though this does not preclude a significant difference in *emphasis* between individualistic and collectivist regimes).

The most rigidly inegalitarian of traditional social systems still extant is the one characterized by the hierarchy of caste, that of present-day India. It is difficult for someone unaccustomed to the mind-set of an environment so comprehensive and so rigid in its arrangements to think their way into it; but there are good if somewhat exaggerated guides, and they help to point up by the very extreme character of the contrasts they make: the novelty of an egalitarian perspective.

> As opposed to modern society, traditional societies, which know nothing of equality and liberty as values, which know nothing, in short, of the individual, have basically a collective idea of man, and our (residual) apperception of man as a social being is the sole link which unites us to them, and is the only angle from which we can come to understand them.[6]

De Tocqueville catches the distinction very clearly indeed. As a member of a strictly segregated society, he observes, the individual is still part of an organic social whole, and moreover one with a deep sense of temporal continuity. As an egalitarian, the feel for familial heritage and social patrimony is lost, and the ultimate effect is alienation.[7] And though the concept of aristocracy is easily idealized, and that of democracy rendered correspondingly bleak, there is enough in this difference for us to suspect that something *is* lost perhaps, however much we gain from attempting to realize equality for all.

As it is, traditional values and deep habits of mind are not so readily dispatched anyway, and the "fear of equality," like the "fear of freedom," remains quite palpable in even the most modern of social environments. "Many members of the working classes," Lane argues (from a tiny sample of 15 white, married, male, East Coast Americans), "do not want equality. They are afraid of it. . . . Equality for the working classes, like freedom for the middle classes, is a worrisome, partially rejected, by-product of the demand for more specific measures."[8] How far we can generalize such parochial conclusions is hard to say—Lane thinks them true for "most of the world most of the time"—but advocating equality is likely to conjure up common problems wherever it occurs. A regime that offers greater equality of *opportunity,* for example, will need to find an explanation of any new status hierarchies that emerge and for the low-rank status with which some are consequently lumbered. "Lower status people generally find it less punishing to think of themselves as correctly placed by a just society than to think of themselves as exploited, or victimized by an unjust society."[9] They also tend, Lane says, to look down on those beneath them, as a way of giving their own comparative advantage, however slight, the seal of superior virtue; caring less, that is, about "equality of opportunity than about the availability of *some* opportunity. . . . A man who can improve his position one rung does not resent the man who starts on a different ladder halfway up."[10]

There are, of course, examples of societies so eroded by the avarice of the privileged or the despair of the dispossessed that the pernicious aspects of prevailing inequalities are exposed and there is revolt, but they are much more rare than the exploitive realities of the world would lead one to expect. In countries like America, competitive consumption *within* classes becomes a surrogate for conflict *between* them, and questions about the pattern of capital accumulation and what sort of society this creates come a poor second to claims for incremental reform and increased pay—which leads one to ask: just who does espouse equality today, and what socioeconomic clout do they possess?

WHO ESPOUSES EQUALITY?

In the European tradition the intelligentsia have often spoken and taught on equality's behalf. Though mixed, their contribution has proved most significant in the past. Whether they can convey such a value into the future is another question again. The finest such contributors[11] also point up the self-help qualities of egalitarian rule, and the fact that, given the chance, most people will opt for less inequality rather than more. As Stretton remarks, not only can the poor use what the rich hoard, but the most important inequalities feed off themselves in a host of disadvantageous ways:

They affect government usually in the direction of reinforcing themselves . . . [they] probably bias social and political research and persuasion . . . [they] encourage corruption . . . and to the extent that they do so they limit society's collective political, administrative and economic options . . . [they] degrade many human relations, intensify most social conflicts and . . . do nothing for growth, productivity, conservation or any other good thing. . . .[12]

Who else might support the cause? Liberty, as phrased today, was the catch-cry of early industrial and commercial entrepreneurs seeking greater economic freedom and political power; equality was one way the poor such enterprise produced could ask, like Oliver, for more. In the industrialized societies of today, however, neither owners, workers, managers, bureaucrats, nor government personnel seem as deeply concerned as they once were to establish their egalitarian credentials or to see equality extended. What of those in nonindustrialized states? Third world elites argue for reduced disparities in the international economic order, and their outcry draws attention to the gross inequalities in productivity, power, and human welfare provisions that prevail. Generating change has proved problematic, however. In poor states, leaders who argue for more (for pay-back reparations or for global redistribution), or for the chance to get their countries out from under some rich state or corporate heel, do so as often as not for their own elite advantage. The impoverished peoples they ostensibly serve come a poor second. The ideology of the state itself, perhaps the most potent in the present-day world, also gets in the way:

. . . it is one thing for those who have long played a salient role in history, largely by virtue of having achieved that independence and solidarity for which the state has been indispensable to invoke today the imperative of human solidarity. It is quite another thing for peoples who have been the objects of history rather than its subjects to respond to this imperative.[13]

In fact, greater equality *between* states would have no necessary effect on what the ladder of privilege looks like *within* them, and strategic attempts to equalize global patterns of production and distribution, such as the New International Economic Order, would likely founder on the selfish character of most particular regimes. *Some* such strategy would seem indicated to lift the constraints on poor societies that effectively prevent them doing anything much at all. But how one provides the most effective way of extending life's chances to all earth's people is not self-evident. Since the desire to do so, furthermore, does not seem endorsed by any rising global stratum an egalitarian ideology could likely prove very difficult to sustain. Indeed, to achieve success would seem to require "three revolutions [at least]: one in the rich world, one in the poor world, and one in the relations between them."[14] There are also certain preconditions—material and cultural ones—that make equality possible and without which it probably is not. Poor countries typically lack some or all of them. When one considers that any regime actually interested in providing for its people must cope *as well* with rich states who command most of the world's aid, trade, and investment opportunities, plus the bulk of its productive resources, while actively pressing for the rest, the outlook is grim. If Stretton is right and equality *is* a "first condition of contentment" and of "any general environmental self-restraint," then "it is likely to be the first condition of any willing sharing of surplus resources, on a significant scale, across national boundaries, for the benefit of the billions still fighting nature and each other to scramble nearer to a tolerable minimum of material security."[15] It is also likely to be a condition long delayed.

The pivotal process will probably remain, as it has been for the last hundred years, that of industrialization. Industry has typically required new kinds of social organization. These have had to force their way out through the hereditary hierarchies of those countries where the industrial means of making things has been seriously applied. Such societies have then had to come to terms with, or capitulate to, the emergent identities of socioeconomic class. New criteria of performance, pitched at the capacity of the individual rather than pandering to family status, push prevailing institutions into comparative decline. And just perhaps there is a universal solvent here that will eventually undermine the more impervious of humankind's social systems, since: "The soil grows castes," as Young puts it, but "the machine makes classes."[16]

The discussion so far has focused on equality as an *economic* ideal. This is understandable in an industrializing world where human productivity has increased by an unprecedented amount, and levels of material well-being unheard of in human history have become possible for a greater number of people than has ever existed before. In the industrial societies, the majority of the populace now enjoys standards of ease and public order superior to that of all but the most favored of traditional communities and the most privileged of historic elites, and any desire to extend those standards makes economic equality an obvious issue. The traditional notion that the poor deserve their plight because this is due to their indolence does not disappear, but it does become harder to deny a fairer share to those who manifestly work for it, especially when the ones suffering are made aware of what Marx in particular pointed out—of the extent to which their conditions might be prevented by a deeper understanding of its causes and by the exercise of collective will. The proposition that some minimal material provision be made legally available to all has become, for richer countries at least, a real and practical one.[17] Spurred on by the salutary experience of periodic depressions, the working classes have wielded the power of their trade unions to make such proposals into democratic policies. The Russian revolution produced a ruling group committed, as none in that nation before it had been, to an egalitarian philosophy of such a sort, while Mao Tse-tung attempted to secure the same in China for a poor, fragmented, and largely peasant community that had an even more modest industrial base to build upon. This doctrine eventually made its way into world society in the form of the argument for fulfilling basic needs; for socioeconomic development of a sort that might meet the fundamental, individual necessities of any and everybody, and particularly, but not exclusively, those of the very poor and those of a material kind.[18] And many constitutions and lists of rights have been produced that establish the moral sanctity of these needs, specifying what they mean.

POLITICAL EQUALITY

Much of what has been won in the battle for equality as an economic ideal, however, has followed from its realization in political terms. As a political principle equality assumes that any adult human being, not obviously dangerous or deranged, is able to decide what is the best for him or herself; can consequently choose between rival representatives; and has the opportunity, if he or she should want to use it, of going up for political office. When English liberals first sought such rights, they wanted what the landed aristocracy had to apply to themselves—to the rising bourgeoisie who owned and controlled the new wealth-producing factories, the merchants, and the men of means. The advent of an industrial proletariat, however, concentrated in towns and therefore much easier to organize, strengthened the social case for an even wider franchise, including *all* men, and finally all women too.

The idea of universal suffrage, we might note, held out to those who fought so hard for it the promise of profound social change, of something more radical than material gain. Such promise was soon frustrated, however. Though incremental reforms *were* effected, and across Europe and its settler domains the foundations of the contemporary concept of the welfare state began to appear; though the extraordinary notion that however modest their means or however addled and ill-informed they might be, ordinary people should be allowed to have a say in the way their lives and ways of living were determined, and in doing so could foster in a practical fashion both order and justice, became commonplace ("Only the wearer knows where the shoe pinches," it was said, "and should not suffer in silence;"[19] no *classless* society was ever achieved.

Political equality owed much to European conceptions of *religious* equality and of *legal* equality too. Religious reformists for their own reasons had urged the primacy of a personal rather than an institutionally mediated faith, thus helping to legitimize a sense of the individual as standing outside established hierarchies on good ground of his or her own. The individual, it followed, should be able to revere whatever deity his or her spiritual sensibilities might prefer, or to worship several of them or, indeed, none at all. In the Church-ridden context of post-Renaissance Europe, these were highly controversial concepts, and indeed, prizing the clerical away from the political proved to be a painful process. Yet it did expedite other prospects, and socialist states like the Soviet Union see it as a necessary precursor in this respect. (A devout citizenry has not prevented a country like Poland from putting ostensibly socialistic policies into practice, which suggests that the secularizing tendency of industrial culture need not always prevail, nor need such culture be the sole vehicle, as in the Chinese experience already mentioned, for such reforms, Many religions, furthermore, have an egalitarian ethic of their own, the fatherhood of God implying the brotherhood of man. On the whole, however, it is secularism and political equality that seem to be closely allied.)

LEGAL EQUALITY

Advocates of legal equality defend the principle that society's authoritative rules and sanctions not be arbitrarily applied. Deciding precisely what is more or less capricious or reasonable in this regard requires reference to other values, and historically these have been those that a society serves at large. We find growing appeals to more abstract criteria, a more comprehensive concept of equality defined in terms of social justice and human rights, and it is this value-content that has come to prevail today. This has been made possible, in turn, perhaps, by an aboriginal human sense of fairness and the feeling that human beings have personalities and wills and are significant in themselves.

In medieval Europe legal equality as we may know it now did not exist. Since human distinctions based upon hereditary factors, the possession of property, social status, profession, or faith were not considered improper by those with the power to endorse them, such disregard ought occasion no surprise. The concept of a common law—equally applicable to every one of the state's population—came later; it had to follow the success of strong monarchs in centralizing their lands and unifying their subjects. It had, on the whole, to await the Industrial Revolution and the opportunity this gave for the expression of democratic sentiments and a leveler's concept of the commonwealth. Mere ideals had to be given teeth by enabling laws that allowed those to whom equality was meant to apply actually to enjoy it. As developed by the English, for example, the "parliamentary representative system, . . . non-political civil service, and . . . non-military police force were ultimately devices for insuring the civil liberty and legal equality of democratic citizens. Behind all three lay the notion that all citizens have certain rights of liberty and equality, and the infringement of these rights . . . could never henceforth be regarded as compatible with democratic government."[20]

EQUALITY AND FRATERNITY

Having looked, very briefly, at how egalitarians have argued their case for various sorts of social change, we return to our discussion of what it means as a human virtue, as a universal ideal. Implicit throughout is again an assumption about human nature; in this case about our common humanity and our basic identity as something that is not culturally specific. Such an assumption depends in turn upon a preference for talking across to other human beings rather than up to or down to them. This is the link between fraternity and equality, since a sense of the former makes it possible to think or feel oneself into the place of some other, which is "essentially to regard him [sic] as a being like yourself, whose aims and purposes are as valid as your own . . . to grant him equal scope and equal powers with yourself. . . ."[21] If the values of the other are ones I would consider bad or wrong, illegitimate or unreasonable, then the identity is more difficult to establish. He or she is less like myself. His or her aims and purposes are different, even perhaps, by my lights, completely invalid, and I might be reluctant as a result to grant equal competence and power to someone I see as actually evil. At which point the value divergence ceases to be amenable to rational discourse. Short of this, however, there remains scope—not inconsiderable—for rational and empirical argument and clarification.

THE SOCIAL RELEVANCE OF HUMAN INEQUALITIES

It is in this realm that we might be able to decide the relevance or importance of particular human inequalities (rather than just asserting them and taking our behavioral cues from there). It is here that the debates of biologists and psychologists impinge, and I am in accord with Wilson for once:

> Nobody who takes morality or politics seriously can afford to disregard those disciplines. . . .
> For even though they have not reached their maturity as sciences, the mere attempt to follow
> them . . . will help to prevent us lapsing into one of the almost infinite number of myths about
> "human nature," myths which in this century have lost some of their currency.[22]

We might merely manufacture new ones, of course, or refine and refurbish the old rather than rendering them obsolete, but we can watch for that while we seek something superior. New knowledge will not be enough by itself. New facts alone are never sufficient to sustain or destroy a particular value or ideal. Human conviction can (and sometimes, one may argue, should) prevail despite what particular "facts" reveal. At any rate, facts are subject to human selection and interpretation—which is not to say we should ignore them, but only to suggest that they will not do their work alone.

As one such human conviction, equality presents problems. While it affirms the significance of characteristics common to us all—our basic needs, our human dignity, our human worth—it must somehow confound the effects of our differences, where we vary and are not the same. These effects manifest themselves in social hierarchies, and those who benefit most from such arrangements are apt to prefer them and to select their arguments accordingly. Philosophers like Plato and Aristotle, who wrote in defense of the hierarchic structure of Athenian society against the democratizing demands of city artisans and laborers, have been used repeatedly in the West to sanctify such a preference.

> At the core of the shared outlook of the Socratics was an ethical ideal incapable of being realized by the common man, presupposing a freedom from the world of material necessity in a practical as well as a philosophical sense. This practical and philosohpical "idealism" was reflected in an authoritarian political design.[23]

Equality entails the distribution of similar shares to social equals; the concept of redress, however, of *equal* shares to those who are *unequal* through no fault of their own, was not one these Greeks ever entertained. Social hierarchy was seen to be essential (as they and many since have argued) for sound social health.[24] History could only be a "process of degeneration," characterized by the "steady growth of appetite," and "due to culminate in universal materialism and envy."[25]

INEQUALITY OF TREATMENT

In applying egalitarian beliefs, the fact that people *are* different may mean they have to be *treated* differently. The utilitarian ideal that each person counts as one, and nobody as more than one, obviously depends on whom we think of as a person. Does the category include, for example, women, slaves, nonwhites, children, or trees? Does the principle require that anybody counting *less* than one be granted special privileges to allow him or her to do so? It certainly seems that way. Anything else would discriminate in favor of the strong. Thus various members of a society may have to be compensated for the disadvantages that accrue from some special hardship or need, from their insufficient merit, from their inferior ability, or from their meager contribution to the general good.[26] Given such compensation, the social, economic, and political *outcomes* may still be unequal, but they will be less so when allowed for than otherwise; and only by allowing for them can equal opportunity be said to exist for each to make the most of his or her individual endowments. There is a very practical paradox, in other words, in the way equality can lead to its own negation. A truly equal chance for different individuals will insure different results, and, to prevent these differences from becoming the basis for persistent social inequalities, ways will have to be found to give each new generation something like an unprejudiced chance. And that is not easy, threatening personal "freedom" and much else. Compensation of this kind can reflect the devious assertion of hierarchy too. Take the case where the deficiency is seen as a socially accidental rather than an individually inherited one. Reactionaries have always been able to attribute the reason for the subordinate status of the lower orders to intrinsic inferiority and to leave it at that. In these more egalitarian times they may be called upon to deplore the way a social system operates, but if they are subtle enough they can still "blame the victim." In debates about socioeconomic underdevelopment, for example, they can decry a particular culture's failure to teach a sense of personal achievement or commercial acumen. The fact that the cause lies as much if not more in well-defended patterns of bourgeois behavior that make global modernization and mass mobilization very difficult indeed, where they do not preclude it altogether, is conveniently ignored. Everyone concerned may have the most splendid of intentions, but the consequences seem distorted nonetheless: "In order to persuade a good and moral man to *do* evil . . . it is not necessary first to persuade him to *become* evil. It is only necessary to teach him that he is doing good."[27]

EQUALITY AND LIBERTY

As a general value, equality must compete with other such ideals. While the liberal concepts I am discussing do tend to support each other in ways I have not here described, it may not always be possible to make the most of them all. To create these conditions of social sameness where no one can argue that he or she lacks, for no good reason (the qualities of goodness are obviously important here) what others do not, may not only require enforced inequalities of various kinds but may require constraints on liberty that are galling indeed. The exploited female may positively enjoy her plight, and granting her equality of opportunity may make her much unhappier than she is. The egalitarian can say that the coercion is justified or that the grant is good in its own right, which is to place equality prior to freedom or happiness. It is possible also to argue that more equality makes for *more* liberty and *more* joy, and though this may not be immediately obvious, we can at least look to see if it is so, and if we think it is, then they are mutually reinforced.[28] If not, then we either lay down the law (if it be in our power to do so and if we want equality enough) or we compromise, buying a "less or more uneasy compromise" between "principles which in their extreme form cannot co-exist."[29]

Any compromise occurs under particular historical circumstances and will be much influenced by them. Marxists argue that the influence is a determining one and that abstracted ideas about human nature are irrelevant. We should look, they say, for the concrete class interest that lies behind the analytic disguise. This did not prevent Marx himself, however, from assuming that human beings have basic needs and that a *communist* society ought to meet them. Therefore, though human natures must be historically placed as expressions of prevailing modes of production, they are also, by his admission too, something more than that: something historically constant, unalienated, universal, predictable, and prime.

In twentieth-century Britain, Tawney argued that the compromise could best be effected by eliminating social impediments to individual development, and he recommended progressive taxation, pooling the community's surplus resources, expanding social services, and democratizing education in this regard. Thomson[30] has traced equality's progress from its original, rather literal restatement in revolutionary America, England, and France as a doctrine of political and legal rights, through its enactment as a way of organizing social and economic life, to its status as the sensible quality in assertions of global fraternity, documenting (so he thinks) real progress in human freedom too. Plamenatz put it this way: "some kinds of inequality are fatal to freedom, others are conditions of it. The equality that really matters is equality of freedom, or in other words, equality of opportunity."[31] Real opportunity, that is, denotes freedom of choice. To do what? At this point we may recall the dichotomy between individualist and collectivist regimes. Should we have, as Wollheim puts it, a "right to equal property" or rather an "equal right to property," which is quite a different thing?[32] To a *liberal*, equality means an "equality of rights which would not include the right to a majority to trample on the rights of individuals" (this idea of *equal freedom*, as Lakoff indicates, makes a separate concept of liberty actually *superfluous*);[33] to a *socialist,* equality means rather an equality of needs to be served by common use of the fruits of productive labor. Here freedom denotes material well-being as secured through collective action, and individual liberty comes in a poor second to that of the collective. Lakoff adds a third conception, that of the *conservatives*, but they are not egalitarians at all. The stratified societies they prefer they see as threatened on the one hand by anarchy, and on the other by autocracy. To them equality is anathema, and for that matter (except as it obtains to themselves) so is liberty. Social gradations, conservatives argue, are essential for social stability and allow us to make a virtue out of what seems naturally necessary anyway. "For Socialist, Liberal, and Conservative," Lakeoff asks, "could we not write Optimist, Meliorist, and Pessimist?"[34] as befits their divergent assumptions about human nature (as altruistic and communal, self-centered and willful, or appetitive and irrational), as befits their preferred conceptions of social structure (organic, atomistic, hierarchic), and as befits their preferred social objectives (harmony versus consensus versus order)?

The above would suggest that it is fruitless to look for a single idea of equality. Nevertheless, sorting through the diverse meanings, we can probably agree, if not on a specific philosophy, then at least on a dominant mood. An egalitarian looks out on a world where inequalities abound. He or she will ask for justification for the differences that occur there and will deplore the persistence of those that cannot be reasonably supported in a general way. It is enough to deny the significance of particular distinctions. To promote egalitarian values, one does not have to urge a positive homogeneity upon humankind, and it would seem preferable, if only out of respect for human variety, not to do so anyway.

Those who recommend uniformity of some sort can broach the subject in two ways: by fastening upon a particular characteristic such as the possession of reason or of will; or by exalting one omnipotent truth, such as our equivalent status in the eyes of God (or Nature or History or Law). Equality is sought here by limiting options or enlarging a singularity, and a society built upon either would, one suspects, not last. If we do not share the requisite trait in the right amount, if our sensibilities are not informed by the requisite vision, life under such a regime would likely prove an impoverished experience indeed.

The more modest request—for justification, that is—represents a significant advance over the sort of traditional circumstance where the hierarchic order goes unquestioned. Justification implies reasons, and ones that are relevant and practical, and this will destroy any sense, should there still be one, that the prevailing state of affairs is simply necessary or inevitable as such. When a social order is opened up to question in this way, then it is opened up to change. Once the social order itself becomes an object of inquiry, its members can examine their understanding of it, of the source of the authority that rules over them, and of their obedience to it. And they may think again about accepting the status quo.

The simplest inequalities to justify are the ostensibly natural ones—in particular those of age, strength, race, sex, and what is broadly termed intelligence. Philosophers have dodged around these distinctions in various ways. ''Nature hath made men so equal,'' Hobbes says, ''in the faculties of the body, and mind; . . . [that] when all is reckoned together, the difference between man, and man, is not so considerable, as that one man can thereupon claim to himself any benefit, to which another may not pretend, as well as he.''[35] Some express a sense of ''ultimate and outrageous absurdity'' when forced to contemplate the notion that *moral* worth be judged by some *individual* capacity rather than by what we share. Those better endowed with a particular trait can be as ''gifted,'' they observe, ''for vice as for virtue.''[36] (As Greenberg says in a way reminiscent of an earlier tradition, perhaps ''we should learn to think of human beings not as 'equal' but as 'sacred.' ''[37]).

Social, economic, and political conditions can be changed if the creative consciousness exists to do so. The quality of human existence is comparatively plastic. Natural distinctions are much less so. As a consequence, proponents of equality have not, except in the most general fashion (pointing up our common requirements for food, shelter, and affection, for example, or our shared aversion to physical pain and mental anguish), based their claims upon biology. At their most extreme, they consider a biological or a psychological comparison as ethically irrelevant: "The only sense in which it can be said to be factual at all is that men [sic] do, as a matter of fact, feel the imperative to regard moral claims of other persons as in some important sense equal to their own."[38]

This begs the question: *why* do they have that sense? Some consideration of our biological and psychological identities would seem to me to be part of any answer. It is significant, too, that those *antagonistic* to egalitarian values say something else. As one might expect, they sheer away from social causes and give reasons for their defense of human hierarchies in terms of the superior qualities inherent in being white, for example, or male, or mentally adept (being old or strong or upper class is less relevant, under modern conditions, at least). Whiteness *alone* is only a symbol for a whole bag of better things, which specify for the speaker what it means to be human and what one may do with that. This is the entry point for argument, since if it can be shown that whiteness is not a meaningful category *in fact*, or, if it is, that it cannot be used *objectively* to predict other qualities, then the stratifier is seen by reasonable people anyway to be a dogmatist, and his or her rationalizations can be shown up as not argument but excuse. Thus: "The Nazi 'anthropologists' who tried to construct theories of Aryanism," for example, "were paying in very poor coin, the homage of irrationality to reason."[39] No debate with them could change their racist convictions, nor did argument prevent a human holocaust, but in the teaching of the generations these arguments are important and they contribute, where this occurs, to moral progress. "There is an element of myth in all . . . systems of dominance . . . it seems to be a rule, at least at one stage of development, that societies are organized more easily if people think they are more different than in fact they are."[40] In disabusing such beliefs, however, one *can* make it that much harder to justify the sort of distinctions used to distribute social resources to pernicious effect.

This is one feature of a much larger process to do with the human capacity to be objective, and the way human reason has been used to detach the self from the environment the better to understand and to manipulate it. This capacity, which is the key characteristic of science and of modern modes of cognition, not only puts the individual over and against the natural universe, it abstracts him or her from society too. It is the necessary mental step that makes an individualistic ethic conceivable. Once the step is taken, the idea that large complex communities are *necessarily* dependent upon ordered social hierarchies, buttressed by the belief that this is divinely inspired, is impossible to sustain. People will make do and get by; they will accept society's premises because it provides them with a place; they will accept extreme inequalities as long as real privilege for them remains so remote as to seem irrelevant. There is all the difference in the world, however, between habitual dependence and natural servility. The latter is preordained. The former is not. And once we are sensitive to this distinction, the possibility exists for a definition of civilization not in terms of its artifacts but in terms of its human concern, and for a collectivist ethic not predicated upon strict stratification.

Let us look a little more closely at some important ideas about natural distinctions that have been used historically to defend social differences and political and economic hierarchies. How immutable are they? How seriously do they affect ideas about equality? How much credence can be given the arguments for structured inequality that proceed from what is known about the sort of beings we are?

INEQUALITY: THE VISUAL PREFERENCE FOR VERTICALITY

The most general biological proposition in this regard is the one put forward by Laponce.[41] Social hierarchies derive, he says, from what we "see." Regardless of competition for scarce resources, the functional requisites of the system, or even our inherent propensities for dominance or dependence, humankind has a penchant for "marking" space and, particularly, for the dimension of "verticality," for up and down. Presumably because of the influence of gravity and the way we are physiologically constructed, "upward" has a positive connotation that downward lacks. What is more, the same preference colors not only our physiological perceptions, but our social and cultural ones too. As a result humankind "cannot but perceive" society "in terms of an up-down hierarchy. . . . Morally he [sic] looks above to the notion of an abstract good, perceived to be higher than the self; religiously he links himself to divinities located high up, preferably in the sky; and politically he links himself to an authority perceived to be above the self."[42] Hence the static concept of society as a ladder. Hence the psychological effect of "images of ascent," manifest in the "liberative," even "curative" power of any ideology that promises progress. If we legislate against such predispositions as we may well choose to do, then we will incur suitable costs. We will have deliberately to craft semantic alternatives since our choice will be, quite literally, an unnatural one. "We do not have to teach that power comes from above, but we need to teach that power comes from below"[43] if this is where, in fact, we want to "see" it coming from.

All of this is quite plausible until we reflect upon those cultural disciplines that reject the concept of the individual as radically divorced from the cosmos. The oriental idea of the centered self, for example, that locates the individual within a mental domain without spatial bias, within a sphere, that is, makes verticality obsolete. Closely linked with such a concept is usually one of intrinsic "energy" (Indian *prahna*, Chinese *ch'i*, or Japanese *ki*) that is difficult for occidentals to visualize but is every bit as viable as a social, political, and cultural philosophy, and every bit as convincing as an expression of our mental preferences. What Laponce has done, I suspect, is to note his very Western awareness of verticality and ascent, seek some possible natural explanation for it, and then derive that awareness from what he then claims actually precedes it. He has reversed the real sequence. Had he been raised elsewhere, I would venture to suggest that verticality and ascent would seem significantly less natural to him in these terms. He would have felt more at home with a sense of "heaven and earth," with a sense of a dynamic center located within himself (usually in the abdomen; in Japanese, for example, called the *hara*), and any biological preference for up and down would have seemed far less self-evident. Like some endless loop, this center contains the cosmos at the same time as being contained by it, along a single continuum that links all. Is such a concept merely traditional, "primitive," a culturally infantile attempt to cope with our highly differentiated life environment by crawling back into the womb? If so, this makes Laponce look pleasingly modern. However, when we describe evolutionary history in terms of growing spatial awareness, we first find creatures with not much of a dimensional preference at all; then come those conscious of up and down (verticality); then those with the added sense of front and back (horizontality); and finally, as in humankind, all the above plus some (often incomplete) comprehension of left and right as well. On this sequence *verticality* and *ascent* are only one step less primitive than the most basic of locational senses. Could we not also posit an additional stage to the series that recovers the sphere, only this time informed by the other sorts of awareness as well? This would make of the oriental approach not the ultimate atavism but an emergent ideal. Carried through from the biophysical to the sociopolitical domain, the implications could be interesting indeed. Instead of "hierarchy," we would then have "sphericity." Not that oriental systems themselves have ever really made this extension (the Middle Kingdom perhaps?), but it is no accident that the ethic of *aikido,* for example, involves both the concept of self-integration and that of universal love.'[44]

INTELLIGENCE

One quality that *has* come to loom large in an age of complex technology and burgeoning bureaucracy is that of our mental quickness, our grasp, our problem-solving capacities, and teachability. These qualities have been grouped together under the term intelligence.[45] Very generally, the concept of intelligence refers to the intellectual skills we use in negotiating our immediate environments, both natural and contrived. Anything more particular soon encounters the fact that what is intelligent behavior in one culture does not necessarily appear to be so in another. Indeed, "there are as many ways of being intelligent as there are technologies; intervention of new technologies will create new ways of being intelligent . . . technologies have [thus] the effect of making some particular underlying abilities critical, or at least relevant, to intelligent performance."[46]

Despite such differences, we find the widespread association of ingelligence and mental acuity with the capacity to apply both social and cognitive rules in novel ways. The intelligent person "knows" or "sees" when exceptions will do better work, a notion developed at great length by Stenhouse—the P-factor he calls it—in terms of an individual's power not to respond in the usual fashion to a typical situation that would otherwise have a typical behavioral outcome,[47] for withholding responses that is, or delaying them in a relevant way. And indeed some such capacity would seem necessary if we are to find adaptive variability in behavior. With it we can contravene our instincts, or the force of habit of culturally acquired beliefs, attitudes, and values, and this should increase our ability to endure.

We must never forget, that is, that the

> human brain is a very extravagant organ. It seems capable of responding to anything, sometimes very predictably, sometimes very unpredictably (if the stimulus is interesting enough) and it can put itself into the service of virtually anything that demands it to function—from creating personal illusional systems to building practical models of physical phenomena, constructing theories to justify political action, or [for that matter] satisfying test psychologists.[48]

Though it has proven so far impossible to dissociate environmental opportunity and individual initiative from what might naturally obtain (we inherit both our constitutions *and* our environments in complex, nonadditive ways), there are many differences in human performance that *are* felt to derive from differences in personal aptitude that we cannot ignore. Capablanca was a natural chess player. He was born with the gift, a "talent," that he then trained; he was clearly extraordinary from a very early age. Mozart was a natural musician in the same way. And though very few of us are so obviously outstanding in anything we do, the feeling persists that some people are inherently better endowed than others and that this includes a quality we call intelligence. The latter is not a skill at a game, nor some special bent of an artistic sort. It is a reasoning power. We do not speak of an intelligent carpenter, however much he or she excels at his or her craft. He or she must also demonstrate competence of an analytic as well as a physical kind, as manifest, for example, in the thoughtful design of a piece of his or her work, to win this much-vaunted adjective. Again, not all reasoning capacities denote intelligence, since we reserve for the rather more narrow (and usually less altruistic) ones the concept of shrewdness or cunning, and for the more comprehensive the word wisdom. The concept has proved sufficiently discrete, however, to allow the intervention of the "intelligence test;" and for psychologists to rank people, like cognitive light bulbs, as bright or dim. This has led in turn to speculation about the possibility of a new sort of political hierarchy, redolent of Plato's utopia but recast in terms of contemporary modes of social organization—a *meritocracy*.[49] (Those who would highlight what they see as the "powerful trend" towards the "advancement of people on the basis of ability . . . measured objectively,"[50] that is, by "IQ," are the main protagonists here.)

Let us elaborate. If intelligence is largely inherited, as Herrnstein says, and if one's success in societal terms and consequently one's status and material rewards are dependent thereon, then social standing will "to some extent" reflect genetic endowment too.[51] The danger in this is that egalitarian political and social reforms will then produce a class system based upon intellectual merit. When individuals are allowed to find their "natural" station in society (in *intellectual* terms that is), then the dominant class will inevitably be the more able one. Not so implicit in Hernstein's argument are others however: that "complicating factors" (as he coyly calls them) like racial discrimination, and discrete sorts of social inheritance, might be actually *necessary* to prevent the advent of a class-bound society of this sort based upon genetic difference;[52] that the status quo really is, in the long run, for our own good; that equality of opportunity tends to eliminate other sources of individual difference, allowing only intellectual ones to prevail; that it portends its own negation, prompting us, Herrnstein hints, to look elsewhere for our preferred values. A technologically advanced age implies a new hierarchy of castes, and "sooner or later, if and when technology has truly replaced the drawers and the hewers and the other simple vocations, the tendency to be unemployed may run in the genes of a family about as certainly as I.Q. does now."[53] The mediocre will merely beget more of the same, and their mental unequals (i.e., superiors) will command the social heights unassailed.

The sorry social vista sketched above is too impressionistic to be very reliable. There is a much contested issue, for example, in that of *heritability*, since this concept only makes sense in a particular group context, being different for diverse peoples at different places and time. It also denotes qualities that in human beings are far from fixed.[54] (I will return to this question in a moment.) What is more, the fact of *regression* makes any allusion to meritocratic caste very misleading indeed. If mating were totally controlled, groups of men and women with the same mean IQ would have offspring with their own intellectual capacity. Otherwise, there is a range that drifts toward the average for the breeding population as a whole.[55] Both the children of meritocrats and the children of mediocrats tend toward whatever the mean intelligence might be for the breeding stock as a whole. They do the same in height, weight, and any other variable trait, and for "anyone wishing to perpetuate class or caste differences, genetics is the real foe; there is no way (except wholesale slaughter) of preserving the status quo.''[56] Genetic leveling is marked on the one hand by capable and socially privileged parents who use their power to protect their less able young from falling down the social ladder, and on the other by less privileged parents who try and prevent their progeny from getting ideas above their station. Do away with such impediments and individual mobility is much enhanced. Innate "merit" alone might then be allowed to determine who goes where. Human breeding patterns, however (or rather, the lack of them), would prevent any socially divergent outcome arising, at least on genetic grounds, and happily so.

Eysenck, who has also put the advent of "mediocracy" up against the case where the "best" people have the top jobs and inhabit the most intellectually taxing professions, encounters difficulties in defining "best." He says it is those who "by nature" are most able to learn necessary and complex skills and efficiently to perform the socially most important tasks.[57] "Experience," he argues, shows that "intelligence" is "vitally necessary" in this regard, and "the facts" demonstrate that IQ tests can predict with considerable accuracy who they are. Now, no one, we may say, wants an idiot for a doctor, lawyer, or academic mentor. But it is by no means obvious that the brilliant but obviously indifferent surgeon, for example, is to be preferred as a practitioner over one who is basically competent but is also concerned. The former is highly proficient but the latter may prove superior simply because he or she cares about patients as people and the other does not. In other words, intelligence thus defined is only one human quality, and though modern society requires and rewards many of those who can crudely be characterized as "bright," over a certain difficult-to-define point, "brightness" becomes positively counterproductive. There are other traits that a society needs if it is to be a sustaining one, and that it systematically denigrates only at significant cost. Practically any physically competent person can pick peas. Considerably less are likely to be able to pass medical school exams or acquire any of the other taxing intellectual and practical skills a modern society pays most for. This does not mean, however, that those who do best at exams are "best" in some more comprehensive and more humane sense of the word. (Nor does it mean, for that matter, that picking peas is unimportant, though modern societies will inevitably tend to favor those who possess the skills needed to coordinate them, to command their industries and services, and to improve upon these over time.)

Behind the criticisms above lies the thought that the good society is not individualistic and competitive but pluralistic, classless, and cooperative, and one must be explicit about this. Young puts the point as part of an imaginary manifesto:

Were we to evaluate people, not only according to their intelligence and their education, their occupation and their power, but according to their kindliness and courage, their imagination and sensitivity, their sympathy and generosity, there could be no classes. . . . Every human being would then have equal opportunity not to rise up in the world in the light of any mathematical measure, but to develop his [sic] own special capacities for leading a rich life. . . . The child . . . [would be] a precious individual, not just a potential functionary of society. The schools . . . [would] be devoted to encourage all human talents, whether or not these are of the kind needed in a scientific world . . . [and] by promoting diversity within unity, they would teach respect for the infinite human differences which are not the least of mankind's virtues.[58]

Not all human talents are preferred. The general principle of favoring diversity is a liberal one. In nurturing the "good" traits along with talents for what we feel is "bad," however, we may get more than we bargained for, hence the supplementary rule that enjoins consideration for other people. This leads to traditional questions about the difference between self-regarding and other-regarding acts, about whether the former are possible, and, ultimately, the difference once again between an individualistic ethic and a collectivist one.[59] If biology is to enter the argument, however, we must remember that *no one* in fact can know how to compare the superiority of particular traits, since what will prove superior in the long run is not known until we get there. We can make a guess, but we have as yet no grounds for more than reasonable predictions.

To Eysenck this sort of thing is wordy and woolly where it is not downright irrational. Human diversity must be quantified, he says, and fed into the "proper predictive equations" before we can really say what is going on and decide what is best to do.[60] How good at quantifying human ability, then, is the most common measure today—the I.Q.? The debates over this issue are very extensive. It does seem, however, that the IQ test, despite significant attempts to arrive at a general factor of intelligence with it, is a much more limited tool than is often supposed; and any conclusions based upon it will reflect the limitations of the instrument itself and must be treated with great care.

Originally developed by French educational authorities at the turn of the century as a practical device for separating the goats who could cope with school from the sheep who could not, it rapidly became, in American hands, a very broad device for sorting out the more or less educable, the more or less employable, and, in terms of American values, the more or less worthwhile.[61] In recent times many doubts have been expressed about what IQs actually do, to what extent they are inherited, and to what extent they can be used to make significant statements on differences in race and sex. They have always been open to ideological abuse. On the one hand, we have those who serve some privileged status quo who would locate the basic cause of social injustice in biological fact. On the other, we find researchers seeking to establish that those designated defective are better described as socially deprived. With this sort of divergence in mind, it would seem prudent to remember that IQ is a psychometric artifact, and that psychologists and biologists tend to approach the human phenomenon of intelligence in a rather oblique way. IQs do change over an individual's life; they can be modified by modifying the test conditions; and they are too closely associated with the educational values that determine success or failure in Western schools (with the test subject commonly having to *converge* on a singular truth by a process of analytic reasoning) to be seen as an adequate means for doing more than predicting individual differences in the narrow (however necessary) capacity for achieving success in Western institutions of learning. "[O]ne might almost be moved to suggest," one critic asserts, "that lack of success on such tests should be seen as a sign of superior qualities."[62] Hence low IQ may reflect rather less inferior intrinsic ability and rather more a student's success at learning his or her socially programmed position in life.

Attempts to complement the IQ with tests for *divergent* thinking, which is one possible way of arriving at a CQ (a *creativity* quotient), have had mixed success. The qualities involved are so intangible: "There is," it seems, "no ideal intelligence"[63] in this regard. No one to my knowledge has found ways of allowing for temperament or for levels of personal interest and motivation. No one either has tried to find an AQ (*aesthetic* quotient) or an EQ (*ethical* quotient) or an SQ (*spiritual* quotient), though all of these might prove just as important in deciding what sort of a society we want to reproduce. The fact that educational achievement is important (though not in fact either necessary or sufficient) for one to succeed in material, prestige, and power terms in an industrial or industrializing society sould not be allowed to obscure the extent to which this and the conventionally favored IQ restrict our understanding of other sorts of human excellence and originality—or, indeed, of what being human actually means.

The idea of heritability, which is the "proportion of the total variance in . . . [intelligence] attributable to genetic factors, in a particular population at a particular point in time,"[64] is also more difficult to establish than might be assumed. Some would say that it is not a plausible quantity at all and put the whole burden upon our different life experiences.[65] Though the study of genetically similar children who are reared apart is said to reveal the existence of similar IQs regardless of the different environments in which they have grown up (which is good evidence for heritability of the capacity to do IQ tests, and hence of intelligence, too, if one does not buy the criticisms made above); and the IQs of genetically dissimilar individuals reared together do not usually converge; can we establish anything more precise than this? The empirical study of separated identical twins and the attendant critique of them is a minor academic industry in its own right, and I shall not even attempt a review of it here.[66] Suffice it to say that twin-study findings are inconclusive where they have not, as in the case of one eminent British psychologist, actually been faked.[67] The existence of academic fraud does not destroy the argument for heritability, of course, though

Burt's contribution was so important in this debate that it has certainly modified its force. Burt provides an extreme example of experimental bias. Kamin suggests that the effect is also evident at less exalted and less conscious levels, however, and that other factors, like allowing for the age of the subjects concerned, must also be taken into consideration.

> The intraclass I.Q. correlations of separated MZ (monozygotic or identical twin) pairs would in fact be an estimate of the heritability of I.Q. *if* some key assumptions were made. First, the twins would have to be a representative sample, genetically, of the population in which we are interested. Then, the range of environments to which the twins have been exposed would have to be fairly representative of the range of environmental variation in the population. Third, and perhaps most critical, there must be no tendency for the environments in which twin pair members were reared to be systematically correlated.[68]

There is no experiment of which I am aware that observes these stringent conditions, and until one is done, we just do not know. The empirical evidence, in other words, is very far from being all in, and until it is the tools we use to measure intelligence remain relatively imprecise.

The concept is also singular. When we talk about it, "we imply that there is one principal kind of cognitive ability. It sounds wrong to speak of 'intelligences' in the plural . . . we can talk of different 'kinds of intelligence,' but we still tend to imply one overriding capacity. . . ."[69] Within this rubric, much ingenuity has been expended on trying to define what the general range of our abilities to select, integrate, and coordinate mentally might be, both between people and within any one person as they develop and grow. There has been much debunking of the pretensions of experimenters. The notion that some people are born brighter than others persists, however, as does the sure conclusion that "genetic potential uncontaminated by the effects of experience" is "impossible to assess."[70]

What can we conclude? The genetic differences between human beings does *influence*, it seems, the mental capacity to perform such basic cognitive tasks as remembering and reasoning; but it is not yet established, and it seems increasingly likely that it never *will* be, that differences in intelligence are *primarily* due to genetic endowment. Intelligence has been called the "psychic analogue of physical endurance,"[71] and whether that is a good comparison or not, like endurance, it can be improved. It can also be impeded; people can be taught to be stupid too. In the human case, environments are particularly important in this regard because they are cumulative. Environmental deprivation, for example, will deplete any human potential, especially when the neglect is systematic and sustained, because it preempts the personal acquisition of those mental skills that require progressively more complex learning experiences. (The relationship, one must remember, is an intimate one. A genetic endowment is evident only after it has responded to an appropriate environment, and the environment can only act upon what genetically obtains.) Environmental deprivation does not, however, seem enough to undermine group capacity over time. As

> The caste system in India was the grandest genetic experiment ever performed on man. The structure of the society endeavoured for more than two millenia to induce what we would now call genetic specialization of the caste populations for performance of different kinds of work and functions. Such specialization has not been achieved . . . and although modern India has far to go to abolish inequalities of status and opportunity, all castes have produced persons of ample competence to acquire non-traditional education and to engage in non-traditional occupations.[72]

In the name of spiritual merit, and in the interests of the established order of Brahmanic privilege, the caste system continues deliberately to waste the sort of talents that a meritocratic society would ostensibly seek out and use. From the point of view of the "inferior" Indians, or that of the human project as a whole, the waste is woeful. So are the effects of conditions of life in large parts of the contemporary world, where basic needs of a physical, let alone mental, kind are not met. It remains sheer hypocrisy, however, to assert that the plight of those afflicted is genetically deserved.[73] While genetic variation may account *to some degree* for different people's different abilities, we can say no more than this. The extent of that "some" degree has not yet been established as either "large," "important," or "significant," and, given how our environments and endowments interact, it will probably continue to defy quantification in this form.

RACE

The second biological discriminant that inegalitarians offer as grounds for perpetuating hierarchic social structures is that of *race*. Any discussion of intelligence will overlap that of "racial" difference, so I shall move on to this difficult debate next. The idea that peoples without white (rather, pinko-grey) pigmentation are innately less intelligent than the latter has found particular favor in the United States where, not coincidentally, testing for intelligence has been most widespread. Though all human races are to some extent mixed, and American "blacks" notably so since their ancestors came from a number of tribal groups and, more importantly, interbred in the New World with the "whites" there, we find persistent differences in their test quotient scores that do not disappear, it is claimed, when allowance is made for the culturally unfair nature of the test questions and the test situations themselves. The difference is then ascribed, despite the persistence of unequal social treatment, to *heredity* (though we might note that the average gap cited—15 points—is no greater than that between the children of any particular human family; and furthermore that the average differences between large groups of people are always less than those between individual members of any one of them). There have been some attempts, albeit not very systematic ones, to arrive at global comparisons along these lines, and different average IQs have been established for various human populations. No one can fairly claim to know what this means,[74] however, which suggests that we should look more closely at the bases of this controversy, and in particular, at the concept of race itself.

Biologically the word refers to specific patterns of genetic variation within a species as a whole, a definition that reflects advances in the study of population genetics made over the last fifty years. As a species we can interbreed if we want to, our progeny will be viable, and the differences between us will be very small compared with the differences between a human being and anything else. If and when we do breed, our children inherit a shuffled sequence of the parental genes, which are fundamental units of heredity and are passed on, except for the occasional mutation, without being modified themselves. The shuffling is so effective that the outcome, except in the case of identical twins, is always genetically unique, which means that in this sense practically every individual is too. This is why there is such a variety in human potential and such a diversity of personal endowments. Mating opportunities are not everywhere the same, however, since comparatively few realize the biological possibility of breeding with someone far removed from where they live, either geographically, or by socioeconomic, linguistic, or religious distance. Other environmental influences vary, too, causing natural selection and adaptation. Hence, within the common gene pool that all humans share, there are eddies. The eddies are not very large—Lewontin argues that only 6 percent or so of human genetic diversity is "racially" derived, 8.3 percent being due to differences between the more local populations within any one "race," which leaves by far the largest fraction (85.4 percent as a mean proportion of the total species) due to the difference between individuals as such.[75] That racial 6 percent can include obvious differences in terms of skin color, for example, facial form, teeth type, or hair, which is why we can loosely link a people's common descent and their diverse physical qualities. Does it also include "intelligence," however?

Traits like those listed above do not always come in readily recognized combinations, and there are others, like blood grouping, for example, that confuse the picture further. Putting all of them together highlights the anomalies in the patterns of their distribution and makes the attempt to classify us by appearance alone highly problematic. While we *can* broadly identify what seem to be particular human types inhabiting particular geographic areas, such groupings are not discrete. They shade off into each other along gradients or *clines*, as they are called, the frequency with which particular traits appear tailing away as one traces a particular population across the map, while others build up in their place. Human variety does not occur along sharp lines, and any stratigraphic approach that would shovel off the accumulated wealth of human breeding to reveal the hard-edged outlines of what are supposed to be foundation stocks underneath would thus seem certain to fail. Furthermore, because of the importance of culture in determining how we do things, what seem to be characteristic *behavioural* qualities contribute nothing further to our understanding in this respect. So the human picture must remain highly confused.

Human beings have a penchant for categorization. Indeed, ''one can suggest that this tendency to reduce the graded variation of the world to finite symbolic form is as close to being instinctive as anything in the human behavioral repertoire.''[76] Given the obvious, and the now not-so-obvious differences in human populations, there has been ample opportunity to exercise this instinct on ourselves, and the range of categories arrived at has been very broad. So indeed has been the response to ''race'' itself. We have, for example, those who would dispense with the term altogether (sometimes called *ignoracists*), who argue that a true appreciation of human variety will come about only when what people believe to be true is finally decreed, in the light of current science, to be patently false. ''Where racial categories are concerned,'' Brace has said,

despite the vast amounts of information now available, those groups which are accepted as being valid races still reflect the stereotyped impressions of seventeenth and eighteenth century European merchants. Both to the scientist and the average man, what are considered the significant dimensions of human biological variation owe more to the location of the ports of call of the old European mercantile system than to the average biological differences between major geographical and populational centers.[77]

Advance agents of a handful of countries in the process of a new kind of consolidation, these traders eventually had to share the field with those sent to make and administrate competing empires. The Industrial Revolution generated a set of particularly potent regimes that did not hesitate to arrange their understanding of the world, and other people's places there, in such a way as to legitimize their own sense of power, privilege, and superiority. ''Race'' was a convenient way to mark the comparative stations. The more remote from European preferences a population appeared to be, the more sufficient the cause for considering it naturally inferior and the more fit to serve a foreign purpose. This went well with the concept of human races as ''discrete'' and ''archetypal,''[78] a competing view to that above developed as such in the contemporary context by Carleton Coon.[79] Though Coon admits the dynamic nature of raciation, he suggests that it is possible to trace through the fossil record five basic types of *homo sapiens*, along lines that remain quite distinct. This would be plausible, particularly if we did not expect the typology to be too precise, if it did not contradict our understanding of the extent to which human genes have flowed around the common pool.[80] The evidence from Africa suggests that the modern diversity of human form and physiological function are not of ''any great antiquity."[81] Furthermore, human diversity is so great, so multidimensional, in fact, that it proves impossible to find a listing of groups where the variation within each category is less than the differences between it and the next. There are no populational nodes which can be used to map "as the foci of maximum genetic distance" the space between, let us say, the three main "races"[82] (normally called Caucasoid, Negroid, and Mongoloid). The word can produce only "infinite confusion."[83] Thus Lewontin concludes, in the spirit of the first perspective, that: "Since . . . racial classification is now seen to be of virtually no genetic or taxonomic significance . . . no justification can be offered for its continuance."[84]

Montagu, the most intransigent of the antiracists, recommends the use of "major groups" as a replacement term, each such group being made up of smaller "ethnic groups" (defined by him as part of a species population in the process of splitting off from the common stock, though still capable of breeding with other members of it). Given its cultural and linguistic connotations, this latter term raises problems of its own since "ethnic" traits may be shared by peoples very different in their genetic endowment, and, likewise, those genetically similar may be riven by acquired beliefs. Over the years, however, Montagu has consistently argued that "race" is a myth, or rather an ideology serving the cause of privileged groups in rationalizing, even sanctifying, the fact that they prevail.[85] How would his opponents reply? Physical and mental attributes are related, they would say. And the "non whites" are inferior.[86] To which Montagu would say that while some groups of people do share among themselves certain similarities in form and function of a sort others do not, that is all that we can say. Anything more would be a mischief. Hence his assertion that:

> a *scientific* typology of races *either* on morphological *or* on gene frequency grounds seems to be ruled out. All that can be usefully discussed by scientists are the processes by which racial differentiation comes about, and the environmental and social circumstances which lead to an increase or decrease in such differentiation over time . . . the isolate concept *a race* has no explicit "objective" meaning whatsoever.[87]

Less troubled analysts, a third group, would rather keep "race" in the scientific vocabulary, while carefully defining each time the way the word is used. Dobzhansky, for example, while admitting that drawing distinctions between intrabreeding subgroups of the human population and calling them "races" will always involve arbitrary assessments about where the boundaries fall, argues that one trait often shades quite quickly into another thus providing points in the human landscape where we *can* put a line.[88] Arriving at a specific number of major groups will depend entirely upon how many traits we measure and the purpose of our inquiry. The fact that our maps of the distribution of human traits fail to converge on a limited number of separate categories may frustrate the typologist, he says, but it does not negate the concept of "race." It merely refines it, enabling us to see more readily the "transitional populations" between race groups and the way genes percolate through the whole.[89] In similar vein it is argued that:

> we cannot understand fully the evolutionary history of mankind either in terms of individuals alone, or in terms of the species as a whole, because individuals do not evolve, and the details of the evolutionary process are not necessarily the same for all regional and other subdivisions of the species. This is why it is of theoretical importance to recognize races or subspecies in evolutionary biology whether or not they are considered descriptively important.[90]

The geographical variety in genetic patterns is considerable. The patterns are also not static since they are, as evolutionary episodes, quite temporary.[91] Therefore they can be no more scientifically suggestive. (Genetic similarities indicate shared heritage. Widely separated populations, genetically alike, may have got that way by other evolutionary means such as natural selection or genetic drift; i.e. "Congo Pygmies seem to be simply short Africans and Papuan Pygmies short Papuans.")[92] In such a view there *are* patterns nonetheless, however, and, though no classification of races as discrete categories seems possible, and "there is no denying man's genetic variability," populations are linked by a series of clines, and each possesses a "unique constellation of inherited biological attributes."[93] As a consequence, most of this intermediate group will talk in a way the first does not of the possibility of racial differences in intelligence (though the liberals among them do not see this as relevant to a discussion of *equality*).

Yet such a compromise conclusion does seem rather specious. "Race," it can be said, is one of the most trivial of human discriminants and one of the most profound in its social consequences. If that triviality is demonstrable as such, scientifically so, then we have direct support for the ethic of equality. If it is *not* trivial, especially in terms of what a society values, then to sustain an egalitarian ethic we have to assert a more general argument about our common human dignity or the value in allowing equal opportunity *despite* human diversity, which is far less convincing to those who have an interest in the sort of ethos social hierarchies sustain. How far apart should we hold the fact and the value? On the one hand, Dobzhansky argues that, biologically, each individual is "unique and unrepeatable"[94] and *therefore* should not be treated in terms of the stereotype of the group he or she belongs to; on the other, he says that the same observable fact has no relationship at all to social policy. This is a confusion. As we have seen already, the doctrine of equality does not depend on establishing our biological *identity;* hence, we can talk of equality whether we believe in one human race or many. However, in discussing those human *in*equalities that are relevant to what a society and its governing group esteems, it is necessary to bring biological facts back into the equation if only to clarify what the empirical scope of the problem seems to be. The fact (1) that human genetic diversity is evolutionarily advantageous and we should celebrate it as such since we simply do not know what qualities will prove most adaptive for any future stage of our species in part or whole; (2) that human genetic diversity is most evident within the major groups that might be made of mankind, rather than between them, the latter proving problematic anyway because of the way in which human races form a genetic continuum; and (3) that our genetic diversity as a species is so extraordinarily rich that under "most systems of equal opportunity and equivalent selection, any numerically significant segment of the human species could . . . probably replace any other with respect to behavioral capacities,"[95] seems to me to be particularly important. Any debate about human values ought to be informed by such empirical understandings which, while ultimately inconclusive in themselves, are nevertheless far from irrelevant. And where we find examples of what are commonly called racial antagonisms, antagonisms that feed upon typological stereotypes about human variety, then it may not settle any arguments but it does remain appropriate to point out that advances in biological knowledge have, in fact, made this sort of thinking obsolete.

The *least* troubled analysts like those of the first group simply assume that there is "undoubtedly a high correlation" between social and biological definitions of race, [96] and get on with the business of establishing the differences between them. They flatly reject the findings of both their extreme and more modest antagonists; hence, it is on the second proposition above that debate is still likely to stick. Jensen, for example, has argued that intelligence is inherited; that statistics show American "whites" and "blacks"—classified as such by "common social criteria"—perform differently on tests of their abstract learning, reasoning, and verbal abilities, and that this is most likely because of their unequal genetic endowments. Controlling the data to allow for environmental variations in socioeconomic status does not eliminate the gap. It is "hard to imagine," he says, "that there have not been different selection pressures for different abilities in various cultures and that these pressures would be as great for intelligence as for many physical characteristics which are known to differ genetically among racial groups."[97]

Is it in fact so hard? Intelligence, one can argue, is a different sort of trait (or collection of traits) from any other. If we choose to breed people in a selective fashion, as we do with mice or dogs, then we could no doubt develop innate capacities for running mazes or chasing rabbits and consolidate family lines skilled or unskilled in the appropriate abilities. Intelligence, however, is not the same as running down a maze or chasing a rabbit or, perhaps, passing exams. As a general human attribute it may have put us by now in a quite different league than that of any other terrestrial species. It relies not only on organic endowment, though, but on cultural competences of a highly developed kind.

We can assume, too, I think, that reasoning capacity has proved adaptive in all human environments, particularly given the extent to which we create our own.

Thus less challenging or less severe life situations do not denote, as some assume, less selective pressures for intelligence. Can we discriminate as readily as Jensen seems to suggest between the intellectual skills of a nomadic Australian aborigine and those of a sedentary European-style suburbanite in one of that nation's coastal capitals? Just how significant *is* the distance between the educated, presumably intelligent Western anthropologist and his or her ''primitive'' subjects?[98] We may document legions of culturally acquired discrepancies, but can they be used to support statements about comparative mental capacity? I have already expressed reservations about IQ testing wherever it takes place. The correlations that exist between high scores and educational or occupational success are also liable to mislead (which is hardly surprising given the importance in determining one's personal prospects of familial socioeconomic or professional class, and the way money and authority accrue to those who are ''ruthless, cunning, avaricious, self-seeking, lacking in sympathy and compassion, subservient to authority, [and] willing to abandon principle for material gain''[99]—qualities that may or may not be accompanied by those of intelligence per se). Hence the specific conclusions Jensen comes to are highly suspect.

This need convince nobody since, as one shrewd observer puts it, even if ''we'' (white, supremacist, racist) had *proof of superior* ''negro'' intelligence, we would still have a long way to go to overcome contemporary prejudice; and ''any white reader who doubts this should simply ask himself [sic] whether he would trade the genes which make his skin white for genes which would raise his I.Q. 15 points.''[100] IQ studies among various global populations suggest in fact that the highest mean scores are to be found among peoples of Chinese and Japanese descent, and the Japanese in particular score well over ''white'' Britains and Americans,[101] which on a racist scale of world worth would suggest Mongoloid superiority. Again, this is not a conclusion one expects many ''whites'' would prefer to accept.

The only truly decisive test of genetic difference would require the creation of a uniform global environment in which individual capacities could flourish unchecked. To aspire to same would seem somewhat utopian (though the *attempt* might be well worthwhile given what it could mean for those less well off). When we consider the problems involved in testing intellectual abilities, plus those involved in standardizing environmental influences, there is very little we can say with certainty about genetic difference; and we do well simply to admit that diverse capacities will show up in various human groups under different test conditions, and leave it at that. Racial identification (or socioeconomic class, for that matter) is *not* a very useful piece of information to have for predicting in advance what any individual's abilities will be, hence group labels like this, while generating averaged expectations in general, have to be abandoned in the particular if we are to give scientific understanding its due. If genetic endowments are as sensitive to environmental stimulus as some suggest,[102] developing only where conditions are favorable and remaining irrelevant where they are not, this would reinforce the point. Environments may mask individual potential in more profound ways than we yet suspect, and it is a real problem realizing the freedom to be different (individual *and* collective) while securing rights to be the same. We can sort our way through this dilemma only by keeping in mind the importance of individual variation *and* what Tawney has called the "capital fact" of our common humanity.[103]

As the world moves toward one overarching industrial culture, it becomes irrelevant who first produced contemporary technology. *All* human groups possess the genetic means to adapt and improve on what others have done. "The essential point at issue is whether the abilities of large populations are so different that their capacity to participate in modern technical culture is affected. Remember in the first place that no race has evolved to fit the selective pressures of the modern world. Technical civilization is new. . . ."[104] Or, as the 1967 UNESCO statement on race puts it, "Current biological knowledge does not permit us to impute cultural achievements to differences in genetic potential. . . . The peoples of the world today appear to possess equal biological potentialities for attaining any level of civilization."[105] That knowledge is part of the process of defusing racial confrontation at large,[106] and the general attempt to reduce the importance of a pervasive human contradiction. There are, sadly, plenty more.

SEX

If race allows no reasonable predictions about individual behavior (unless defined not in biological but in cultural, and hence in much more mutable terms), what of *sex*, which would seem a most natural distinction for human society to make?

When Stephen, the nineteenth century British conservative, asked himself if sexual inequality was "real," he was able to reply:

> There are some propositions which it is difficult to prove, because they are so plain, and this is one of them . . . men are stronger than women in every shape. They have greater muscular and nervous force, greater intellectual force, greater vigour of character . . . [a] general truth, which has . . . in every age and country led to a division of labour . . . the general outline of which is as familiar and as universal as the general outline of the differences between them. [107]

So important is this inequality, he declared, that it makes any blanket argument for giving human rights to all simply inadmissable. Furthermore, it suggests that any attempt to change the present situation would prove fruitless, nay destructive, since it contravenes basic biological facts that will prevail. The sensible course would be to work within the limits these facts provide, since any attempt to extend them could only constitute an unnatural act.

In direct opposition to this point of view we find those who argue, equally deterministically, that human beings are born with no marked difference in potential except their reproductive and lactative ones, and that society alone decrees all else. It is natural for us to be unnatural, and we are renowned for ignoring our biologically given capacities or adding to them in culturally acquired ways.[108] We come into the world psychologically neutral, they say. Our natural propensities are highly diverse, and people become creatures of their natures "only if society enters into nature's conspiracy."[109] Men and women do, after all, share 45 of their 46 chromosomes, and the hormones that are specific to sexuality are present, albeit in different proportions, in both. In this view, how sex roles emerge depends upon whether one emphasizes a comparatively passive social-learning and reinforcement perspective ("I want rewards, I am rewarded for doing boy things, therefore I want to be a boy"); a cognitively active and developmental approach ("I am a boy, therefore I do boy things, therefore the opportunity to do boy things [and to gain approval for doing them] is rewarding");[110] or a psychoanalytically based identification theory like the one Freud built with his often bizarre "ethnography" of "bourgeois, turn-of-the-century Vienna."[111]

Between the two lie a range of possible positions. We can, for example, admit both a degree of biological programming *and* a capacity for countermanding genetic endowment that leaves the issue open for whatever particular parents and their culture might, wittingly or unwittingly, decide to do. Cultural socialization would then only "reflect" important biological determinants, or exacerbate what are only minor differences, or it might actually manufacture them.

It is often tempting, when confronted by such a welter of ideas, to assume that the truth lies on (or under) the middle ground between them. If we harbor such preferences, we should resist them, however, until we have reviewed the evidence more closely. (A question as important as this rarely receives a definitive answer anyway; it rather gets relocated in some more contemporary place.)

Three things can be said at the start: that sexual identity is a highly significant psychological and social fact in every human society now or ever known; that there is no recorded case of any such population being governed predominantly by women (bearing in mind that our understanding of other societies has been advanced mostly by men, and Western ones at that, on the information of other men, and will as a consequence be radically biased);[112] and that the notion of equality, as applied to the way the sexes act and can expect to be treated, is one of the "few truly revolutionary ideas in human history,"[113] winning general currency only recently under the general rubric of *human* equality as such.

It seems particularly difficult to sustain the point that in men and women we do not find irreducibly different sorts of being, and, if we do, that they merely constitute complementary components of the human enterprise, rather than competing ones. The whole realm is fraught with passion and paradox.[114] "Male and female are biological categories; masculinity and feminity are social definitions;"[115] but whether the former determines, predisposes, or can be shown to be actually irrelevant to the latter, and whether the former explains the recurrence of male dominance in human society at large—these things are far from clear.

What do we know about the average differences in attributes determined by sex? Here we must discriminate between *physical* and *psychological* factors. In the former case, the distinctions are both obvious and obscure. Elaborate attempts have been made to move from child-bearing, for example, to much more remote human activities to which it does not apply, such as whether or not females may join a society's governing elite. In the latter, psychological case, there seems to be surprisingly little to go on (which does not mean that the little we do find is not also highly significant).[116] Let us look at each set of factors in turn.

Physically, we can identify genetic, hormonal, and structural differences between the two human sexes. The structural differences include primary features (as these pertain to reproductive organs) and secondary ones (height, strength, body hair, susceptibility to disease, and so on). Secondary qualities vary widely across our species, and it proves very difficult to tell an individual's sex from these alone without knowing the actual physical range for the particular group to which he or she belongs. The primary qualities, however, are just that. Anomalies do occur, but usually the same sexually discrete syndrome happens at once. The obvious identification (by genitalia) is established anatomically. The hormonal and chromosomal distinctions are not so readily discerned, and must be established by technical means. When conception occurs the ovum of the female (with its X chromosome) is fertilized by the sperm of the male which, bearing either an X or a Y chromosome, thus determines the sex of the subsequent fetus. The basic mammalian "template" is a female one and, if the male-making process initiated by the XY combination does occur, then female differentiation takes place "by default."[117] More precisely, for the first few weeks the fetus has no sex (or rather, has the basic ingredients for both), and any difference can only be determined genetically. The critical influence is that played by the male sex hormones (androgens), and once these are present (provided by the mother, at first, in response to the Y chromosome, and then once the gonads differentiate, by the embryo himself), a male baby begins to develop. If androgens do not appear, the fetus is female. To be female, in other words, there need be no strategic intervention. The same hormones establish sex differences in that part of the brain (the hypothalamus) that eventually controls body cycles, and the presence of androgens in sufficient quantities will end (for the male) any capacity for the recurrent release from the pituitary gland of those biochemicals that regulate the monthly female round. This process is a complex one, however, and we do well to note that "the initial completeness of inhibition of feminine behavioral potential, in the course of normal differentiation, varies across species. . . . In man . . . it is probably not very complete, and is perhaps individually variable as well."[118]

What has this to do with behavior? Can we say that this *physiological* divergence has a direct effect *psychologically?* Does the presence or absence of androgens confer upon the human unit sexually specific neural characteristics that act ever thereafter on what the individual may do? No one can yet say with any certainty (which does not of course prevent them from doing so),[119] and what we might be able to deduce from those cases where the system "goes wrong" is ambiguous too.[120] There is no straightforward sex-based difference, for example, between "brain cells, sex-hormone uptake, and behavior"[121] and, though individuals of one sex may be more easily urged to act in a particular way, such as exerting their dominance or nurturing the young, such responses are difficult to establish as general, sex-specific ones. Hence, it is of considerable significance that a large part of the process of laying down sex identities takes place after birth, under the auspices of society at large.[122] And any argument that biologically male and female predispositions that induce male and female behavior are built into our basic "wiring" must be understood in this light.

Determining human sex is a process. What happens if we start at the other end, as it were, considering behavior and ability first and working back from there? Can we define mean differences that might denote deeper determinants that occur in all cultures and give us a clue as to where to look for cause? The comparative cross-cultural literature is sketchy,[123] and any biological commonalities are soon lost when we begin to consider other variables. Societies differ widely as well in the sort of moral prohibitions and life possibilities they offer individual men and women. Nonetheless, female child-care functions and male strength and assertiveness do seem very generally dispersed, and they do seem to predispose characteristic ways of dividing up human tasks and prompting characteristic patterns of human behavior. (Some might argue the case for an evolutionary logic at work here—warfare, for example, proving a male preserve simply because men have proved more expendable—though selective advantages that have worked thus far need not do so for the future, nor need they be necessarily resistant to cultural modification.) If women have to meet their needs through men, to some extent they will tend to learn to act in a fashion that fits their situation. If they are assigned thus in the first place because they are born women, the circle is closed, which explains a good deal about the way sexually discrete sorts of behavior get passed on.[124] The same sort of logic informs both racist and sexist ideologies in this respect: prevent a human group from enjoying equality of opportunity and then, because it does not fare as well as some *superior* social sector by their privileged standards of performance, declare it *inferior*.

Stereotypes persist and the typical judgment, despite every qualification and exception, seems to consider women as more

> passive (less active, less overtly dominating and aggressive), dependent (helpless, conforming, obedient, suggestible), nurturing (helpful to others, sympathetic, and empathetic), highly verbal, affiliative (sociable, popularity-oriented), and sexually restrained, [and men as more] achievement-motivated (for power and fame in political and economic activities) and, in adulthood, . . . [more] physically aggressive, emotionally inexpressive, and assertive about displaying and utilizing their intelligence.[125]

Most people have a clear idea about what gender they belong to and see themselves behaving accordingly. As such they are different simply because they think they are. They are more alike than they usually assume, however, and in listing attributes like those above we inevitably suggest differences that are categorical rather than points on a set of moving and moveable scales. Absolute distinctions are misleading since the overlaps *are* important, and what are only *averaged* qualities at best do not permit more than the most limited and probabilistic expectations about any particular person, and whether he or she actually represents the group mean.

In their comprehensive review of what is, admittedly, a culturally monocular literature, Maccoby and Jacklin found limited distance between the psychological propensities of women and men. From infancy on, or so the American evidence suggests, there are in fact close similarities in how we perceive, learn, and remember things, in achievement motivation, in sociability (as distinct from the nature of particular social relationships—boys more than girls tend to move in large groups that have dominance hierarchies), suggestibility, and sense of self-esteem. Males are more overtly aggressive (though, as Bardwick reminds us, "to measure the true levels of aggression in males and females one must include verbal aggression, interpersonal rejection, academic competitiveness, gossip . . . deviation from sexual standards, passive aggression . . . manipulation . . . will power, withdrawal, tears, and somatic complaints—as well as fighting, hitting, and biting").[126] Males also tend, on average, to perform better on visual-spatial tasks in mathematics. Females show greater average verbal ability, and though males are more dominant, females are not, paradoxically, very submissive. They are just "easier to exploit."[127] On such behavior traits as fear, timidity, and anxiety; physical activity; competitiveness; compliance; and propensities for "mothering"; the American evidence is mixed.

Females seem least susceptible to exploitation when they have a comparatively significant degree of control over the process of producing what society consumes and the material product itself.[128] In hunter-gatherer communities, what women glean from the land is more important for sustaining the group than what men kill. Not coincidentally, perhaps, any picture of the "dependent, pregnant female, huddled in the cave awaiting her provider's return from the hunt, trading sex for food,''[129] is patently false. Human equality under these circumstances is *relatively* well realized. The advent of agriculture, and of more predictable resource supplies, has historically allowed for larger families and the evolution of differences in kin group and ultimately class wealth. Women then tend to lose control of economic power, losing as well their tenuous claims for equal treatment too. They are no longer indispensable as material producers, and only with the invention of industry do they find substantial employment again as productive laborers in demand.

Though the discriminatory mores of agrarian living persist in today's industrial states, modest advances have been made in improving the relative status of women and in expanding their possible options; and industrially inspired ideologies like socialism have enabled the subject of sexual equality to be broached in such largely preindustrial countries as the People's Republic of China. The legitimacy of male dominance has been brought into question, at least, and that, in historical terms, is extraordinary enough. There is still the problem that a ''predominantly masculinity-oriented equality may facilitate an increasing similarity between the sexes, without a parallel change in societal institutions,'' which may be unequal in other ways.[130] But there is point to getting to base one first.

To the extent that the sexes are alike—and we can say that in many ways they are—then arguments for their inequality do not apply. Where they are unalike we can envisage a range of possible responses. Some, like Stephen, would see women as different, regardless, *and* inferior and would simply celebrate the status quo. Differences can also be deliberately exaggerated. Thus one could argue that societies should teach girls to submit gracefully, so as to facilitate their adult encounters with their naturally more dominant male partners. Such differences could also, conceivably, be reduced by cultivating greater male passivity. If the latter really did contravene an innate male propensity, then it could only be done at cost, measured, as Wilson puts it, in the ''added energy required for education and reinforcement and in the attrition of individual freedom and potential.''[131] Against this, of course, one would need to count the *increase* in *female* freedom and potential, so long and so successfully denied.

Debates about equality of this kind are closely bound up with a whole series of revisions taking place in the world that are making over ''traditional'' societies, so-called, into urbanized, industrial ones. Contemporary concepts of the male and female role tend to get redefined in the process in terms of the social circumstances that are coming to prevail, and these in turn reflect profound changes in the global mode of production. Where the changes have gone farthest, individual identity has often become problematic. No longer is it conferred by birth. It must be bargained for, on the sort of personal basis that presumes considerable self-awareness and self-confidence. No wonder so many people view such changes askance, preferring to stay within their gender-drawn boundaries rather than moving out to defend either more human or more personally oriented ones.

This says far too little about the history of subjugation that otherwise civilized philosophies have allowed. As world society comes to require more people with whatever are deemed to be the appropriate capacities that make it work, however, then it is likely to prove more difficult to keep the able members of half the human species habitually hobbled. Since scientific evidence does not indicate any genetically based difference that need matter in this respect, it is sociocultural conditioning that stands in the way.

EQUALITY OF HUMAN WORTH

The concept of equality is based in the end on the idea of human dignity and worth, on the prescriptive recognition of individuals, as Kant argued, as ends in themselves.[132] While we know that what some people do in the particular will be better than others, we can also acknowledge that this applies to their performance (their doing) and not their person (their being), i.e., that superior or inferior performance does not in general denote a superior or inferior personality.[133] Confusing the two has significant consequences, for we then find ourselves unduly honoring some human beings while "gratuitously" humiliating others, and much of the ground for advocating human rights and social justice gets lost as well. The confusion is common, where it is not positively promoted, since in competitive societies like our own, and increasingly world society, those who do well are always apt to congratulate themselves on their competence at large. And those who fail find it hard not to see in that a reflection on their whole selves. To counter this tendency, we have to force such evaluations apart and find what is of value in the individual that we ought to respect. This means concentrating not on our specific capacities, which will differ, but upon those that we all share (our capacity to act autonomously, for example, to exploit a "private space," and to further our self-development).[134]

Individualism of any sort can be taken too far. As radically social beings, an individualistic ethic is ultimately a rather arid one for human beings to bear. The belief in equality does not have to be pushed to this point, however. Society, as I said earlier, precedes[135] the individual, and equality is a social attribute to be achieved collectively or not at all. Equality means nothing except in terms of social comparisons, and since respect for a person requires the recognition of both his or her individual *and* social properties, the attempt to achieve the sort of equality that nurtures the individual will of necessity consider how supportive and permissive the collective is too. Which brings us back to where this chapter began. Like the Klein bottle, each seems to contain the other, and it is little wonder we are bemused. The visual ambiguity has its philosophic analog. We confront a closed surface, and it has a single side.[135]

NOTES

1. *Equality* and *identity* are not synonymous, however. For a discussion of this and the conceptual dimensions of the concept, see H. Bedan, "Egalitarianism and the Idea of Equality," in J. Pennock and J. Chapman, eds., *Equality* (N.Y.: Atherton Press, 1967).
2. M. Lewis, *The Culture of Inequality* (Amherst: University of Massachusetts Press, 1978) pp. 3–4.
3. J. Gardner, *Excellence—Can We Be Equal and Excellent Too?* (New York: Harper and Bros., 1961) p. 3.
4. L. Dumont, *Homo Hierarchicus* (London: Weidenfield and Nicolson, 1970), p. 11.
5. Ibid., p. 4.
6. Ibid., p. 8.
7. Ibid., p. 9:

> . . . there are two mutually opposed configurations. . . . In the first, as in Plato's Republic, the stress is placed on society as a whole, as collective Man; the ideal derives from the organization of society with respect to its ends (and not with respect to individual happiness); it is above all a matter of order, of hierarchy; each particular man in his place must contribute to the global order, and justice consists in ensuring that proportions between social functions are adapted to the whole. In modern society, on the contrary, the Human Being is regarded as the indivisible, "elementary" man, both a biological being and a thinking subject. Each particular man in a sense incarnates the whole of mankind. He is the measure of all things (in a full and novel sense). . . . What is called "society" is the means, the life of each man is the end. . . .

Cf. A. de Tocqueville, *Democracy in America* (Alfred Knopf, N.Y., 1953), vol. 2, pp. 90–92:

> Among aristocratic nations, as families remain for centuries in the same condition, often on the same spot, all generations become as it were contemporaneous. A man almost always knows his forefathers, and respects them: he thinks he already sees his remote descendants, and he loves them. . . . Aristocratic institutions have, moreover, the effect of closely binding every man to several of his fellow-citizens. . . . As in aristocratic communities all the citizens occupy fixed positions, one above the other, the result is that each of them always sees a man above himself whose patronage is necessary to him, and below himself another man whose cooperation he may claim. . . . It is true that in those ages the notion of human fellowship is faint, and that men seldom think of sacrificing themselves for mankind; but they often sacrifice themselves for other men. . . . Amongst democratic nations new families are constantly springing up, others are constantly falling away, and all that remain change their condition; the woof of time is every instant broken, and the track of generations effaced. . . . As each class approximates to other classes, and intermingles with them, its members become indifferent and as strangers to one another. . . . Thus not only does democracy make every man forget his ancestors, but it hides his descendants, and separates his contemporaries from him; it throws him back forever upon himself alone, and threatens in the end to confine him entirely within the solitude of his own heart.

8. R. Lane, "The Fear of Equality," *American Political Science Review* 53, no. 1 (March 1959): 35–6.

9. Ibid., p. 49.

10. Ibid., p. 50.

11. See, for example, R. H. Tawney, *Equality* (London: George Allen and Unwin, 1964); H. Stretton, *Capitalism, Socialism and the Environment* (Cambridge: Cambridge University Press, 1976).

12. Stretton, *Capitalism, Socialism*, pp. 171–3.

13. R. Tucker, "Egalitarianism and International Politics," *Commentary* 60, no. 3 (September 1975): 31; also his extended treatment in *The Inequality of Nations* (N.Y.: Basic Books, 1976). Also F. Ajami, "The Global Logic of the NeoConservatives," *World Politics* 30, no. 3 (April 1978): 450-68.

14. Stretton, *Capitalism, Socialism*, p. 180.

15. Ibid., p. 181.

16. M. Young, *The Rise of the Meritocracy* (London: Thames and Hudson, 1958), p. 21.

17. We might note large-scale preindustrial examples of such provisioning, like that of the Inca Kingdom of Peru. The impetus here was paternalistic, as one might expect of an absolutist theocracy. This should not be allowed to detract from what were considerable achievements, however, particularly in view of the plight of the modern descendants of those once so ruled. See W. Prescott, *The Conquest of Peru* (N.Y.: Mentor, 1961).

18. J. Galtung, "The New International Economic Order and the Basic Needs Approach," *Alternatives* 4, no. 4 (March 1979): 455–473.

19. D. Thomson, *Equality* (Cambridge: Cambridge University Press, 1949), p. 73.

20. Ibid., p. 40. In England we also find pre-Industrial Revolution precursors of this historical push, e.g. the Diggers and the Levellers of Crommellian times.

21. Ibid., p. 158.

22. E. Wilson, *On Human Nature* (Cambridge: Harvard University Press, 1978), p. 56. Cf. B. Williams, "The Idea of Equality," in P. Laslett and W. Runciman, eds., *Philosophy, Politics and Society* (Oxford: Basil Blackwell, 1952), p. 148:

    Most moral thinkers in the past, and not a few in the present, assume that the only rational justification for a moral opinion must, so to speak, extend outwards and upwards, away from the choosing self. I believe that X is wrong: I justify this in terms of a rule: this in turn is justified in terms of a higher rule, and so on: until perhaps I find myself building a watertight system of metaphysical morality, a giant framework of absolute and externalised rules, or even a political utopia in which all my desires, or what I believe to be my desired, find full expression. But there is a kind of rational justification which moves in a different direction, inwards, and downwards into the human psyche: and it is to this that we have to turn, retracing our steps down the pyramid of moral criteria . . . back to the self.

23. E. and N. Wood, *Ideology and Ancient Political Theory: Socrates, Plato and Aristotle in Social Context* (Oxford: Basil Blackwell, 1978), p. 260.

24. "I think that wise and good men ought to rule those who are foolish and bad"; J. Stephen, *Liberty, Equality, Fraternity* (Cambridge: Cambridge University Press, 1967), p. 212; this is an unexceptional statement until we come to specify which is which, and from where we might recruit the former. To Stephen, as a good nineteenth-century British conservative, "equality" was the "most emphatic" and the "least distinct" of the modern values and in a "vast number of cases . . . [was] nothing more than a vague expression of envy on the part of those who have not against those who have, and a vague aspiration towards a state of society in which there should be fewer contrasts than there are at present between one man's lot and another's." (p. 179) The argument from envy is, as Stretton says, "absurd." Envy of this sort exists, of course, but to call it the prime impetus of the egalitarian is to parody that position; it cannot disguise the pernicious aspects of privilege nor the fact that "whatever the rich have, the poor could use" (Stretton, *Capitalism, Socialism*, p. 170). When it came to *political* equality,

Stephen had a more interesting case to make. Universal suffrage would not change the configuration of political power, he said. This might assume a new "shape" but not a new "nature": "The result of cutting it up into little bits is simply that the man who can sweep the greatest number of them into one heap will govern the rest" (p. 211). Again, however, we find the undisguised advocacy of social elitism. (Note the contempt in the domestic analogy of an electoral broom.) The rhetoric is splendid nonetheless:

> Equality, like liberty, appears to be a big name for a small thing. The enthusiasm about it in recent times seems to me to have been due principally to two circumstances: the invidious position of the French privileged classes before the Revolution, and the enormous development of wealth in the United States. . . The case of the French privileged classes certainly was as gross a case of a distinction without a difference as has ever occurred in the world, and the French are just in the mood to become rhetorical about it. . . . The success of equality in America is due, I think, mainly to the circumstances that a large number of people, who were substantially equal in all the more important matters, recognised that fact and did not set up unfounded distinctions. How far they actually are equal now, and how long they will continue to be equal when the population becomes dense, is quite another question. It is also a question . . . whether the enormous development of equality in America, the rapid growth of an immense multitude of common-place, self-satisfied, and essentially slight people is an exploit which the whole world need fall down and worship. [P. 220]

25. S. Lakoff, *Equality in Political Philosophy* (Cambridge: Harvard University Press, 1964), p. 174; the reference is again to De Tocqueville.
26. G. Vlastos, "Justice and Equality," in R. Brandt, ed., *Social Justice* (N.J.: Prentice-Hall, 1962); W. von Leyden, "On Justifying Inequality," *Political Studies* 11, no. 1 (1963): 56–70.
27. W. Ryan, *Blaming the Victim* (London: Orbach and Chambers, 1971), p. 19. See also my chapter six.
28. The question is "whether the range of alternatives open to ordinary men [sic], and the capacity of the latter to follow their own preferences in choosing between them have or have not been increased by measures correcting inequalities or neutralising their effects. If an affirmative reply can be given, liberty and equality can live as friends; if a negative one, they are condemned to be foes" (Tawney, *Equality*, p. 229).
29. I. Berlin, "Equality as an Ideal," in F. Olafson, ed., *Social Policy* (N.J.: Prentice-Hall, 1961), p. 149.
30. Thomson, *Equality*, p. 139.
31. J. Plamenatz, "Equality of Opportunity," in L. Bryson, et al., eds., *Aspects of Human Equality* (N.Y.: Harper and Bros., 1956), p. 106.
32. Olafson, *Social Policy*, p. 112.
33. Lakoff, *Equality in Political Philosophy*, p. 7. Also W. Gallie, "Liberal Morality and Socialist Morality," in P. Laslett, ed., *Philosophy, Politics and Society* (Oxford: Basil Blackwell, 1956), pp. 123–28.
34. Lakoff, *Equality in Political Philosophy*, p. 238.
35. T. Hobbes, *Leviathan* (London: Fontana, 1962), p. 141. The Greeks would have included here "social class". See p. 23.
36. Williams, "Idea of Equality," p. 115.
37. Greenberg, "Commentary," in L. Bryson, op. cit., p. 110.
38. F. Johnson, "The Concept of Human Equality," p. 25.
39. Williams, "Idea of Equality," p. 113.
40. P. Mason, *Patterns of Dominance* (Oxford: Oxford University Press, 1970), p. 5.
41. J. Laponce, "Relating Biological, Physical and Political Phenomena: The Case of Up and Down," *Social Science Information* 17, no. 3 (1978): 385–97.
42. Ibid., p. 391.

43. Ibid., p. 393.
44. In the West we find a standard conservative riposte here. Thus Stephen, "the Gruffian," declares that "a man who has a disinterested love for the human race—that is to say, who has got a fixed idea about some way of providing for the management of the concerns of mankind—is an unaccountable person . . . capable of making his love for men in general the ground for all sorts of violence against men in particular" (*Liberty, Equality, Fraternity*, p. 239) What, however, of a philosophy that as its "fixed idea" would defend humankind *in the particular* from social abuse? Tricky, what?
45. W. Sombart, *The Quintessence of Capitalism* (London: T. Fisher Unwin, 1915), pp. 203–4.
46. D. Olson, "Culture, Technology and Intellect," in L. Preswick, ed., *The Nature of Intelligence* (Hillsdale, N.J.: L. Erlbaum Associates, 1976) p. 199.
47. D. Stenhouse, *The Evolution of Intelligence* (London: George Allen and Unwin, 1973), p. 69.
48. W. Charlesworth, "Ethology: Understanding the Other Half of Intelligence," *Social Science Information* 17, no. 2 (1978): 246.
49. Young, *Rise of the Meritocracy*.
50. R. Herrnstein, *IQ in the Meritocracy* (London: Allen Lane, 1973), p. 1. Eighty percent is the figure he cites.
51. Ibid., p. 129.
52. Ibid., p. 163.
53. Ibid., p. 142.
54. P. Vernon, *Intelligence: Heredity and Environment* (San Francisco: W. H. Freeman, 1979), Ch. 13, "The Interpretation of Heritability."
55. H. Eysenck, *The Inequality of Man* (San Diego: Edits, 1975); T. Bouchard, "Genetic Factors in Intelligence," in A. Kaplan, ed., *Human Behavior Genetics* (Springfield: Charles C. Thomas, 1976).
56. Eysenck, *Inequality of Man*, p. 220.
57. Ibid., p. 223.
58. Young, *Rise of the Meritocracy*, pp. 135–6.
59. D. Spitz, ed., *On Liberty: John Stuart Mill* (N.Y.: W. W. Norton, 1975).
60. Eysenck, *Inequality of Man*, p. 261.
61. N. Block and G. Dworkin, *The IQ Controversy* (N.Y.: Pantheon, 1974) for the Lippmann/Terman debate where the basic issues were originally rehearsed. Also L. Kamin, *The Science and Politics of IQ* (New York: Laurence Erlbaum, 1974), Ch. 1.
62. A. Gartner, et al., eds., *The New Assault on Equality: IQ and Social Stratification* (N.Y.: Harper and Row, 1974), p. 5; also C. Fischer, "Intelligence contra IQ," in K. Riegal, ed., *Intelligence: Alternative Views of a Paradigm* (Basel: S. Karger, 1973).
63. D. Robinson, "If You're So Rich, You Must Be Smart," in C. Senna, ed., *The Fallacy of IQ* (N.Y.: The Third Press, 1973), p. 23. Also H. Butcher, *Human Intelligence: Its Nature and Assessment* (London: Methuen, 1968), Ch. 4, "Creativity and Intelligence."
64. Kamin, *Science and Politics of IQ*, p. 34.
65. Ibid., p. 176.
66. See Vernon, *Intelligence*, Ch. 11 (noting the frontispiece disclaimer); Kamin, *Science and Politics of IQ*, Ch. 3.
67. L. Hearnshaw, *Cyril Burt, Psychologist* (London: Hodder and Stoughton, 1979).
68. Kamin, *Science and Politics of IQ*, p. 34. Also J. Blum, *Pseudoscience and Mental Ability* (N.Y.: Monthly Review Press, 1979), pp. 13–19.
69. Butcher, *Human Intelligence*, p. 40.
70. Ibid., p. 49.
71. J. Kagan, "What is Intelligence?" in Gartner *New Assault on Equality,* p. 114.

72. T. Dobzhansky, *Genetic Diversity and Human Equality* (New York: Basic Books, 1973), pp. 31–2.

73. Ibid., p. 49.

74. P. Vernon, *Intelligence and Cultural Environment* (London: Methuen, 1969); R. Lynn, "Ethnic and Racial Differences in Intelligence: International Comparisons," in R. Osborne, et al., eds., *Human Variation: The Biopsychology of Age, Race, and Sex* (N.Y.: Academic Press, 1978).

75. R. Lewontin, "The Apportionment of Human Diversity," in T. Dobzhansky et al., eds., *Evolutionary Biology* (N.Y.: Appleton-Century-Crofts, 1972), vol. 6, p. 381:

    It has always been obvious that organisms vary, even to those pre-Darwinian idealists who saw most individual variation as distorted shadows of an ideal. It has been equally apparent, even to those post-Darwinians for whom variation between individuals is the central fact of evolutionary dynamics, that variation is nodal, that individuals fall in clusters in the space of phenotypic description, and that those clusters, which we call clines, or races, or species, are the outcome of an evolutionary process acting on the individual variation. What has changed during the evolution of scientific thought, and is still changing, is our perception of the relative importance and extent of intragroup as opposed to intergroup variation.

76. C. Brace et al., eds., *Race and Intelligence* (Washington: American Anthropological Association, 1971) p. 4.

77. Ibid., p. 5.

78. F. Ebling, ed., *Racial Variation in Man* (London: The Institute of Biology, 1975), p. xiv.

79. C. Coon, *The Origin of Races* (London: Jonathan Cape, 1963). Thus Coon's definition of a race is that of a human population, physically unique. See C. Coon et al, *Races* (Springfield: Charles C. Thomas, 1950), p. xiv.

80. A. Alland, *Human Diversity* (N.Y.: Columbia University Press, 1971), Ch. 4, "The Fossil Background and the Origin of Races."

81. M. Day, "The Evolution of Man," *Racial Variation in Man*, p. 7.

82. Alland, *Human Diversity*, p. 55. Also S. Washburn: "There are no three primary races, no three major groups. The idea of three primary races stems from nineteenth-century typology . . . (p. 523, in his "The Study of Race," *American Anthropologist*, vol. 65 (1963).

83. Alland, *Human Diversity,* p. 62.

84. Lewontin, "Apportionment of Human Diversity," p. 397.

85. A. Montagu, *Man's Most Dangerous Myth* (N.Y.: Oxford University Press, 1974), 5th ed. See also M. Banton and J. Harwood, *The Race Concept* (London: David and Charles, 1975).

86. "The average person in our society [and many a creation myth provides parallels] observes that certain other persons belonging to different ethnic groups possess physical and mental traits which differ from his [sic] own." He concludes that these physical and mental traits are somehow linked together, and these traits are inborn and immutable. Vague notions about a unilinear evolution "from monkey to man" encourage him to believe that such "races" are "lower" in the "scale" of evolution than is the group to which he belongs; that there is a hierarchy of "races." From such a starting point as "prehistoric man," he envisages a continous progression upward, culminating in the final development of his own "race" as a group. Between "prehistoric man" and himself stand, in an intermediate position, "all other peoples of mankind. . . ." "There are," however, as Montagu maintains, "no scientific grounds for this conception" *Man's Most Dangerous Myth*, p. 101. See also S. Rose, "Scientific Racism and Ideology," in Ebling, *Racial Variation in Man.*

87. E. Leach, "Cultural Components in the Concept of Race," in Ebling, *Racial Variation in Man*, pp. 30, 54.

88. Dobzhansky, *Evolutionary Biology*; see also P. Kilham and P. Klopfer in M. Mead et al., eds., *Science and the Concept of Race* (New York: Columbia University Press, 1968).
89. Dobzhansky, *Evolutionary Biology*, p. 72.
90. J. Loehlin, et al., *Race Differences in Intelligence* (San Francisco: W. H. Freeman, 1975), p. 24.
91. F. Hulse, "Social Behavior and Human Diversity," in R. Osborne, ed., *The Biological and Social Meaning of Race* (San Francisco: W. H. Freeman, 1971), p. 77.
92. Leach, "Cultural Components," p. 29.
93. E. Sunderland, "Biological Components of the Races of Man" in Ebling, *Racial Variations in Man*, p. 24.
94. T. Dobzhansky, "Race Equality" in Osborne, *Biological and Social Meaning of Race*, p. 14.
95. B. Ginsburg and W. Laughlin, "The Distribution of Genetic Differences in Behavioral Potential in the Human Species" in Mead et al., *Science and the Concept of Race*, p. 34.
96. A. Jensen, "Can and Should We Study Race Differences?" in Brace et al., *Race and Intelligence*, p. 17. See also the peculiarly anachronistic "morphologist," J. Baker, *Race* (London: Oxford University Press, 1974).
97. Jensen, "Can and Should We Study," in Brace, *Race and Intelligence*, pp. 18–19.
98. These differences emerge in an amusing way from Laura Bohannan's account of *Hamlet* to a group of Tiv elders. Only after rearranging the play as she related it to suit their own cultural precepts were her listeners satisfied. In this they were not notably less adept than Bohannan herself, despite the general way the anecdote serves the patronising ethnocentric calculus: "anthropologist" = objective, aware, superior; "native" = quaint, ignorant, inferior: "Sometime," concluded the old man, gathering his ragged toga about him, "you must tell us some more stories of your country. We . . . will instruct you in their true meaning, so that when you return to your own land your elders will see that you have not been sitting in the bush, but among those who know things and who have taught you wisdom" (P. Boch, ed., *Culture Shock* [N.Y.: Alfred A. Knopf, 1970], p. 300). Also T. Kroeber, *Ishi in Two Worlds* (Berkeley: University of California Press, 1961).
99. N. Chomsky, "The Fallacy of Richard Herrnstein's I.Q.," in Block and Dworkin, *IQ Controversy*, p. 296.
100. Robinson, "If You're So Rich," in Senna, *Fallacy of IQ*, p. 41. See also K. Liungman, *What is IQ?* (London: Gordon Cremonesi, 1975), Ch. 23.
101. Lynn, p. 283.
102. S. Scarr-Salapatek, "Race, Social Class and IQ," *Science* 174 (1971): 1285–95.
103. Tawney, *Equality*, p. 197.
104. Washburn, "Study of Race," p. 527–8.
105. L. Kuper, ed., *Race, Science and Society* (Paris: UNESCO, 1975), p. 360; also M. Gluckman, "New Dimensions of Change, Conflict and Settlement," ibid.
106. Given particular credence by H. Tinker, *Race, Conflict and International Order* (London: Macmillan, 1977), p. 135; also G. Shepherd, et al., eds., *Race Among Nations* (Lexington: D. C. Heath, 1970).
107. Stephen, *Liberty, Equality, Fraternity*, pp. 193–4: "Strength, in all its forms, is life and manhood. To be less strong is to be less of a man, whatever else you may be. . . . The greater part of our humanity appears to me to be a mere increase of nervous sensibility in which I feel no satisfaction at all" (p. 199). This leads Stephen to the somewhat tautologous conclusion that it is the "strongest man in some form or other who will always rule."
108. R. Fox, *Encounter with Anthropology* (Harmondsworth: Penguin, 1975), p. 43.
109. B. Rosenberg and S. Sutton-Smith, *Sense and Identity* (New York: Holt, Rinehart and Winston, 1972), p. 36.

110. L. Kohlberg, "A Cognitive-Developmental Analysis of Children's Sex-Role Concepts and Attitudes," in E. Maccoby, ed., *The Development of Sex Differences* (Stanford, Calif: Stanford University Press, 1966), p. 89. Cf. W. Mischel, "A Social-Learning View of Sex Differences in Behavior" in the above.

111. P. Van den Berghe, *Age and Sex in Human Societies*: A Biosocial Perspective (Belmont: Wadsworth Publishing Co., 1973), p. 46. Also I. Frieze et al., *Women and Sex Roles* (N.Y.: W. W. Norton, 1978).

112. S. Goldberg, *Male Dominance*: The Inevitability of Patriarchy (London: Abacus, 1979):
     Patriarchy, male attainment, and male dominance are social manifestations of the fact that male physiology is such that the environmental presence of a hierarchy, high-status role, or member of the other sex makes the male, more often and more strongly than the female, (1) feel feelings of competitiveness and need for attainment and dominance, (2) suppress other feelings and sacrifice other rewards, and, therefore (3) exhibit whatever behaviour is necessary in any given society to attain position, status role, and dominance in male-female relationships. [p. 72]
     . . . There is not a single other nontrivial hypothesis in all sociology for which one can invoke [as Goldberg argues one can here] both anthropological universality and direct neuroendocrinological evidence. [p. 137]

113. Van den Berghe, *Age and Sex*, p. 52.

114. C. Tauris and C. Offir, *The Longest War* (New York: Harcourt, Brace, Jovanovich, 1977), p. 3.

115. B. Yorburg, *Sexual Identity* (N.Y.: Wiley, 1974), p. vii.

116. E. Maccoby and C. Jacklin, *The Psychology of Sex Differences* (Stanford, Calif.: Stanford University Press, 1974), particularly Ch. 10. Also M. Wittig and A. Petersen, eds., *Sex-Related Differences in Cognitive Functioning* (San Francisco: Academic Press, 1979), particularly the Epilogue.

117. C. Hutt, *Males and Females* (Harmondsworth: Penguin, 1972), pp. 17, 18.

118. J. Money and A. Ehrhardt, *Man and Woman, Boy and Girl*: The Differentiation and Dimorphism of Gender Identity from Conception to Maturity (Baltimore: Johns Hopkins University Press, 1972), p. 91.

119. See for example, Goldberg, *Male Dominance.*

120. Money and Ehrhardt, *Man and Woman.* Also S. Weitz, *Sex Roles:* Biological, Psychological and Social Foundations (N.Y.: Oxford University Press, 1977), Ch. 1.

121. Money and Ehrhardt, *Man and Woman*, p. 247.

122. Ibid., p. 18.

123. P. Rosenblatt and M. Cunningham, "Sex Differences in Cross-cultural Perspective," in B. Lloyd and J. Archer, eds., *Exploring Sex Differences* (London: Academic Press, 1976).

124. J. Williams, *Psychology of Women*: Behavior in a Biosocial Context (N.Y.: W. W. Norton, 1974), p. 388.

125. B. Yorburg, *Sexual Identity* (N.Y.: Wiley, 1974), p. 15. Note also J. Bardwick, *Psychology of Women* (N.Y.: Harper and Row, 1971), p. 100:
     The male mind discriminates, analyzes, separates, and refines. . . . "Masculine" is objective, analytic, active, toughminded, rational, unyielding, intrusive, counteracting, independent, self-sufficient, emotionally controlled, and confident. The feminine mind knows relatedness, has an intuitive perception of feeling, has a tendency to unite rather than separate. . . . "Feminine" is subjective intuitive, passive, tenderminded, sensitive, impressionistic, yielding, receptive, empathic, dependent, emotional and conservative.

126. Ibid., p. 134.

127. Maccoby and Jacklin, *Psychology of Sex Differences*, p. 371.

128. R. Blumberg, *Stratification*: Socio-economic and Sexual Inequality (Dubuque: Wm. C. Brown, 1978), Ch. 3.

129. Ibid., p. 7.

130. H. Holter, *Sex Roles and Social Structure* (Oslo: Universitetsforlaget, 1970), p. 279.

131. E. O. Wilson, *On Human Nature* (Cambridge: Harvard University Press, 1978), p. 134.

132. S. Lukes, *Individualism* (Oxford: Basil Blackwell, 1973), p. 125.

133. G. Vlastos, "Justice and Equality," in Brandt, *Social Justice*, pp. 70–71.

134. Lukes, *Individualism*, pp. 131–3.

135. By which I mean that for most people, to be born is to enter a social context at once. Even should the parent or parents be quite alone he or she or they will bear the imprint of the culture from which they have come, even where they have chosen to repudiate it. The idea of an individual born outside such a context is conceivable, but the human product, as in the few documented cases of the phenomenon, will be a feral one. The individual, in this sense, *assumes* the social.

136. Ibid., p. 149:

> For, on the one hand, such respect requires us to take account of them as social selves—moulded and constituted by their societies—whose achievement of, and potential for, autonomy, whose valued activities and involvements and whose potentialities are, in large part, socially determined and specific to their particular social contexts. On the other hand, it requires us to see each of them as an actually or potentially autonomous centre of choice (rather than a bundle composed of a certain range of wants, motives, purposes, interests, etc.), able to choose between, and on occasion transcend, socially-given activities and involvements, and to develop his or her respective potentialities in the available forms sanctioned by the culture—which is both a structural constraint and a determinant of individuality.

4

Freedom from Hunger and Freedom to Choose

Liberty, as applied to humankind, denotes specific spheres of individual or collective action and the extent to which they are conditioned or unfree. We speak of those with liberty as those who are unfettered in some way, hence the semantic net that surrounds the idea seems to be centered upon the notion of nonconstraint. That is only a beginning, however. Who are these people precisely? From what are they free? What do they do? For how long? And at whose expense? Constraints are many and so are the possible sorts of liberty their absence predisposes.

The concept makes for fine phrases, but we soon learn to be cynical of how such words are used. Their catch-all quality obscures in this case a very mixed bag indeed.

"Liberty is really a vague collective for a host of social and moral dilemmas and conflicts. Some liberties are good, some are bad, some are indifferent. People disagree which are which. Some of the disagreements can be resolved by agreeing to generally liberal institutions . . . [some] can't . . . liberty is a conflict-of-interest problem . . . a class or a race problem . . . an efficiency problem. . . . Some liberties-to-prey belong in the jungle and are just as deadly anywhere else. Very poor people haven't many options: [then] liberty can be a problem of economic growth or redistribution. Most liberties have to be institutionally created and protected: [then] liberty is a constitutional, administrative, design-and-construction problem. Though valued as equally free, different societies may offer differently detailed patterns of choice . . . [then] liberty is a shopping problem. Liberties are unreal unless people have will and skill to use them: [then] liberty is a hearth-and-home, educational, character-building problem . . . many freedoms for me impose constraints on you . . . [for this] then and a great many other reasons liberty is always a problem of power. Freedom, power and subjection can easily be three people's impressions of the same relationship: then liberty is a question of definition," and of what we value as right, good, true, useful or dear.[1]

LIBERTY DEFINED

Can we pattern the analytic mesh to give us a more coherent understanding of the confusion of issues caught above? Several notable attempts have been made to do so, and they range across the same socialist/liberal/conservative spectrum mentioned in the previous chapter. A typically *liberal* conception of liberty would see the good society as, above all, an efficient one, where we are each free to get what we deserve in competition with everyone else. The good government in this view is the one that allows as much individual choice and as much of the interplay of competitive merit as possible. The *socialist* creed would tend to defend the liberty to be ("whatever is worth being for its own sake") rather than to acquire ("that so-called 'fair reward,' which is so often got by snatching it from under the nose of one's neighbor"). Societies and governments are judged in terms of their capacity to secure the material welfare of all and the necessary practical conditions of any good or truly human life.[2] A socialist would do this by eliminating *collectively* the waste and insecurity that is seen to follow from liberal competition. Which brings us to the *conservatives* who consider liberty the particular privilege of those, because of their socially superior status, who happen to inherit it, or those upon whom the paternal patronage of some superior is bestowed.

Each of the above depends predictably upon specific assumptions about human nature, and the analysis of the genetics of altruism *versus* self-interest is as relevant here as it was earlier on in this work. What else can be said in a general way? Among the less obviously ideological accounts of the concept, Mason, for example, distinguishes between the conventional categories of *legal* liberty (the ruling rulers), *economic* liberty (the ways we have of realizing a fair return for work done), and *social* liberty (how we insure opportunities for individual achievement, mutual respect, and communal esteem).[3] Adler is more analytical, placing primary emphasis upon liberties or freedoms as natural, circumstantial, or acquired. *Natural* freedoms are "(i) inherent in *all* men, [sic] (ii) regardless of the circumstances under which they live and (iii) *without regard* to any state of mind or character which they may or may not acquire in the course of their lives";[4] *circumstantial* freedoms are those contingent upon the particular arrangements under which we reside and strive to act;[5] and *acquired* freedom denotes the development of a "certain state of mind or character"[6] or the attainment of designated traits that can then be used to identify the liberated person or group. He draws secondary distinctions between *self-realization* ("an individual's ability to act as he wishes for the sake of the good as he sees it");[7] *self-perfection* (which distinguishes the "acquired freedom of being able to will as one ought from the circumstantial freedom of being able to do as one pleases";[8] and *self-determination* (by which he means "an individual's natural ability to determine for himself what he wishes to do or to become")[9].

Combining these two dimensions—the three modes of possession and the three changes in the self—and allowing for two particular variations on the major themes, namely, *political* liberty (that freedom we may attribute to the individual "in virtue of his political status as a citizen")[10] and *collective* freedom ("which the human race will enjoy collectively in the future when it has achieved the ideal mode of association that is the goal of mankind's historical development")[11], Adler can classify a very wide range of ideas indeed. He formulates a single definition that he claims incorporates them all[12] and concludes by arguing that *un*freedom is "to lack the power whereby the self can make what it does and what it achieves its own, *or* to be overpowered by another" (so that what happens to the self, for instance, is the work of somebody else).[13]

Adler's framework allows of much finer detail than the summary above suggests, and he is able to show very clearly the extent of the agreement and the disagreement between diverse historical and contemporary commentators. Despite, or perhaps because of, the complexities he so carefully articulates and displays, there seems something rather too straightforward about the ultimate conclusion, something too unheeding of past time and place. To regain a feel for the former, we must turn to someone like Malinowski. The latter sense is best restored by attending to analysts like Marx or Fromm.

Writing for a nation at war, Malinowski was concerned to find in freedom sufficient doctrinal force to counter the anticulture, as he saw it, of America's antagonists and to prevent them placing such an ideal at the service of their totalitarian beliefs. He considered any use of the word that described it in terms of the willing submission to constraint as plainly perverted, and, consequently, in the middle of his map of meanings, he depicted liberty as the absolute absence of all restraint.[14] This idea has two dimensions, he argued: a *transcendental* one where the human spirit becomes either indifferent or impervious to mortal strife (a conception that is essentially antilife as we know it), and one that can be defined in terms of *culture*, and the compensatory phenomena like conscience and magic that we use in our attempts to resist fate or control the play of happenstance. Three further antinomies (those between the negative and the positive, the subjective and the objective, and the release from versus the acceptance of law) suffice to bring the plethora of surrounding ideas into an ordered array. As one moves along the last continuum toward freedom *from* laws, Malinowski thought, one moves through liberalism and a sense of the increasingly unencumbered individual into anarchy. In the *other* direction, one encounters greater overt discipline, the creative use of authoritative rules that attempt to "force people to be free," and, ultimately, where the individual has been totally absorbed by the collective milieu, tyranny outright.

Malinowski railed against transcendentalists and all those who would cast the concept in personal, "free floating" terms, and he emphasized the need for a positive and concrete definition that allowed for specific social and cultural traits.

Real freedom, he concluded, is "always an increase in control, in efficiency, and in the power to dominate one's own organism and the environment," which means the "breaking down of certain obstacles . . . [the] compensation for certain deficiencies . . . [and the] acceptance of rules of nature, that is, scientific laws of knowledge, and of those norms and laws of human behavior which are indispensible to efficient cooperation."[15] It involves, as does any viable act, a degree of restraint, of unfreedom. Here the danger lies, he realized, in the way particular persons or groups can coopt the disciplinary means to serve their own desired ends, rather than those of the community or of humankind as a whole; in exalting constraint as an end in itself. "Claim too little for freedom and you leave scope for slavery. Claim too much and you allow its foes to prove that it cannot exist anywhere"[16] (or that it is *always* undesirable, or that it flourishes under conditions where we would do well to suspect that it does not). What are these "obstacles" that deserve to be destroyed, and why? What deficiencies must be made good, and how do we do so? What are the "rules of nature" that Malinowski enjoins us to accept? Despite the desire to forge a practical and tangible weapon worth wielding against the fascist foe, his answer to these very important questions amounts to little more than a sustained rhetorical flourish. We must move on.

The last assertion, that of obedience to scientific knowledge, recalls the Marxist-Leninist argument that "man is free when he becomes conscious of the necessity of his actions" and when he chooses thus to make a virtue out of what seems preordained.[17] Might he not, however, set a human purpose over and against a natural constraint if he deems it worthwhile and the cost of opposition seems justified? Nature is neither good nor bad. We are the ones who make such distinctions. We may give prior credence to what seems preordained because it is less presumptuous to do so, or we may not. Our modest acceptance of the inevitable may be well founded, but there is also often a good case to be made for attempting to transcend or subvert what we believe to be our "natural" limitations.

Marx himself, while concerned that humankind work *with* their natural propensities (in particular, their penchant for society and for creative productive endeavor) rather than *against* them, did not see individual actions as ultimately determined in quite the way many historical materialists were and still are wont to do. Humankind choose their own history, he argued, though the choosing is always done within specific social contexts conditioned in turn by whatever particular means are employed to produce what the society needs to subsist. This context comes down to us from our predecessors; we do not construct it for ourselves. It is a historically specific one, however, and so, therefore, is the bondage it imposes. Each such effect will be relative and impermanent, and furthermore, "if we can be allowed to generalize from the tenor of Marx's texts, it would seem that an individual would be more directly and fully determined in his economic relationships than in those remotely connected with his labor activity. . . . A more or less determined subject does not have to be unfree."[18]

The broad currents shaping human history work upon entire class structures, which leaves ample scope, Marx held (at least within his general evolutionary/revolutionary schema), for personal voluntarism. The historical context remains crucial. Thus under *capitalism*, he continued, people are made subordinate by the nature of the productive process. This subjects the laborer, in particular, to a system of manufacture that not only alienates him or her from whatever it is he or she makes, but also from the laboring process as such, from his or her fellow workers, and from humankind as a whole: "In the system of wage labor the properly human life of man loses its free and self-directed character; as it becomes a means, the very species-life of man is transformed into a mere means of physical existence. Man suffers the unfreedom which is a loss of himself"[19]—a judgment that may be applied to all industrial societies, of course, and not just the capitalist ones.

Capitalism is the outcome of an extended historical process. Humanity has won, with the advent of science and industry, an extraordinary degree of control over its environment. We possess now significantly enhanced productive (and destructive) powers. The effect has been to liberate as well as to inhibit. We have won our freedom from the world in this way by learning how to subordinate it to human ends. We have also generated social formations that place superior controls in the hands of only a fraction of our number. Marx argued that capitalism was the main problem in this regard, and, once this way of organizing the world was abolished, industrial "machinofacture" could be used to provide for everybody's basic requirements without resorting to inequitable social hierarchies for doing so: "this *historical* concept of freedom, as power, does not contradict or even replace the *anthropological* concept, freedom as self-realization. The two are complementary to each other. The self-realization of man is impossible so long as he is not able to control his environment. On the other hand, the possession of power itself is not an end but only a means . . . for . . . perfection."[20] This brings us back to Marx the voluntarist, since by his lights the whole point of the enterprise was to enjoy our creativity and our versatility unchecked by natural or social constraints. Knowing about the causes of unfreedom and the underlying character of historical change would not necessarily provide the conditions for this; things had to get worse, he thought, before they would get better, but the way events were moving pointed in the right direction toward a world beyond necessity where humanity could come at long last into its own.

The notion of "coming into its own" has both collective and individualistic dimensions. As indicated already, socialist philosophies lay more stress on the former. Taken to extremes, we find the individual completely dissolved in his or her social solution, incapable as such of autonomous activity, a mere "moment" in the "social whole."[21] Somewhat less absolute is the concept of freedom in *relational* terms, as the particular quality of a process of social interaction;[22] as a social quotient that political and economic systems can distribute more or less equally or not at all. As something pertaining to *individuals*, liberty is the property of the person and as such is part of a most important historical process:[23] that far-reaching change whereby particularly influential sections of humankind have come to recognize their separate selves as the "primary unit of human life"[24] (a change that has gone hand in hand with the development of another equally significant category—that of the *cosmopolitan*).[25]

Fromm contends that this invention, while removing some of the constraints that social life and a sense of oneness with nature create, has also taken away the sense of security that these provide. Nothing constructive has been put in their place. As a result we, the invented, tend to live out lives that are solitary, helpless and afraid. On the one hand, particularly under the influence of protestantism and capitalism, there is the "growing strength and integration, [the] mastery of nature . . . [the] power of human reason, and . . . solidarity with other human beings." On the other hand, however, "growing individuation means growing isolation, insecurity, and thereby growing doubt concerning one's role in the universe, the meaning of one's life, and with all that a growing feeling of one's own powerlessness and insignificance as an individual."[26] We find progressively more of those whose options exceed their ability to order them in "hierarchies of preference"; who become "confused and disoriented, haunted by boredom and frustration, eager once more simply to be told what . . . [they] must do."[27] Rather than forge new or more robust conceptions of the self, we submit to demagogues, to the anonymous authority (the "compulsive conformity") of collective opinion, to the dictates of conscience or of duty, (all of which are devices that tend to eliminate the self). Or else we simply cease to care.

NEGATIVE AND POSITIVE FREEDOM

This historic progression has made all the more evident the difference between *negative* and *positive* freedom—freedom *from* constraint as opposed to the freedom *to* do something else. The former reflects the discovery of human singularity. The latter one can cast in terms of the spontaneous and active realization of that fact. In political life this corresponds to the distinction between a state that stands over and above the individual, securing a specific domain within which each citizen may move, and one in which all join the community enterprise to shape and direct it.[28] This common dichotomy provides productive pegs to hand arguments about liberty on, and I see no reason not to use them here. There has, however, been one notable challenge to such a formulation that we should consider first.

MacCallum has argued that a less confused and more pertinent approach to the subject is to say: "Whenever the freedom of some agent or agents is in question, it is always freedom from some constraint or restriction, or interference with, or barrier to doing, not doing, becoming, or not becoming something. Such freedom is thus always *of* something (an agent or agents), *from* something, *to* do, not do, become or not become something; it is a triadic relation."[29] If we keep this *relation* in mind, he thinks, we are not tempted to view liberty as *either* positive *or* negative, a difference that does not, he says, describe "genuinely different kinds of freedom" but rather serves "only to emphasize one or the other of two features of *every* case . . . freedom is always *both* freedom from something and freedom to do or become" something else.[30] We ought to talk, in other words, less about competing concepts or kinds of freedom, less about which is the right or correct or most desirable form of it, and more about people themselves and what counts as constraints to them. A *dichotomy* is pointless at best. At worst it distorts. We do well to resist counterposing categories in this way and to turn our discussion to the much broader range of possible human situations that the concept usually implies.

And yet Fromm, for example, uses exactly this dichotomy to neither reductionist nor pointless effect. He is acutely aware of agents or persons and of particular life contexts. There is no assumption (Malinowski explicitly denies this, as does Mill) that human beings might be free absolutely, universally, and without limitation. He does not argue that the question is *either* negative *or* positive. Rather he suggests that the process of moving from one to the other has got stuck in the middle and that the possible consequences are dire indeed. MacCallum, keen to avoid any discussion of liberty that might fail to do it justice, must distort the case of those who talk in terms of freedom "from" and freedom "to" in order to make them appear unclear. This is not well observed. Indeed, it is not even self-evident that the triadic relationship he identifies always applies. While there is no form of liberty that does not presume prior constraint, as Berlin says: "A man struggling against his chains or a people against enslavement need not consciously aim at any definite further state . . . [nor need] classes and nations."[31]

As a point of entry the two-step distinction remains a good one then, and, while we may readily accept reminders about the range of issues liberty implies, it is not at all obvious that those who have fastened upon its positive and negative dimensions have done the concept the marked disservice that MacCallum suggests they have. Like the nature/nurture or the is/ought dichotomies, we push these poles apart only the better to appreciate the patterns they make in the real world, where they almost invariably appear together. When we speak of our freedom *from* something, we do refer, even if only implicitly, to a contrasting and more constructive state of affairs, that the *absence* of the specified constraint would presumably then permit us to enjoy. This is evident when we consider that: "We congratulate ourselves on being free from care, poverty, and fatigue; but cannot correspondingly complain that we are free from nourishment, riches, or rest . . . unless as a way of revising accepted standards of what is in a man's interest."[32] And when we consider that freedom never means just a lack of constraint but a lack of *injurious* restraint, at least where "injury" is understood in terms of the particular values that are used to define well-being.[33]

The two dimensions are interwoven, then, something that comes clear when we attempt a closer definition of "constraint." Feinberg distinguishes between negative constraints (or "absences," like lack of money, strength, skill or knowledge) and positive ones; between internal constraints (sore muscles, headaches, refractory "lower" desires) and those external to us (using a broad definition of the self). He arrives thus at a four-part matrix that includes internal positive constraints (obsessive thoughts, compulsive drives); internal negative constraints (ignorance, weakness, deficiencies in talent); external positive constraints (barred windows, locked doors, pointed bayonets); and the external negative ones (like lack of transportation or lack of weapons).[34] The issues are complex but they are still, as displayed here, discrete, and I would like now to consider the basic dichotomy more closely, taking each dimension in turn.

NEGATIVE FREEDOM AND MALNUTRITION

Negative freedom, as indicated above, has been most widely used to define the private domain of the individual; a realm within which we may act unrestrained and unobstructed, where frustrations are few: "The only freedom which deserves the name," Mill said, "is that of pursuing our own good in our own way, so long as we do not attempt to deprive others of theirs, or impede their efforts to obtain it. Each is the proper guardian of his own health, whether bodily, *or* mental and spiritual."[35] Undue interference from others in this regard must ultimately incur unacceptable costs to humankind. We want as large a personal domain in this respect as the complementary need to sustain society can stand.

Stephen accused Mill of overestimating the human capacity for harmony, fraternity, and good works[36] and emphasized instead the part habit and coercion play in promoting "character." "Originality" and "vigor" are early victims, he argued, of any society that puts a "high level of comfort easily within the reach of moderate and commonplace exertion."[37] A fair proportion of the contemporary world's population would probably be prepared to run this risk, of course, but then they are not on the whole well-fed conservatives like Stephen, which suggests an important addition to Mill's list.

Among the liberties Mill recommends (of conscience, thought, and feeling; of taste; of self-determination; and association), there is no mention in other words of one very specific impediment to human choosing and, indeed, to the very desire to formulate intentions and to exercise choice—that of inadequate nutrition. And yet what more impelling constraint could there be than the biologically imposed handicap, socially preventable, of insufficient food? There are fundamental physiological threshholds involved here that no amount of philosophy can avoid. Their coercive effects are real, however indirect they may be, controlling individuals by controlling the material conditions under which they subsist, and decisively influencing their opportunities by influencing their physical capacity to entertain alternatives and to decide between them. There is no more pervasive way of depriving human beings of their capacity to learn to "respond with advantage" to what their environment provides.[38] It is no accident, the Beadle declares, that Oliver Twist becomes stroppy once his diet has been improved.[39]

There are obviously other factors necessary for human development—nurturing first, and then leisure, health, a coherent cultural context, and some measure of incentive and encouragement—but we do need adequate physical nourishment if anything else is to be possible at all. This is not to neglect the importance of *social* malnutrition, and the fact that the environment must possess the "vocabulary," the "imagery," the "accent of intelligence"[40] and of emotional support if the individual's genetic capacity is to be successfully realized. But that capacity can be impaired by biological insult alone.

Precisely how significant might such material deprivation be? It has proved difficult to ascertain the quality and quantity of food that is really necessary to establish and preserve health and human vigor. Scientific evidence suggests fairly conclusively, however, that not enough protein (whatever the limit is) at decisive points [41] in the diet of a pregnant mother and/or in the first years[42] of a baby's life is enough to cause damage to the latter's central nervous system and brain sufficient to impair intellectual capacities and both the ability and the willingness to learn ever thereafter, and this regardless of the quality of the food the child later receives (assuming, of course, it actually survives). Subsequent undernutrition has the effect of further increasing the individual's susceptibility to infectious diseases like tuberculosis, pneumonia, and acute diarrhea, and promoting (along with the associated consequences of anemia, poor health care, poor public hygiene, poor sanitary provisions, and parasitic infestations) a general condition of apathy, lethargy, and irritability.[43] Diets radically deficient in calories and protein do not in fact allow more than the most basic and limited of human activities. Those who so suffer simply do not have the energy for anything else, and the more deprived and the longer deficiency prevails, the more listless and debilitated and susceptible to ill health they become. This may affect in turn individual feelings of social potency, compounding the reluctance to act in ways that might cut the cycle and successfully combat the conditions that induce such a state.

"The political consequences in nations where attempts are being made to bring about a positive belief in the ability to build new social patterns, and to achieve new forms of group cooperation are obvious."[44] Altruism gives way to more selfish and hostile behavior, or to indolence and fatalism. Neither syndrome will contribute much to the collective effort that is necessary to relieve a national, regional, or socially sectional famine. People become preoccupied with their own subsistence needs and they tend to lose their capacity for cooperation and hence for any group achievement up to and including revolt. There thus occurs a "spiral of defeat,"[45] one that grows deeper and does not dissipate. This must certainly handicap any country concerned to involve its inhabitants in large-scale socioeconomic change and deprive it of some at least of the human talent and potential it needs to sustain that process. Thus Stauffer argues: "Especially as a result of the devastating childhood years . . . a permanent distortion of the distribution patterns of all physical and mental values are effected in the populations of most underdeveloped nations."[46] This not only exacerbates the developmental disadvantages they already suffer, further inhibiting industrial productivity, agricultural output, and the prospects of mass education, but it can ultimately defeat itself, a biologically induced sense of hopelessness breeding more of the same in a quite literal as well as metaphoric sense.

There are at least forty known nutrients that must be present, alone or in specific combination, for the human unit to develop in the way it can do, and arguably ought to do. The precise amounts of all of the ingredients that make up a balanced diet have not yet been specified and they seem to vary somewhat between particular populations. Hence the threshhold of insufficiency is difficult to define. In most cases, however, this problem is wholly gratuitous since the quality of what gets ingested is so poor as to render scientific precision largely irrelevant. Less severe cases of malnourishment may have a less severe influence on physical growth or mental capacity. They may have none at all if such effects are only manifest beyond some threshhold where the brain is no longer capable of sparing itself, and where that threshhold is not reached. Again, for very large numbers of people this debate is of academic significance only.

It is interesting in this regard that there is no established standard yet to gauge what constitutes protein deficiency from the time of birth up to adolescence, a period in a person's life when the available protein[47] "is clearly critical to the development of intelligent behavior."[48] Reservations also remain about the dietary importance of substances like zinc, magnesium, and vitamin E, and how a diet lacking these materials would affect the way we act and feel. There is no doubt, however, regarding many other substances or their importance in promoting physical and mental development and well-being. To the extent that the structure of contemporary world society promotes this state of affairs, it promotes a massive organic assault on the physical and mental potential of much of humankind. Given the technical capacities of the contemporary global populace taken as a whole, this appalling situation need not exist. Nothing can be done for those who survive, permanently mentally maimed, to undo the damage. Nor, it has been suggested—the effects are so pervasive—may the second and third generations beyond them escape harm. Yet much *could* be done under the appropriate socioeconomic circumstances to better their chances. The task is daunting given the power of the privileged to defend their chosen status quo. The scientific debate makes the moral case well-nigh irresistible though:

> May we now beg paediatricians, and more especially politicans, to accept the whole of the human brain growth spurt period, from mid-pregnancy well into the second postnatal year, as a period not only of brain vulnerability, but of *opportunity* actively to promote proper growth by providing the best possible environmental conditions? There is evidence that this opportunity is chronologically determined and it only knocks once.[49]

Or, as Vitale avers, "If certain nutritional requirements are not being met, then let us meet them."[50] The concept of a good diet is after all, in comparison with other aspects of "modern" culture, a comparatively neutral one. What more basic *human* right could there be?

Nutritional investment alone, I repeat, is not *sufficient* to produce optimal mental development since this depends upon early nurture and social learning as well, which implicates the individual child's social surroundings in a much more comprehensive way. It is *necessary*, however. There may in fact be some sort of inverse relationship at work here since, as "the degree of malnutrition declines, the importance of the environmental factors increases, as does the significance of how the child himself [sic] responds to or generates stimuli from the environment around him."[51] Environmental stimuli are never irrelevant and, indeed, it appears much might be done at local levels—that is, within the house and home—to prevent severe malnutrition in nonindustrialized countries, even without the political and economic revolution that would seem to be the most obvious prerequisite today.[52] (Though all of this does assume that we agree with Montagu that the "greatest evil" and the "most enduring of all tragedies for the individual and society [sic] lies in the difference between what he was capable of becoming and what he has in fact been caused to become.")[53]

POSITIVE FREEDOM AND THE BIOLOGY OF CHOICE

Positive freedom is more problematic. It suggests not just the absence of what may inhibit us, but the presence of enabling conditions that allow whatever is valued to come into effect. We move from the minimalist's conception of what we might do to a more ambitious concern with whether or not we have the means or the power to attain what we choose to consider virtuous or true. This is a much more open-ended approach, and we should conceivably resist extending the concept so far lest it end in a crude disguise for despotism, or a mere label that affirms whatever we happen to like or want. In this latter case we have to remember that ". . . freedom is one thing, and want-satisfaction (or contentment) another."[54]

Those who would maximize freedom see it as subordinate to no other value. "Freedom," they argue, "is not to be justified because it brings happiness or anything else in this world greater than itself." Any such justification will either prove circular, they say, or lead to conclusions perilous to freedom itself.[55] We do need, however, to constrain the idea in some way if only because where "*some* incapacities are not considered to be unfreedoms, perfect freedom itself will be an utterly empty and unapproachable ideal."[56] One way to do this might be to limit our liberties to those that do not conflict. But here we are only likely to succeed in setting "new standards" in "slavery."[57] We could also focus upon what it is that we actually desire, defining specific freedoms, and more or less freedom, in terms of our power more or less to enjoy them or it. A technological and instrumentalist age like our own, so deeply imbued with the idea of progress, might find such an approach a quite sensible one. A similar effect, of course, is also achieved by simply scaling down our expectations ". . . through religion and the moralization of human nature; through the release of the soul from the tyranny of vain desires; through self-examination and the cultivation of contentment."[58] This, however, and the preceding ploy would put the meaning of freedom in jeopardy again. They are suggestions to be treated with great care. We might cope with our *frustrations* in some such fasion, but any *objective* constraints would remain the same regardless. And we would remain to that extent *unfree*.

A third option would be to focus upon the very capacity to choose and to initiate individual or collective acts itself. One is tempted, in fact, to rest the whole case here, with the individual as subject, not object; with the active agent deciding for him or herself *what to do*. "Custom," Mill observed, ". . . does not educate or develop . . . any of the qualities which are the distinctive endowment of a human being. The human faculties of perception, judgement, discriminative feeling, mental activity, and even moral preference, are exercised only in making a choice. . . . The mental and moral, like the muscular powers, are improved only by being used."[59] Yet any choice that is meaningful to us will entail more than merely making up our minds. It implies a *decision* between real alternatives, a decision that is not stage-managed in some way or taken out of fear. Freedom of choice implies "real" personal ability, "real" environmental opportunity, "real" equality. This implies other things again about our level of awareness, about whether we know what each possible course of action involves, what the range of the possibilities might be, and whether the society in which we live and those who dominate or lead it are prepared to allow sufficient diversity to give choice a chance.

The distinction between positive and negative freedom is something that applies at the global level too (and may well have found its original inspiration there).[60] A people who fight for freedom from a metropolitan power can discover, once they are self-governing, that they are hemmed in by new forms of dependency more subtle and no less, perhaps even more, pervasive than the old. Negative constraints may remain, doubtless changed in form but still substantial. Sovereignty can prove a mere mask for continued external manipulation, even control. Freedom for such a population, that is, genuine autonomy and meaningful self-determination, will then require a more cogent and perhaps revolutionary concept of *positive* freedom, plus supporters prepared to defy the exploitive logic of the capitalist world economy and the selfish interests of rich countries and of local liaison elites; national liberators with a radical sense of purpose who are prepared to push the necessary sacrifices to get their compatriots out from under and to meet mass rather than minority needs.

The costs would lie in the necessary constraints. Under a revolutionary regime (as long, of course, as it remained uncorrupted), these might be justified in terms of the doctrine of basic needs. Poverty, such a doctrine declares, which was once considered an inevitable evil ("the poor are always with us") *can* be abolished. A seemingly perennial, well-nigh natural aspect of human society can be redefined if not as *un*natural, then at least as amenable to sociopolitical improvement. And given greater understanding of what can be done, any specific society should then be able to choose more effectively how to conduct its affairs in this regard. Quite simply, we know more now about the range of global sociopolitical structures. And this matters. There are more options and, in this sense, greater potential freedom too. "Unfreedom is created by the restriction of choice, by physical restraints that prevent any choice because they prevent any action whatsoever, . . . by the loading of choices, so that some become, for ordinary practical purposes, ineligible,"[61] or else because the possible range of options has not been appreciated before.

We are very deep here in the contemporary camp, very close indeed to the essential "theology" of liberalism and rationalism—the feeling that liberty is truth and that knowledge and knowing makes us free;[62] that progress issues from the pursuit, and the enlightened application, of what is true; and that our choices expand as we know more. Ignorance binds us to erroneous beliefs that a burgeoning science of nature and of society can dispel. There is no "depth" in "mere darkness."[63] Cast the right light and we no longer need attempt to do what is demonstrably beyond our competence. We can clarify the limits, the conditions, and the constraints that operate on how we may act. We can learn thus to work *within* the realm of the possible rather than *without* it, which is the doctrine of "liberation by reason."[64] What are the truths, the limits, as we know them to be today? Are they worth looking for or do we, as the existentialists say, transcend them altogether simply because we happen to *be*?[65] Is the human will only one mental manifestation of our "original ontological freedom"?[66] Is human existence something over and above the natural being; are we truly *exceptional* so that natural laws no longer apply to us in the way they do to lesser entities?[67] Or are we *determined* somehow too, our actual choices explainable, even predictable, in the light of causal physical laws?

This brings us to the question raised in chapter 1, and a hardy perennial it is too: how free are any of us in this regard? How rigidly programmed are the things that we value and do? And in knowing what the programs are, if programs there be, can we account for them so as to be further free? What conclusions flow from contemporary discussions of the biology of our intentions and of our capacity to choose?[68] Is the whole debate misplaced, perpetuating a liberal distaste for the way in which arguments about human nature have been used to oppose human liberation and social change? Or is it enough to recognize that freedom and change presume human characteristics able to *resist* social conditioning *regardless,* and that these characteristics can be biologically as well as culturally derived? If this were not the case, could the call for reform ever arise? And should it do so in some aberrant way, could it ever meet with a nonsocial, that is to say, individual response? The sense persists that if "man is indeterminate . . . [and] entirely the product of his [sic] society, [this] must . . . destroy all the central arguments for freedom."[69]

The *biology of choice* is a particularly interesting area of scientific concern. When we speak of human values and more particularly of human morality, we stand, it would seem, at a point furthest removed from biological evolution. Values, morality, and ethics are not genetically transmitted. They are the particular constructs of particular cultures and are not passed on in any physiological way as are other of our vital ingredients. We assume the capacity for them and that, to be there at all, they must have had some demonstrable evolutionary advantage. We can also assume that we have inherent qualities that are best served by some sorts of moral choices rather than others. But our *specific* concepts of good and bad, right and wrong—these depend upon the idea of the human unit as demonstrably free of biological predispositioning. This is their truly creative character.

Such an idea is also fairly remote from what is popularly supposed to be the case, and this has been used to argue highly conservative conclusions. The "ordinary man" today, it has been said, "wants to be a supermarket statistic, in his own way."[70] That is a comparatively modest desire, and it seemingly has little to do with values and morality. Tucked into the second clause about having "his own way," however, is a good deal more than the average cynic might suppose; a general sentiment that has been made into much larger arguments—on the one hand for the "wisdom of the past" and the sense, contra Mill, that we are better served by custom than rationality,[71] and on the other against the "comfortable, smooth, reasonable, democratic unfreedom" that industrial societies generate in the name of what seems technologically most efficient, productive, and fair.[72]

Hayek concludes, in defense of the first, that cultures carry within them rules "never deliberately made . . . obedience to which builds more complex orders than we can understand."[73] Supermarkets are abstracted phenomena, he would argue, and they are *necessarily* so; they are part of the market process that makes large open societies possible. They are products of an economic order that is now very extensive indeed; of a complex division of labor that can only be coordinated by such "impersonal signals" as profits and prices. The solidarist ethics appropriate, he says, to earlier, smaller, and more intimate societies no longer obtain; nor does the utilitarian preference for maximizing personal pleasure. He defines freedom, therefore, not in terms of the realization of some particular communal purpose but as obedience to the rules of market exchange; of competitive costing and the impersonal information this conveys about how we should behave. The system may never have been planned as such, but it has proved, he maintains, extraordinarily productive. Its critics are ingrates. They are victims of their frustrated and most primitive emotions. The intellectual alternatives they parade before us must not be allowed to distract from the strengths of moral tradition and the self-regulating economy it sustains. They make too much of reason and too little of those foundations, neither accidental nor capricious, that allow reason to prevail.

Marcuse by contrast is not concerned, like Hayek, to defend the capitalist system and the "open society" from the effect of primordial sentiments that lurk in the human psyche, but from the extension of the logic of modern culture to the social and political realms where it results, he argues, in servitude more subtle and pervasive than anything seen heretofore. Again, reason is the villain. It has gone too far. Industrially advanced civilization promotes productive largesse, rational efficiency, and a restricted concept of choice. True freedom has disappeared. "Under the rule of a repressive whole, liberty" paradoxically "can be made into a powerful instrument of domination."[74] What value are free elections when elites prevail regardless? "Free choice among a wide variety of goods and services does not signify freedom if these goods and services sustain social controls over a life of toil and fear—that is, if they sustain alienation. And the spontaneous reproduction of superimposed needs by the individual does not establish autonomy;"[75] it merely bears out the potency of contemporary constraints. What we really need is denied us, or rather we are taught and we learn to value and to conform to what the untroubled activity of this sort of a society actually requires. Rather than living free from want, from governmental interference, and mass indoctrination, we find ourselves still bound by "material" and "intellectual needs" that "perpetuate obsolete forms of the struggle for existence'';[76] we enjoy a sort of ''euphoric unhappiness'' that may be the mode of our ultimate manipulation and the final cost of a fundamentally static way of life.

> The techniques of industrialization are political techniques; as such, they prejudge the possibilities of Reason and Freedom . . . as all freedom depends upon the conquest of alien necessity, the realization of freedom depends on the *techniques* of this conquest. The highest productivity of labor can be used for the perpetuation of labor, and the most efficient industrialization can serve the restriction and manipulation of needs. When this point is reached, domination—in the guise of affluence and liberty—extends to all spheres of private and public existence, integrates all authentic opposition, absorbs all alternatives.[77]

(In a *pre*industrial context, the pattern Marcuse describes is mirrored by the sort of phenomenon that analysts like Freire have observed. There the oppressed, ''having internalized the image of the oppressor and adopted his guidelines, are fearful of freedom. Freedom would require them to eject this image and replace it with autonomy and responsibility.'')[78]

Neither Hayek nor Marcuse give choice its due. We are built, Hayek thinks, to consume culture, rather than produce it. To want to change things as they are, he argues, particularly if this means attempting to construct a planned, collectivist society, is to surrender to the regressive instincts of our hunting and gathering forbears, instincts that cultural selection has systematically suppressed. And yet how does cultural evolution occur if not, as Hayek himself admits, because of individual and collective norm-deniers and traitors to tradition? Exceptions only make sense in a context of regularly observed rules, but exceptions do succeed, contra Hayek, by means other than popular acceptance and incremental reform. Simply because culture *is* learned, and as organisms we do learn so well, we can redesign a culture in a single generation if there is the political will and the circumstances allow us to do so and if we do not cut too deep across any innate species-specific predispositions. To call this presumptuous would be to miss the point. The possibility is a real one and, indeed, in many parts of the world today, it is public policy put into practice. And it is one that works. Why, otherwise, would Hayek be so afraid? Whether we approve the end product or not is a different question entirely, and one that he has confused with his desire not to see some established principles of human conduct that are dear to him actually change. *His* choice—which is to emphasize the importance of one moral tradition while demeaning our capacity to imagine alternatives, to demean our capacity for cultural opportunism in general—is not a scientifically informed one. Inherited customs define all we do, but they can change, and they can *be* changed, both quickly and completely—either by conversion or specific direction or some combination of the two. Depending on what we think of the challenged tradition, we may deplore or approve this fact, but we cannot dismiss it out of hand.

Marcuse, by contrast, is too impressed with the shape and significance of the contemporary sociocultural milieu to acknowledge the extent to which other individuals, like himself, are capable of seeing through it. Human beings are not on the whole as gullible as he presumes, and as a consequence their capacity to make meaningful choices is not so restricted either. In other words one must "trust in the oppressed," as Freire says, "and in their ability to reason."[79] (There is the additional argument here that while industrial society may foster restraint, it is possible that in some circumstances the evil done can be justified in terms of the greater good produced. This judgment depends in turn on what we think it means to be human, and, ultimately, on our conception of human nature. Too far along this line and we come, as indicated earlier, to the concept of freedom defined as the blessed state of the slave. Not far enough, however, and we surrender any chance whatsoever—dangerous doctrine though it be—of achieving good ends by bad means. We can all cite examples of beneficial constraint, and particularly those where we are not able, for instance, to predict accurately the consequences of our acts. Here, paternalism may have a point, since without some such protection we invite the rule of the strong and a society that is free only for those with sufficient might to be so. Who, on the other hand, cannot conceive of cases "where the good produced is so slight and the interference to produce it so widespread that legislation would be wrong?")[80]

Both authors, one conservative and one socialist, one who would defend a particular culture and one who wants to see it changed, underestimate for their respective polemical purposes the human capacity to imagine alternatives and their outcomes and to choose. What is the biological basis for such a capacity? The first thing to note is that moral choices are made in the light of moral judgments (though we can always choose a moral course of action for nonmoral or even immoral reasons, and there is always the possibility that what we think of our acts in principle is different from why we do what we do in fact). As I mentioned in chapter 1, moral judgments are not all of the same caliber, and it has proved possible, following Piaget,[81] to arrange such judgments on a ladder that corresponds to distinct steps in the development of our cognitive capacities. As we grow up, that is, our powers of moral reasoning change, and this reflects, perhaps, a *biologically* definable set of stages that seem to occur in a fairly fixed and predictable fashion regardless of the geographic or social realm.[82] Many individuals will get stopped before they reach the top, but the program as such does seem to become more open as we grow more humane.

There are several dimensions to this process[83] (and if we approve the sequence for other reasons, we will see these in terms of an advance as well). We can describe the way the infantile propensity to make assessments with sole reference to the likely *consequences* of a particular act gives way to the more adult trait of accounting for participant intentions. We observe thus how we learn to distinguish between sins of omission and sins of commission, and how we tend to deplore more of the latter as we grow up. Another aspect of the process is marked by our rising sense of the *relativity* of moral outlooks and the realization of the fact, as Berlin is at such pains to point out, that value pluralism is endemic to humankind. There is also growing awareness of the fact that "the *morality of an act is independent of the sanctions applied*," as well as a deepening of feelings of empathy, reciprocity, and personal fairness. Justice is seen less, as we develop, in terms of counteraggression, revenge, or punishment and more as a matter of conciliation. There is greater willingness to give others the benefit of the doubt, rather than simply assuming, when things go wrong, that the antagonist is necessarily bad or worthy of blame.

Strung along life's continuum, these dimensions appear first in the form of such "pre-moral" sentiments as the desire to avoid punishment, or to behave only in ways that bring a tangible return, then in terms of conventional moral conformism (doing good to get social approval, or to prevent being censured by an accepted authority), and finally as the expression of personal moral principles (demonstrating an individual belief in rights, the rule of law, and the common good, or, at the highest level, a belief in a developed and self-determining conscience).

Progress over this range takes place in the order given. It is not possible to jump a stage, though it often happens that someone gets stuck along the way, and does not move any further. As Lane indicates, how we answer the question of "who shall decide what is right and wrong" adds a further dimension to our concept of moral choice, and he distinguishes a "primitive morality" (that abides by external rules) from the intermediate sort ("impression management") and the "mature" morality that is "self-generated" and most self-aware.[84] The more we know what we are doing, the easier it becomes, of course, to rationalize hypocrisy and self-interest: "moral appearance may be more important than moral consequence . . . [and] one's high tone of principled choice can arise from insecurity and serve to silence doubts about one's sorry and sinful behavior.

Without some insights of this kind, morality becomes moralism, and the moralist becomes something of a prig."[85] We do also learn, however, to make moral distinctions that are progressively more creative and which, external restrictions permitting, reconfirm in turn our autonomy and our biologically derived capacity to choose. (Being free in this respect does not mean that our choice will be a good one. The deliberation involved in making any choice does require some capacity for "invention," though, or it would prove impossible to marry acts and values at all. "Analysis, imagination and criticism" are the fundamental features of this process, all of which seem to be manifest in fact in animals other than ourselves.)[86]

The second, and perhaps the most important, point to be made about our capacity to choose is that not only may it follow the developmental steps outlined above, but that it represents, regardless of the stage any particular individual reaches, a truly momentous evolutionary outcome: thus "with life, even with low forms of life, problem-solving enters the universe, and with the higher forms, purposes and aims, consciously pursued. We can only wonder that matter can thus transcend itself by producing mind . . . and a world of the products of the human mind."[87] The knowing pursuit of a particular purpose requires choices and enlightened decisions, plus the capacity to recognize same when made by other beings. Indeed the ability to think through a range of alternatives and to think *forward* to possible consequences in a critical way is one index of consciousness itself. The better we can do these things, the more aware we are of what our acts involve and what they mean. Our consciousness "expands" and evolution becomes a profoundly inventive process.

For a lesser organism a particular behavioral preference, however derived, may place a premium upon some specific faculty that selection then favors to novel biological effect. Some such sequence probably led to *us*. Thus "we could say that in choosing to speak, and to take interest in speech, man has chosen to evolve his brain and his mind; that language, once created, exerted the selection pressure under which emerged the human brain and consciousness of self."[88] The difference is that we can now reflect upon our motives and revise them knowingly should we choose to do so, and to a degree shared by no other species. The fact that we *do* share it, at least to some extent, suggests that it is an "entirely natural" trait.[89] There is clear evidence by now of primate groups, for example, evolving new sorts of behavior because one of their number finds a better way of doing things, that the others have been able to perceive as such and copy for themselves. Our own capacity to innovate and to imitate is so extended, however, as to place us (or, more precisely, for us to place ourselves) in a different league. Genetic diversity and natural selection have come up with a species able to do its own evolving *as well* or *de*volving, as the case may be.

As we have explored the extended range of what we can do with such freedom, the concept of legal and moral constraints has emerged to make our attempts at self-definition less random. Legal and moral programs contain particular preferences, particular choices, about how we ought to behave, that we learn, more or less willingly, to abide by. The fact that we may be more willing in this regard and not less so is obvious wherever we seem to surrender our sense of responsibility and we do what we are told to do; where we become, however reluctantly, the instruments of an authority or an institution rather than the "efficient cause" of our own acts.[90] Abdicating autonomy is easy to do in ostensibly modern societies where group activities are fragmented and divided, and no single individual need face what he or she has helped to achieve, nor acknowledge the consequences as those flowing from behavior that is demonstrably his or her own. Those *less* willing to abide by legal and moral programs do not always prevail in their struggle to assert themselves, and there are plenty of those who find *not* choosing, *not* making a decision, all that they can manage under the circumstances in which they find themselves. They then foster what is usually an illusion—that an act of choice is not possible, or not meaningful, and they are invariably confused. Indeed, "nothing is bleaker than the sight of a person striving yet not fully able to control his [sic] own behavior in a situation of consequence to him."[91] Yet those adept in this regard do exist, and they are the ones against whom we measure the rest.

To determine *oneself* how to behave is to offer a judgment about what one believes. The same may be said about cultures as a whole. Not all such beliefs and judgments are equally successful or good, however, hence the perennial debate about what is right and useful and what we should do. We look for new information to better shape and guide our choices, and when all is said and done about intrinsic genetic predispositions and constraints, there remains that part that describes and explains *itself*. We may, that is, have no kind of ultimate nature at all. "Indeed . . . because of the way in which humans are able to create and select their own values, *Homo sapiens* can only be defined . . . as being for better or for worse . . . *self-defining*. . . ."[92] This is the result of a natural process that has favored adaptability and hence consciousness, and the species inherits this singular outcome as a whole.[93]

At this point we revert to the more traditional concern for historical social systems and the evolution of human culture. This is not to deny that there are forces that shape human behavior that voluntaristic analyses in terms of our transcendental capacity for the contrary cannot account for.[94] We tend to choose what gives us pleasure; and what pleasures us, as I shall discuss next, may be as much a result of evolutionary selection as prior choice, perhaps even more so. There *are* such forces, however difficult they may be to define. But they do not make us unfree. Even if we implicate them in what we actually do, our capacity to choose means that they can never be in themselves either a necessary or a sufficient reason for asserting how we *must* or *should* behave. Knowing better what we *are* so we may allow for it when deciding what we might *become* justifies the sort of research I have tried to outline.[95]

Biology allows us to refine our lists of rights and needs, to refine our concept of limits—like that of nutrition. But we will always seek beyond this for greater wisdom. Scientific analysis has given us a much more naturalistic and mechanistic account of a whole range of phenomena that could once only be explained in terms of some hidden purpose or power. Paradoxically, this has only served to point up the unique quality of *Homo teleologos*, the designer, the calculator, the dreamer of dreams, and the student of high resolve. We need no longer appeal to either a mind principle over and above the physical components of the brain, or to a concept of our consciousness as the product of mere "sensations and perceptions."[96] It is possible now to entertain a much more complex view of our higher mental faculties, as the consequence of "complex reflex processes, social in origin, mediate in structure and conscious and voluntary in mode of function."[97] The philosophic penchant for counterposing *body* and *soul* loses its point. The dichotomy turns into a couple of logical "oppositions."[98] We can sensibly talk of values as derived not determined, as open to deliberate rather than merely instrumental control, as not excluded from, indeed as directly accessible to our creative intervention.

NOTES

1. H. Stretton, *Capitalism, Socialism and the Environment* (Cambridge: Cambridge University Press, 1976), pp. 159–160; cf. R. Baldwin, *Social Justice* (Elmsford, N.Y.: Pergamon Press, 1966), p. 17:

   > Liberty . . . in its normal negative sense is the ability to act without the interference of other human beings. What we do with our liberty depends first on our wishes, secondly on our opportunities, thirdly on our powers. Complete liberty includes liberty to pursue our own interests without regard for the interests or rights of others. Equality of liberty . . . is not equal liberty to kill or steal but equal autonomy, that is, equal liberty to live our own life in our own way without molesting or being molested by others. The great problem . . . is the interpretation of this autonomy in the spatio-temporal, material world.

2. See W. Gallie, "Liberal Morality and Socialist Morality," in P. Laslett, ed., *Philosophy, Politics and Society* (Oxford: Basil Blackwell, 1956). As one might expect from the word "socialist" itself:

   > The subject of freedom [here] is man [sic] as a *social* being, in the sense that his proper activity is to relate himself positively to the other members of his species. . . . Since man is essentially a social being he achieves his freedom by positively affirming and developing his concrete social relations, i.e., in the family, the community, the state, etc. . . . One becomes free, not through isolation from other persons in self-centred activity, but, paradoxically, to the extent that one transcends his egoism and makes other human beings the motivating purpose of his actions. Consciousness and self-consciousness are mere pre-conditions for freedom. [J. O'Rourke, *The Problem of Freedom in Marxist Thought* (Dordrecht: D. Reidel, 1974), pp. 20–21].

3. P. Mason, *Patterns of Dominance* (Oxford: Oxford University Press, 1970), p. 27. Note also J. Boyle, et al., *Free Choice: A Self-referential Argument* (Notre Dame: University of Notre Dame Press, 1976), who distinguish (pp. 8–10), between physical freedom, freedom to do as one pleases, "ideal" freedom (to act in accord with an ideal), and freedom as the "emergence of novelty."

4. M. Adler, *The Idea of Freedom* (N.Y.: Doubleday, 1958), vol I, p. 149.

5. Ibid., p. 110.

6. Ibid., p. 134. Cf. Cranston's distinction between freedom as a *faculty* and freedom as "government by reason"; the former, he argues, is a mistake since being free is not the same as having the power to do something (M. Cranston, *Freedom: A New Analysis* [London: Longmans, Green and Co., 1953]).

7. Adler, *Idea of Freedom*, p. 171.

8. Ibid., p. 251.

9. Ibid., p. 168.

10. Ibid., p. 329.

11. Ibid., p. 371.

12. Ibid., p. 616;

> *A man who is able* (A) under favourable circumstances, to act as he wishes for his own individual good as he sees it or (B) through acquired virtue or wisdom, to will or live as he ought in conformity to the moral law or an ideal befitting human nature or (C) by a power inherent in human nature, to change his own character creatively by deciding for himself what he shall do or shall become is free *in the sense that he* (X) has in himself the ability or power whereby he can make what he does his own action and what he achieves his property. [Pp. 5–11].

13. Ibid., p. 615.

14. B. Malinowski, *Freedom and Civilization* (London: George Allen and Unwin, 1947), p. 55.

15. Ibid., pp. 59–60.

16. Ibid., p. 80.

17. O'Rourke, *Problem of Freedom*, p. 7.

18. Ibid., p. 34.

19. Ibid., p. 27.

20. Ibid., pp. 38, 40–43.

21. Ibid., p. 83.

22. See in particular F. Oppenheim, *Dimensions of Freedom* (N.Y.: St Martin's Press, 1961); and, for a review of the Soviet debates on this issue, O'Rourke, *Problem of Freedom*, Ch. 5.

23. E. Fromm, *The Fear of Freedom* (London: Kegan Paul, Trench, Trubner, 1942), Ch. 2, "The Emergence of the Individual and the Ambiguity of Freedom"; Ch. 3, "Freedom in the Age of the Reformation"; also A. Carlyle, *Political Liberty: A History of the Concept in the Middle Ages and Modern Times* (Oxford: Oxford University Press, 1941), Part 1; C. Bay, *The Structure of Freedom* (Stanford, Calif.: Stanford University Press, 1958), p. 83.

24. Carlyle, *Political Liberty*, p. 2.

25. H. Kitto, *The Greeks* (Harmondsworth: Penguin, 1951), p. 159.

26. Fromm, *Fear of Freedom*, p. 29.

27. J. Feinberg, *Social Philosophy* (New Jersey: Prentice-Hall, 1973), p. 15.

28. J. S. Mill, *On Liberty*, (London: J. M. Dent, 1910), is the classic reference here.

29. G. MacCallum, "Negative and Positive Freedom," *Philosophical Review* T6 (July 1967): 312–334.

30. Ibid., pp. 179, 180.

31. I. Berlin, *Four Essays on Liberty* (Oxford: Oxford University Press, 1969), p. xiii.

32. S. Benn and W. Weinstein, "Being Free to Act, and Being a Free Man," *Mind* 80 (1971): 195.

33. J. Stephen, *Liberty, Equality, Fraternity* (Cambridge: Cambridge University Press, 1967), p. 176.

34. Feinberg, *Social Philosophy*, pp. 12–13.

35. Mill, *On Liberty*, p. 75. Also p. 170: "The worth of a State, in the long run, is the worth of the individuals composing it . . . a State which dwarfs its men, in order that they may be more docile instruments in its hands even for beneficial purposes—will find that with small men no great thing can really be accomplished. . . ."

36. Stephen, *Liberty, Equality, Fraternity*, p. 226:

> I believe that many men are bad, a vast majority of men indifferent, and many good, and that the great mass of indifferent people sway this way and that according to circumstances, one of the more important of which . . . is the predominance for the time being of the bad or good. I further believe that between all classes of men there are and always will be real occasions of enmity and strife, and that even good men may be and often are compelled to treat each other as enemies either by the existence of conflicting interests which bring them into collision, or by their different ways of conceiving goodness.

37. Ibid., p. 81.
38. A. Montagu, *Man's Most Dangerous Myth* (New York: Oxford University Press, 1974), 5th ed., p. 382, Ch. 9, "Socio-genic Brain Damage."
39. C. Dickens, *Oliver Twist* (Harmondsworth: Penguin, 1966), p. 93. The memorable cry of "Meat, madam!" is what I have in mind.
40. Montagu, *Man's Most Dangerous Myth*, p. 404.
41. G. Pryor, "Malnutrition and the 'critical periods' hypothesis," in J. Prescott, et al., eds., *Brain Function and Malnutrition* (N.Y.: John Wiley and Sons, 1975). The prediction of just when these occur may depend upon whether one subscribes to a "cell-division" as opposed to a "growth-spurt" hypothesis. Winick argues that malnutrition from birth to weaning influences the process of cell division and permanently reduces the number of cells. Starvation later will reduce cell size, but this phenomenon is in principle reversible (e.g., M. Winick and P. Rosso, "Malnutrition and Central Nervous System Development," in Prescott, *Brain Function and Malnutrition*; M. Winick, "Nutrition and Brain Development," in G. Serban, ed., *Nutrition and Mental Functions* (N.Y.: Plenum Press, 1975).

Dobbing posits points of maximum vulnerability when the brain is growing fastest; points that occur throughout the first several years, in fact, though the earlier ones may be more important. Hence effects vary, since the brain does not develop all of a piece. (E.g., J. Dobbing, "Nutrition and the Developing Brain," in W. Himwich, ed., *Developmental Neurobiology* (Springfield: Charles C. Thomas, 1970)). See also J. Loehlin et al., *Race Differences in Intelligence*, (San Francisco: W. H. Freeman, 1975), Ch. 8, "Nutrition and Intellectual Performance," Appendix M.
42. And perhaps well beyond, though it is not easy then to distinguish nutritional effects from other influences. See B. Kaplan, "Malnutrition and Mental Deficiency," *Psychological Bulletin* 78 (1972): 321–334. Cf. N. Warren, "Malnutrition and Mental Development," *Psychological Bulletin* 80 (1973): 324–8. Also H. Birch and J. Gusson, *Disadvantaged Children* (New York: Harcourt, Brace, World, 1969); F. Mönckberg, "The Effect of Malnutrition on Physical Growth and Brain Development," in Prescott, *Brain Function and Malnutrition*.
43. A. Keys, et al., *The Biology of Human Starvation* (Minneapolis: University of Minnesota Press, Minneapolis, 1956), vol. II, Ch. 36–42; R. Stauffer, "The Biopolitics of Underdevelopment," *Comparative Political Studies* 2 (1969–70): 364.
44. Stauffer, *Biopolitics of Underdevelopment*, p. 365.
45. Ibid., p. 371. Also J. Cravioto and E. De Licardie, "Nutrition and Behavior and Learning," *World Review of Nutrition and Dietetics* 16 (1973): 93.
46. Stauffer, *Biopolitics of Underdevelopment*, p. 379.
47. Absence of which causes *kwashiorkor*, to be distinguished from *marasmus*, which is a disease most common in smaller children (6–18 months) that is induced by severe deficiencies in both protein and calories.
48. Loehlin, et al., *Race Differences in Intelligence*, p. 227.
49. Dobbing, "Nutrition and the Developing Brain," in Himwich, *Developmental Neurobiology*, p. 48.
50. J. Vitale, "Medical and Environmental Aspects," in D. Kallen, ed., *Nutrition, Development and Social Behavior* (Washington, D.C.: U.S. Department of Health, Education and Welfare, 1970), p. 309.
51. M. Read, "Nutrition, Environment and Child Behavior," in Serban, ed., *Nutrition and Mental Functions*, p. 196.
52. J. Cravioto and E. De Licardie, "Longitudinal Study of Language Development in Severely Malnourished Children," in Serban, *Nutrition and Mental Functions*.
53. Montagu, *Man's Most Dangerous Myth*, p. 397.
54. Feinberg, *Social Philosophy*, p. 7.

55. J. Plamenatz, "Equality of Opportunity," in Bryson, et al., eds., *Aspects of Human Equality* (N.Y.: Harper and Bros., 1956), p. 84.
56. Feinberg, *Social Philosophy*, p. 9.
57. Stretton, *Capitalism, Socialism*, p. 159.
58. J. Macmurray, *Conditions of Freedom* (London: Faber and Faber, 1950), p. 22. Also Berlin, *Four Essays*, p. xxxviii.
59. Mill, *On Liberty*, pp. 116–7.
60. Feinberg, *Social Philosophy*, p. 15.
61. Benn and Weinstein, *Being Free to Act*, p. 209.
62. G. Steiner, "Has truth a future?" *The Listener*, Jan. 12, 1978, p. 43; or, more particularly, knowing how to know.
63. Berlin, *Four Essays*, p. 42.
64. Ibid., p. 144.
65. Thus,

> . . . by the sole fact that I am conscious of the causes which inspire my action, these causes are already transcendent objects for my consciousness; they are outside. In vain shall I seek to catch hold of them; I escape them by my very existence. I am condemned to exist forever beyond my essence, beyond the causes and motives of my act. I am condemned to be free. . . . Thus the refusal of freedom can be conceived only as an attempt to apprehend oneself as being-in-itself. . . . Man is free because he is not himself but presence to himself. The being which is what it is [one might want to include here human beings possessed of a bovine consciousness] can not be free . . . for human reality, to be is to choose *oneself*. . . . Thus freedom is not a being; it is *the being* of man—i.e., his nothingness of being. . . . [Or, as a somewhat more opaque passage has it] Freedom is nothing but the existence of our will or of our passions in so far as this existence is the nihilation of facticity; that is, the existence of a being which is its being in the mode of having to be it. [J.-P. Sartre, *Of Human Freedom* (N.Y.: Philosophical Library, 1966), pp. 36–38, 40, from his essay "Freedom To Love, To Do, To Be: Being and Nothingness"]

66. Ibid., p. 43.
67.
> Human reality cannot receive its ends . . . either from outside or from a so-called inner "nature." It chooses them and by this very choice confers upon them a transcendent existence as the external limit of its projects . . . human reality in and through its very upsurge decides to define its own being by its ends . . . which is identical with the sudden thrust of freedom. [J.-P. Sartre in R. Dewey and J. Gould, eds., *Freedom, Its History, Motive and Varieties* (N.Y.: Macmillan Co., 1970), p. 153]

68. Since choice always implicates our actions (even when we choose inactivity), *intentions* are intrinsic too. The conceptual complex is a *dynamic* one, as opposed to that of reverie, wishes and dreams. See Sartre, *Of Human Freedom*, p. 59. Also Boyle, et al., *Free Choice*.
69. M. Midgley, *Beast and Man* (N.Y.: Cornell University Press, 1978), p. xviii.
70. R. Lane, *Political Ideology* (Glencoe, N.Y.: Free Press, 1962), p. 25.
71. F. Hayek, *The Three Sources of Human Values* (London: The London School of Economics and Political Science, 1978).
72. H. Marcuse, *One Dimensional Man* (London: Sphere, 1968), p. 19.
73. Hayek, *Three Sources*, p. 15.
74. Marcuse, *One Dimensional Man*, p. 23.
75. Ibid., p. 23.
76. Ibid., p. 21.
77. Ibid., p. 31.

78. P. Freire, *Pedagogy of the Oppressed* (Harmondsworth: Penguin, 1972), pp. 23–4. C.f. M. Cranston, *Freedom*, on "compulsory rational freedom" (p. 28). "*Rational freedom* finds freedom in discipline . . . [and] is thus individualistic, linked to a private ethos. *Compulsory rational freedom* is political-linked to a social ethic" (p. 29).

79. Freire, *Pedagogy*, p. 41.

80. J. Mabbott, *The State and the Citizen* (London: Arrow, 1958), p. 62.

81. J. Piaget, *The Moral Judgment of the Child* (New York: The Free Press, 1965).

82. L. Kohlberg, "Development of Moral Character and Moral Ideology," in M. Hoffman and L. Hoffman, eds., *Child Development Research* (N.Y.: Russell Sage, 1964); R. Lane, *Political Thinking and Consciousness* (Chicago: Markham Publishing Co., 1969), pp. 192–198. Evidence suggests that the progress we make is not always defined in this way, though the tendency seems to be clear. See R. Tsujimoto and P. Nardi, "A Comparison of Kohlberg's and Hogan's Theories of Moral Development," *Social Psychology* 41, no. 3 (1978): 236.

83. Lane, *Political Ideology*, p. 194. Cf. Hogan's more social dimensions of moral character in his "Moral Conduct and Moral Character: A Psychological Perspective," *Psychological Bulletin* 79 (April 1973): 217–232; "Moral Development and the Structure of Personality," in D. De Palma and J. Foley, eds., *Moral Development: Current Theory and Research* (N.Y.: Erlbaum Associates, 1975).

84. Lane, *Political Ideology*, p. 197: These are given graphic expression in the following statements: 1. "I know the rules: I obey them; they license my actions and thoughts. Indeed, what seems to be selfish is really not that, but rather divine authority, traditional wisdom, authoritative moral law." 2. "As you can see, I am a self-sacrificing, loving, kind person. I give of myself; no one knows the many little things I do to make life better for other people. I am dedicated to the proposition: Others before self." 3. "I am principled, love high standards, live up to them, judge myself more harshly than others. I consult an inner code, and the opinions of others. I often fail, but I am working to make myself a better person."

85. Ibid. "Human frailty consists so much in the tendency to be moved by one's last feeling rather than one's best" R. Neville *The Cosmology of Freedom* [New Haven: Yale University Press, 1974], p. 139.

86. In this sense "personal freedom [as opposed to the social kind] is creative activity in the environment of the given world." Freedom "in creativity" is freedom "to do good" (or bad for that matter), and its heart "rests in privacy." The significance of privacy in turn "is its creative contribution to the public." In this formulation the dimensions of personal and social freedom lie parallel. Beside

> the personal freedom of external liberties is the social freedom of opportunity . . . [beside] the personal freedom of choice between alternatives is the freedom . . . to choose the way to live . . . [beside] the personal freedom of intentional action is the freedom of integral social life . . . [and beside] the personal freedom of creativity is the social freedom of participatory democracy. The freedom of opportunities is a schematic and somewhat empty approach to defining a free society. To that must be added the further dimension of real alternatives to forms of social life . . . But then those . . . are empty if people do not have integral social styles enabling them to take them up in fully human ways. Even those styles are incomplete without a social order in which they can be employed . . ." Neville, op. cit., pp. 186, 192, 197, 203, 207–8.

On the second point, see D. Griffin, *The Question of Animal Awareness* (New York: Rockefeller University Press, 1976).

87. K. Popper and J. Eccles, *The Self and its Brain* (New York: Springer International, 1977), p. 11.

88. Ibid., p. 13.

89. D. Freeman, "The Anthropology of Choice" (Presidential address to the 49th Congress of ANZAAS [Australia and New Zealand Association for the Advancement of Science], 1979), p. 4.

90. S. Milgram, *Obedience to Authority* (London: Tavistock, 1974), p. xii.

91. Ibid., p. xiii. Also I. Janis and L. Mann, *Decision Making: A Psychological Analysis of Conflict, Choice, and Commitment* (N.Y.: The Free Press, 1977).

92. Freeman, *Anthropology of Choice*, p. 19.

93. For a list of the "evolutionary assets of consciousness," see R. Granit, *The Purposive Brain* (Cambridge: MIT Press, 1977), pp. 74–75.

94. L. Tiger *Optimism: A Biology of Hope* (New York: Simon and Schuster, 1979). Why is thinking about the future "good to think," he asks? And further, pp. 33, 35:

    People make cultural norms as inevitably as they make love and, as Piaget has discovered, when they are old enough, i.e., biologically ready, even children invent legal codes of their own. Human culture is not optional though its specific forms usually are . . . [and] one set of forms, pertaining to optimism and the future, are hardly optional at all . . . optimism, not religion, is the opiate of the people.

95. N. Tinbergen, "Ethology in a Changing World," in P. Bateson and R. Hinde, eds., *Growing Points in Ethology* (Cambridge: Cambridge University Press, 1976).

96. A. Luria, *Higher Cortical Functions in Man* (London: Tavistock, 1966), p. 31.

97. Ibid., p. 32.

98. V. Reynolds, *The Biology of Human Action* (San Francisco: W. H. Freeman, 1976), p. 237.

5

States of Happiness and States of Mind

The idea that policy should promote human well-being—should secure individual felicity, the welfare of a society as a whole, or just "good humour" (as Democritus described it)—is a pervasive and potent part of that moral program Europeans put to the rest of humankind. Though this particular cultural tradition has advanced many other notions that tend to contradict such a concept—notions borne out in social, economic, military, and political practices of a decidedly *un*happy kind—it remains a true touchstone of the Western world view and one ripe with ambiguity, rich in promise, and resonant with prescriptive power.

I have lumped together more than one concept here. Happiness and well-being are not the same thing though it is tempting because of their overlap to assume that they are. Wright, for example, cites the former as a *hedonic* and the latter as a *utilitarian* notion. Happiness has "no immediate logical connexion," he says, "with the beneficial," which is what *well-being* implies: "Hence, what is good for one is not necessarily what makes us happy."[1] Wright takes the point too far for my liking; suffice it to say that those who advocate social justice and human rights, who would defend the attempt to focus on the ideas that inform them (ideas like those of fraternity, equality, and liberty already discussed), invariably arrive in the reasons they give at the principle, however defined, of personal or collective "happiness."

HAPPINESS DEFINED

Definitions of human happiness are diverse, documenting mind and body states that range from mere contentment to that of unalloyed ecstasy and bliss, the latter transcending, of course, the descriptive capacities of a prosaic analysis such as the one I am making here. (Though I shall consider the full range, my central

125

concern for the moment remains the emotionally advantaged *mean*—the happy woman or man.) Such definitions include a wide compass of emotional moods and intellectual preferences; feelings and choices that may stem from a wide variety of activities from rose-growing to rape, from patriotic mummery to murder *en masse*. This would suggest the best approach as one that begins by considering not what felicity actually is, but rather what it is not:

> If human beings find it difficult to agree upon the meaning and causes of happiness

[Barrington Moore asserts]

> they find it much easier to know when they are miserable . . . no known human culture has made of suffering an end in itself. . . . It is just not true . . . that human beings enjoy the sufferings imposed upon them by the social arrangements under which they live and justified by that society's moral code. . . . By asking what causes this suffering and is it necessary it becomes possible to escape from the trap of accepting each culture's self-justification at its face value while retaining a capacity for sympathetic insight into its torments and perplexities.[2]

People do despair, but they also possess a marked capacity for making the most of where they are. They can take their measure of pleasure from simple things like domestic life or just a good, fine day. However, the modern concept of material progress has alerted many more now to the prospect of improvement in their life circumstances; and though there are antiutopians who would say that some abiding component in our nature condemns us to unhappiness,[3] and it is commonplace in fact to observe that to free someone from suffering is neither a necessary nor sufficient cause to grant them gladness, the latter does make for a better class of un-ease.

"Better" is tricky, and it is possible to argue, as Kalin does, that Marx, for example, was rather too optimistic on this point, and that he failed to indicate the "limits of progress or the point at which man's powers can no longer match his needs." Indeed, Marx accepted rather too uncritically, it may be said, the human potential for both freedom and prosperity on a world scale.[4] Freud, on the other hand, was too pessimistic by half, civilization being in his view a tenuous attempt to contain the instinctive urges of our subliminal selves, instincts that spring from the "timeless, unalterable id"; that would return us, given the chance, to the state of "tensionless existence" both preceding and succeeding life itself, instincts that find fulfilment only in death.[5] By "better" in this context then, I mean merely more mental and less physical.

It is no accident that the pathology of scientific-industrial societies is most commonly detailed in terms of intellectual or emotional *alienation* and *anomie*.[6] Mental anguish has come to supplant the primary emphasis upon physical deprivation (though one might well consider the shift an achievement in its own right.

Before we condemn too fiercely the inhumanity of modern Western industrial societies, we
have certainly to remember that they do not [at least not nearly so often] leave people to die of
starvation in the streets . . . indeed Western societies are sometimes described as cold and
inhumane for no better reason than that their officials are not [so] readily subject to bribery and
corruption.[7]

Lane has argued in like vein, in defense of modern market economies and their
attendant democratic polities, that the contemporary conclusion that "rationality
inhibits the emotions making human relations coldly calculating"—ostensibly an
ever-more-pervasive phenomenon as the market and mass modernization
spreads—is simply not true. Many nonmodern communities prove as much, if
not more, "tense" and "inhibited" in this respect than commercialized,
democratic ones; and in these cases modernization as such can have a beneficial
effect, actually helping to heighten "warmth and self-disclosure."[8] Market
economics and democratic politics, in other words, can actually make people
"more expressive and more concerned with human relations as it . . . [makes]
them better educated. . . ." And, indeed, "the calculating figure known as
rational economic man has died almost as many deaths as the 'noble savage' and
the heroic proletarian." Furthermore, the loosening of traditional controls over
what individuals assume they can do, a process to which market society and
democratic politics have made their own quite generous contributions, does seem
in general to encourage a less dogmatic, more tolerant, and more capacious point
of view—a state of mind relatively free, that is, from "inner compulsions and
outer immediacy"; arguably more curious and self-conscious and less likely
either to repress or to regress.)[9]

Where happiness is defined as necessary obedience to the collective will,
articulated as such by some ruling group or party in the name of socioeconomic
development or growth, or as the acquisition and consumption of mass-produced
services and goods, it has nonetheless acquired a rather hollow ring, and we are
more wary, now that we have seen a couple of hundred years of putative
progress, of just what this sort of enterprise portends. Market society, and money
economies in general, *have* changed human cognition. Thinking and feeling to a
significant extent *have* been subordinated to material advance. Calculation colors
all, even though the greater range of alternatives made possible, indeed the very
idea that true choice *is* possible, may prove the most important contribution in the
long run. Greater intellectual skills and a more extended sense of the self do *not*
necessarily make us more happy or less depressed, and we must give

some weight to the declining hope that one's life will be better in the future, the sense of
fatalism about social problems, the frustration of dreams of infinite expansion into yet one more
manifest destiny, the rise in suicide attempts, the declining trust in social institutions, all of
which suggest, however ambiguously, the theme of "the age of melancholy" . . . there is
reason to believe [too] that the market economy contributes to this mood, and little reason to
think that democratic politics does much to relieve it. . . .[10]

Contemporary ideologies have a very active quality. Historical thinkers have made many and varied recommendations for alleviating the individual or collective lot, but the ordinary individual has not, until comparatively recently, been wont to ask: what is to be done? Or indeed, to expect that anything can be done at all! The advent of scientific-industrial societies provides powerful lessons that many want to learn, especially in the sociopolitical potential for change.

They provide above all a wide range of new and radical means for making change come about quickly, and growing mastery of the material realm has made the material cause of human misery more gratuitously offensive than hitherto. Noncontemporary cultures have been known to entertain ideas about rapid change, of course, and about socioeconomic (as opposed to spiritual) improvement, but these have typically been the province of particularly desperate minorities. Only in the immediate past has such progress become meaningful for the majority. Only in the immediate past has this come to seem possible at large.

Mastery of the material realm stems from what humankind *knows* (that is, the number of facts it has at its disposal, how many things it can do, and how well it understands what is meant by the good life),[11] and it has been the abiding belief of those still imbued with Enlightenment ideals that *more* knowing necessarily means enhanced control of the physical realm, enhanced capacities to do what one wants, and hence enhanced happiness in the world.[12] Thus the advent of "science" has enabled those who have it and can extend and apply it to expect continual additions to the pile of what they know, and an ever-more-extensive ability to satisfy their felt desires and to add to the heap of their sum happiness.

Depending upon how we define happiness, this will reinforce related values, depending again upon how we define *them*. Thus, if we take the former to mean not just quiescent satisfaction but the active pursuit of what one wants, and one of the latter, such as freedom, to denote the realized self, then clearly they will converge: "The freedom which is precious to man is not mere absence of impediment; it is the opportunity to do what he thinks worthwhile, and he finds his happiness in doing it. And he 'realizes himself' by becoming what he aspires to be, and what he claims the 'freedom' to become; and his idea of what makes for his happiness depends on his aspirations."[13] Different definitions are likely to lead to less compatible conclusions, however. In this case one can only choose the ultimate value one prefers, which is the one found most worth having in and of itself.

This is not to demean the instrumental significance of *what* one knows:

Man, if he is to be securely free or virtuous or happy, must understand himself and his circumstances; he may, if he is lucky, be happy without this understanding, or without much of it. . . . But, if his happiness is to be secure, if he is not to lose it as soon as circumstances change, he must be adaptable; he must know himself and his limitations and must also know something of the "world," of the chances and changes to which men are liable. . . . From Socrates to Kant, nearly all the great moralists have seen a close connection between knowledge, virtue and happiness or whatever else they have considered desirable for its own sake.[14]

(But then, one would have hardly expected them not to. They were philosophers. The folk notion that ignorance might be bliss and that some false notions might be better held rather than dispelled, flatly denies their vocation. Under any such ordinance the need to compose reproving tomes would disappear.) At most, we may simply accept that, Yahweh willing, our command of fact, our competence, and our wisdom will continue to grow and that all good things will consequently come to pass.

Simple acceptance is not possible, however. Human desires, and not just ephemeral ones, either, can be quite dynamic and are not necessarily fixed. They may grow at the same rate as, or even faster than, the ability to fulfill them, and under such circumstances any absolute advance in human happiness will prove illusory. Furthermore, since human beings often flourish knowing comparatively little in contemporary terms, knowing *more* might destroy their comforting myths while putting nothing of moral or spiritual sustenance in the same place. Worse still, it may actually create new myths that the true believers may then have the greater potential to make real, and to heinous sociopolitical effect. The powerful glare of a scientific-industrial society will pass through a "wrong" lens as readily as a "right" one, and, though sufficient wisdom may exist to allow felicity to prevail, the wise themselves may not, and indeed usually *are* not, in a position to rule on which it shall be.

What of the counterpoint: that more understanding can lead to a better appreciation of our human capacities and limitations, a more realistic appraisal of what can be achieved, and readier acceptance of possible loss? "As society becomes more complicated and its members more sophisticated, it may be that happiness is both more precarious and more within men's reach. . . . The happiness which in simple societies costs so little may require a much greater exercise of will and intelligence. . . . For worse and for better, the old innocence (such as it was) has been lost."[15]

Any belief in a natural consonance between the cosmic order above and around us and what is revealed by the moral order and by manipulable social regularities below and within says as much about the human penchant for reason and symmetry as it does about blind faith. Perhaps we should look more closely at the quality of the experience we are trying to describe.

Wright distinguishes between three "ideas" of happiness, which he terms the Epicurean ("having things which please"), the ascetic (having "as few and modest wants as possible, thus minimizing the chances of frustration and maximizing those of satisfaction"), and the activist ("the pleasure of doing that on which we are keen").[16] Whatever we make of this difference, in each case we are talking of a particular feeling, a subjective sense that most of us can readily recognize for what it is, that alleviates anguish and heightens the appreciation of life's worth and both its immediate and long-term prospects. Such a feeling can vary in intensity, as I have indicated already, from quiet enjoyment to the heights of rhapsody (though it is quite possible to enjoy life and find satisfaction in it and not feel happy, or to be so imbued with an ecstatic mood that any conception of "happiness" will cease to apply)[17]. Happiness can also vary in extent, applying to only part of one's life realm rather than all. Thus I can be miserable about my material plight but feel fine in the company of good friends. (Anxiety or despair emanating from a part of one's experience will usually leak through to contaminate other parts, though it depends very much on individual personality how pervasive this will be, and how readily such effects might be reversed.)[18] Held up as *the* way to determine the good life, as the ultimate end of moral action, we have the ethic of *eudemonism* (*hedonism* enjoins us merely to be pleasured or pleased, though the distinction is not always clear). Put about as a political index for promoting collective well-being, or at least as much of it as possible, and we have the *utilitarianism* of Bentham and Mill.

HAPPINESS AND HOW IT IS CAUSED

The *cause* of a feeling like happiness is much debated and reflects many other values.[19] Philosophers, as suggested above, are prone to find rectitude and restraint (variously defined), the right use of reason, and a broad awareness of humanity and the self to be the most conducive to it. Thus "classical happiness," as Jones observes, "is particularly the function of an aristocrat possessing both leisure and intelligence," and, since "contemplation is the highest form of activity because the intellect is the highest part of man's nature . . . it follows that philosophic contemplation is the most pleasurable of all activities in conformity with virtue. . . . Only the philosopher can be truly happy."[20] Mill was a modest exception here, for what *he* valued most in this regard was "diversity, versatility, fullness of life . . . the spontaneity and uniqueness of a man, a group, a civilization"; the very antithesis, it seems, of himself or of the milieu in which he lived.[21] Gourmets, of course, prefer food, while warriors dream of war. Liberals like Adam Smith or his present-day counterparts see happiness resulting from economic free-dealing and the prosperity this is supposed to produce, with a minimum of political and state interference. Economists generally assume that the richer we are the happier we become. Socialists turn the process around and put political intervention first. Personal felicity they define as whatever flows from an increase in the welfare of the collective whole. (The necessary decrees can be so uncongenial that one may well form a presumption in favor of protecting people against predation of this sort. The concept of mass well-being remains important nonetheless, however, and a prudent and humane authority may well be justified in putting the common good before more private pursuits. The difficulty lies not only in the fact that public prudence is hard to define but that forcing, rather than cajoling a people to be happy typically encounters as much resistance and resentment as forcing them to be free. Structuring a society so as to maximize personal potential is one thing. Directly tailoring the individual to suit some prior concept of what pleases the group is another again.)

As with the other values outlined, one may trace the way happiness has moved from the spiritual sphere, to that of law and civic regulation, and, ultimately, to that of individual psychology. How we view what causes it shifts accordingly, from the workings of fate, to the "public life of political science and economics," to the "inner life of impulse and emotion." Just as interesting for our present purpose is the way this reflects changed understandings of "nature"; the way, that is, our ideas have moved from the "majestic deity of the Stoics" through to the great "world-machine" of Newton, to the "terrifying, yet tragic" conception of Darwin and his ilk. In the present time the "problem of happiness" has become, in the West at least, the "problem of adjustment between the primitive subliminal urges of our hidden selves and the drab and practical necessities of every day."[22] The happy woman or man is now seen less as a creature favored by kind or friendly gods, less as a creature trembling on the brink of heavenly transcendence and trying to tumble over by dint of his or her religious faith or karmic distinction, less as a creature sustained by civilized standards of material and political life, and more as the gratified, harmonious human unit, well-off within him or herself. "Perfection" and "pleasure" are the poles of this personal estate, though the notion is considerably more complex than either alone would seem to allow.[23]

HAPPINESS AS THE ULTIMATE VALUE

To fasten upon felicity, then, as the ultimate arbiter of our morals and laws, however commendable this may be, invites confusion. Happiness *is* a good, as human intuition quickly affirms. Is it the *only* good however? The utilitarians thought so, and Bentham produced a kind of felicific calculator to further the point.[24] He simplified the problem though by defining the individual interest in terms of personal happiness, and both or either in terms of pleasure and the absence of pain. Thus he put together "benefit, advantage, pleasure, good or happiness" and claimed that "all this in the present case comes to the same thing."[25] Mill affirmed that these were the only phenomena "desirable as ends," and that anything else one might want was desirable either for the "pleasure" inherent in it "or as means to the promotion of pleasure and the prevention of pain."[26] Bentham was especially adamant: "Nature has placed mankind under the governance of two sovereign masters, *pain* and *pleasure*." Furthermore: "It is for them alone," he said, "to point out what we ought to do. . . . By the natural constitution of the human frame, on most occasions of their lives men in general embrace this principle, without thinking of it. . . ."[27] And Mill averred, suggesting that "human nature is so constituted as to desire nothing which is not either a part of happiness or a means of happiness . . . [and] these are the only things desirable, and good."[28]

Allowing, for the moment, that pleasure and happiness might be the same, what is the empirical status of this observation? By contemporary lights, one commentator has argued that: "If the reader is not a plant, then he [sic] is a pleasure-seeker, for that is what all animals are. . . ."[29] We search, the thorough-going materialist cited here would say, for ways of stimulating electrical activity in those areas of the brain—the limbic system, in particular— that please us when active and prompt patterns of gratifying behavior when not, and this is an "inbuilt property of nervous systems, at least of the complexity of vertebrates."[30] It is *the* "driving force" that explains why "animals do things" and vegetables "do not" and why all our other organs exist. In experiments where humans have been allowed to stimulate their brains directly by means of implanted electrodes, eliciting a range of pleasurable sensations, they have appeared "quite happy to continue doing nothing but this for up to six hours," the maximum period allowed.[31] Our senses permit the same to happen naturally, though human beings are able to engender good feelings by thought alone— which would suggest a capacity for more than mere sensual gratification. We can try and get around such a rejoinder, as Campbell does, by defining pleasure so broadly that it loses most of its meaning, becoming synonymous in fact with *excitation*, but this tells us nothing about the particular quality of the pleasant experiences. At which point, of course, any such theory of behavior becomes circular and ceases to possess explanatory power.

The attempt to derive a physiological basis for Benthamite utilitarianism encounters the same problems that beset the original philosophy itself. Utilitarianism treats happiness

as if it consisted in successfully satisfying one desire after another.[32] But men have not only desires; they have ideals as well, and we cannot go far towards explaining their desires except in relation to these ideals. . . . Social man is a moral and aesthetic animal; he is not just a creature of appetites, whose superior reason enables him to foresee what he is likely to want better than other animals. . . . It matters enormously to man what he is like, both in his own eyes and in other people's. If that were not so, he would not be the tragic, pathetic, and sometimes absurd animal that he is. . . .

And yet "Bentham's . . . fundamental rule, that we should aim rather at helping people get what they want than at making them the sort of people we think they should be, may still be acceptable."[33] (That this can only be a general rule, conditionally applied, is obvious when one encounters individuals like Hitler who "want" to rule the world, for example, or kill every living gypsy and Jew. Ought one not make them into something else more humble or humane? They are, admittedly, the extreme case, but human history has seen many such moral monsters. The argument gets more difficult when we look to draw the line on more marginal cases; but is it not reasonable to suggest that "wanting" is not enough and we should consider *what* people actually want *as well*?)[34]

Bentham and Mill were concerned to generalize happiness over whole human populations. Mill distinguished between different sorts of pleasure, in particular those pertaining to "low" enjoyment of a sensual kind, and those that come from exercising the "higher" faculties of intellect and human imagination.[35] He expressed a clear preference for the latter and argued that this was a qualitative judgment amply supported by practically all those in a position to compare both.[36] Intellect and imagination will respond to very diverse and divergent ideas, however self-engendered or culturally derived. Again, pleasure so defined becomes an all-pervasive concept, and we then lose our capacity to decide what it is. The logic runs: the right act pleasures, pleasure can be invoked by well-nigh anything, hence well-nigh any act is right. Surely we need to specify some other standard for assessing human conduct. If we do this in utilitarian terms, however, utilitarianism becomes a mere disguise for whatever principle such a standard seeks to promote, for whatever particular conception of happiness those who rule prefer. It is not enough, as argued earlier, to promote what makes each happy in his or her own way. And yet, to legislate any particular sort of well-being will make those who do not agree with the legislator more or less unhappy, thus negating the principle itself. By extending the happiness principle to all mankind, by asking that *every* life, as far as this is possible, be led free of pain, fed by a multitude of pleasures with a "decided predominance of the active over the passive,"[37] it is possible to escape this dilemma. But the escape, however worthy in principle, is problematic too. It depends upon prior assumptions about human altruism, and whether as a species we have enough of a capacity for directly deriving happiness from what we do for others, and not only our immediate kin.[38] The biopolitical debate on this has been covered in chapter 2.

The only observation Mill himself makes here is to say that "when people who are tolerably fortunate in their outward lot do not find in life sufficient enjoyment to make it valuable for them, the cause generally is, caring for nobody but themselves . . ."; whereas "those who have cultivated a fellow-feeling with the collective interests of mankind retain as lively an interest in life on the eve of death as in the vigor of youth and health. Next to selfishness, the principle cause which makes life unsatisfactory is want of mental cultivation."[39] This would lead one to believe that Mill, too, in the end, defined happiness as something other than the sensation itself, as the consequence, that is, of altruism and a well-exercised mind. Mill urges these things so strongly that it seems he felt they were moral imperatives in their own right, and not just the means to a pleasant end—which suggests that the utilitarian's definition of happiness is too broad. If we desire freedom, they say, it is because freedom gives us pleasure and *that* is the aim, not self-realization or nonrestraint or whatever else freedom might imply. Yet logic like this is closed. One might just as well argue that there are fairies at the bottom of the garden because those who happen to see fence posts there simply fail to appreciate the true quality of the objects of their perceptions.

This is not to deny that people do have a preference for a sense of well-being and for that deep "appetite" for "possible things" which happiness now feeds upon.[40] Such feelings may well have had a comparatively simple source in that, other things being equal, it was probably the more happy, the more positive, the more optimistic individuals in our evolutionary history who were better able to cope and to reproduce and hence proved more fit to survive.[41] (How one accounts for the recurrent crop of pessimists in these terms is more difficult to do. Did they, as Tiger suggests, help human groups survive too, acting as psychic barometers, perhaps, their distress a warning signal to others of impending shifts in cultural pressure likely to impinge to detrimental effect?)[42]

As a biological predisposition, one can, to some extent, detach the capacity for feeling good or bad from any particular cause of it and can posit such mental moods as intuitive aspects of human experience itself. This provides an interesting explanation or part explanation for positive philosophies as inherent rather than externally derived. If we assume a species-wide and innate urge toward optimism, then progressive sentiments will receive intuitive as well as culturally sanctioned support. "Conceptions of personal salvation which have been historically important in the great religions find their modern counterpart in programs of political and economic modernization,"[43] and though the promise of a more secure and more satisfying life may prove less congenial in practice than many seem to suppose—indeed, anthropologists like Diamond would argue that our universal needs are better served by "primitive" societies rather than "civilized" ones[44]—modern modes of production *are* widely favored, or at least their commodities are, and not least perhaps because of their optative patina and our predisposed preference for them.

BIOCHEMISTRY AND EMOTION

Scientific evidence on human moods and their potential manipulability comes not only from experiments like those with implanted electrodes alluded to above,[45] but also from the controlled infusion of psychoactive compounds into the brain and from what we have come to know about specific chemical balances there. The fact that depression can be treated successfully by administering appropriate drugs would suggest that it can produce (or be produced by—the choice of cause reflect one's position with respect to the mind/body problem)—circumstances of a pharmacologically specificable kind. Conversely, elation would seem to depend on, even perhaps be determined by (and again it is *dependence* or *determination* that betrays the two alternatives), the same equilibrium or disequilibrium, which suggests that there is no warrant for the argument that "neural processes *as such* do not count as the reason for . . . action. . . . "[46] If an individual has a physiologically happy or sad predisposition, with its own biochemical signature, however crude, then surely we do have objective evidence of an internal cause for human action? It may not be the *only* cause, or a *sufficient* cause, but it cannot be excluded just because the ultimate pattern of behavior is voluntarily willed.

Neuroendocrine research suggests that specific hormones (corticosteroids) accompany, and may somehow be implicated in, states of human depression. Some tests suggest there are individuals deficient or defective in this regard who, under severe stress, fail adequately to copy and biochemically cave. A vicious circle develops, with elevated levels of the debilitating substance or substances further inhibiting their capacity to recover. Tricyclics and monoamine oxidase inhibitors are in regular clinical use in Western societies for elevating mood. As to tricyclics, "the mechanism of action . . . is unknown though they are believed to block the reabsorption of norepinephrine in storage sites at nerve endings in the CNS [central nervous system], thus increasing the concentration of active norepinephrine at receptor sites. Serotonin uptake is also apparently blocked and its turnover is increased."[47] Monoamine oxidase inhibitors have a similar effect, increasing the concentration in the brain of the same particular compounds, which are presumably then the ones most directly implicated in the mood-creating or mood-reflecting process. Lithium carbonate, used in preventing and treating the manic phases of bipolar depression (where the afflicted individual swings pathologically from one extreme to the other) is presumed to work in the reverse way, though again the exact effect is not known.

The capacity to induce emotional experiences so directly has profoundly disturbing implications, particularly where the substance has an influence regardless of how we differ one from another and regardless of what our expectations might be.[48] What defense do we have here against abuse? Knowledge itself, if available, is important. And so is the fact that human life-learning provides a private context that makes the exact consequences of this sort of intervention difficult to predict. Indeed, Kety concludes that

it seems quite futile to attempt to account for a particular emotional state in terms of the activity of one or more biogenic amines. It seems more likely that these amines may function separately or in concert at crucial nodes of the complex neuronal networks which underlie emotional states. Although this interplay may represent some of the common features and primitive qualities of various affects, the special characteristics of each of these states are probably derived from those extensions of the networks which represent apperceptive and cognitive factors based upon the experience of the individual.[49]

Emotions are what we feel we want to do. In evolutionary terms they prompt or reflect, more or less closely, whatever the species has "needed to have done" down the lengthy descent of our ancestral tree. In this sense, any emotion, felicity included, "reflects a state of heightened motivation for a behavior pattern that has been critical in species survival."[50] Our personal capacities for conscious appraisal and for coping with intervention are also important: "The more advanced the organism, phylogenetically, the more room there seems to be for flexible control of emotional states and behavior, and the more cognitive processes are involved in such control . . . in a continuous process of give and take with the environment."[51] But this is not the issue I am concerned with at present. If a state of this sort corresponds to a particular though not-as-yet-determined balance of a neurochemical like norepinephrine, such that "relative deficiency . . . at certain central synapses" attends depression, and "relative excess" mania, then the point I want to make is that here we have a *prima facie* case for searching such connections for a possible cause. As Hamburg and others affirm, it is likely that "some severe emotional disorders . . . may be partly based upon genetically determined alterations in normal biochemical processes" and that these "biological predispositions must interact in complex ways with environmental factors."[52]

This covers the various arguments and makes no extravagant claims. It leaves open, however, just how we should define the severity of any specific disorder, and just what normality means. On this score we may say that debilitating depression has little to recommend it, but that more modest bouts of it can serve a positive purpose in the life process. If we do decide biochemically to intervene, we may successfully alleviate distress, but we have left the environmental components in the causal equation untouched. By mitigating *environmental* stress, or providing more congenial life conditions, we might achieve similar results without interfering with our organic substrates and the compounds that mediate our emotional responses. This is not to deny the case for so interfering since under carefully accountable circumstances it has proven possible by biochemical means to break into personal spirals that otherwise promise the most pernicious of emotional consequences. It is, however, the process of accountability that is critical here since in allowing such an exception we lay ourselves open to psychiatric assault or worse. How one defines "pernicious consequences" is open as well to sociocultural or political perversion, and to biased clinical findings or research.[53] Nevertheless, symptoms *can* be so severe that regardless of these dangers treatment is justified, either to rescue an individual from suicide or prolonged psychic despair. Such knowledge as we presently possess will then serve a beneficial purpose. (Alcohol has long been used in a similar way by those not so self-evidently stricken.)

The main point to stress is that psychochemical thresholds *do* seem to exist as such, and though we cannot say yet what puts an individual across any one of them (if only because the human unit is so complex that in any particular case the critical factors will tend to be particular too), nor can we say where precisely they lie, there *are* recognized differences between individuals which seem to coincide with differences in particular hormones and measured concentrations of them in the brain.

THE PHARMACOLOGY OF FAITH

What of those who look beyond mere felicity or mental well-being for a sense of permanent rapport with a deity or two, for a state of detachment sufficiently profound to inure them to the daily round of frustration and strife, or for some more evanescent ecstasy that provides relief from the work-a-world consciousness that we use for regular living but enjoy putting aside? The history of human thought is very rich in subjective accounts of this sort of experience and practically every culture has its preferred techniques for exploiting the remarkable potential of the brain/mind here. The thirst for transcendence they satisfy is clearly opposed to the objectivist aspirations of modern science, though science itself is not above a sip from the same spring. To the mystic and the irrationalist, truth comes from illumination not analysis, and the consciousness of the "mathematician, of the physicist, of the logician or the historian, are of a lower and more mundane kind. They lack the certitude of rapture. . . . They come of secular hazard. . . . They are not eternal."[54] Scientific thought, so abstract and disinterested, annuls a deeper feel for the human condition and the human location, and while science has much to say on both these counts, the dismal profanity it seems to breed systematically denies what the spiritually literate would rather we exalt.

In a very real sense, "the capacity of the brain is the final measure of human ability, and, so, of human ambitions."[55] How are we to assess this capacity and this measure? By the standards of science, of rationality, of the "energies and exact dreams" of logic and inference? Or by blatantly intuitive means, by the apprehension of truths beyond analysis, and experiences that grant the grace and favor of supernatural knowledge and the sense of a realm outside ordinary reality, that is divine? Scientists insist upon public and repeatable facts that have empirical referents as palpable as it is possible to find or make them. Mystics celebrate the intensely private, often unique state of possession that speaks of the ineffable, the esoteric, and the extrasensory, and particularly so, it seems, where the sociocultural milieu is not secure.

All the evidence indicates that the more strongly-based and entrenched religious authority becomes, the more hostile it is towards haphazard inspiration . . . the circumstances which encourage the ecstatic response are precisely those where men [sic] feel themselves constantly threatened by exacting pressures which they do not know how to combat or control, except through those heroic flights . . . by which they seek to demonstrate that they are the equals of the gods . . . [that] proclaim . . . man's triumphant mastery of an intolerable environment.[56]

The difference here, that between *science* and *mysticism*, predisposes rather different ideas about the ecstatic experience. Scientific materialism tends to deny the power of the spiritual perspective, seeming rather to regard it is a sublime joke, the most glorious of the side effects of a particular kind of temporary (sometimes permanent) physiological confusion. A swift kick in the brain chemistry and we get God, or euphoria, or schizophrenia, and it is not incidental perhaps that the "two most important families of euphorigenic drugs" resemble "two major families of endogenous neurotransmitters."[57] The brain is also able to manufacture substances with euphoretic effects itself, from within as it were, and the materialist would rather suppose this renders any subjective sense of faith not real. Perhaps *all* religious and mystical insights, they say, are the consequence of biochemical and physiological stress, externally or internally induced. Such skeptics (and there are religious ones as well) tend to be reductionists and will conclude that we have been pharmacologically hoaxed, either (if they "believe") because such experiences are only valid when they occur as a consequence of more conventional devices like devotion, meditation, or prayer, or (if they do not) because such occurrences can never be a valid description of reality as such. (The brain has a powerful capacity to terminate such effects, regardless of how we interpret them, which suggests that pleasure of this sort "*must* be transient and can only be experienced against the background of its absence."[58] One would certainly expect something of the sort on evolutionary grounds alone. Sustained ecstasy would most likely impede individual and group adaptation and survival since those not *of* this world, for prolonged or even temporary periods of time, would also not be likely to leave many progeny *in* it.) The thorough-going religious position, on the other hand, accepts the authority of divinity. Whether biochemically crafted or a consequence of one of the many regimes for meditation that humankind have created in their bid to focus awareness, to diffuse it, or to deny it outright, the outcome is considered entirely transcendental, a state of spiritual grace.[59]

What happens when the ordinary world ceases to impinge and another sort of consciousness occurs? If this happens gradually, the neuropharmacological parameters may be very subtle indeed. If it does not, as in the case of Kundalini yoga or the ingestion of diethylamide of lysergic acid (LSD), the results can be dramatic and profound.[60] The central nervous system responds, in quite unscientific language, by going bananas. Whether such an effect is exogenously or endogenously derived, any interference with the neurotransmitters noradrenaline and serotonin, and the way they pass information across the gap between conducting cells in the brain, seems to amplify or catalyze its subconscious capacities. Apart from the merely "abstract" and "aesthetic" effects, the experiences that may then ensue, "of death and rebirth, union with the universe or God, encounters with demonic appearances, or the reliving of 'past incarnations,' " are indistinguishable from established reports of religious or mystical rapport.

Why is this so? The scientific explanation points out that our work-a-day awareness does *not* in fact reproduce reality entire; on the contrary, it is a highly selected and simplified version of what impinges upon us, and one that is shaped and interpreted in turn in the light of mental models and images the most important of which are provided by language itself. Our culture makes these for us and many we may manufacture for ourselves.[61] Without this repressive process, we would find it that much more difficult, if not impossible, to maintain our attention. We would have developed most probably another sort of mind, anyway, and one not so readily overwhelmed. Huxley[62] describes the selective mechanism as a "reducing valve." What we know is what we need to know to survive—what makes sense to us—but it can never be more than a partial and metaphorical version of what must "really" obtain "out there." "Our ordinary state of consciousness is not something natural or given, but a highly complex construction, a specialized tool, . . ."[63] and while one might take issue with the definition of what is natural or given that is implied in this statement, under suitable conditions we can receive some sense at least, it is thought, of what raw awareness might be like; without our familiar psychological structures and their physiological supports.

Whether this is something actually better than normal, as Huxley argues, or whether it is "non"-sense, is a much-debated question and is indeed highly debatable. Is revelation any more real than what our seemingly rather restricted modes of thinking and feeling allow? Does the move out of more usual mental conditions reproduce experiences of a *higher* or *lower* kind, or something else again? In striving to make such experiences accessible, must we use restrictive categories regardless, simply because of the language-using, analyzing organisms we currently happen to be?[64] Are the more spiritual of these categories—our sense of the ineffable for example, or eternity or infinity—"the result of the operation of a new perceptual capacity responsive to dimensions of the stimulus array previously ignored or blocked from awareness,"[65] or are they rather the random response of mind systems under siege? A state of ecstasy may enable us to forego the immediate and the obvious, but do we really move then outside it, or rather further within; do we open up to ultimate unknowns, or do we in fact close deeper down? Does any of this matter, since there seems no way at present of deciding one way or the other, or of reaching beyond the whole problem to something else? Both the material *and* the spiritual paths, properly pursued, can lead to similar feelings of "awe, beauty, reverence, and humility."[66] Perhaps, and most simply, when ecstasy strikes we actually witness something quite specific—a rerun of the process of our biological conception, the heat and light of the working brain itself, or some internal mental logic that under normal circumstances remains opaque?[67]

The last point is the most pertinent here, and I shall look at it in more detail because recent research into the way the brain is organized does suggest a particular, if highly speculative, response to questions like those above.

THE PHYSIOLOGY OF CONTEMPORARY COGNITION

Mind can be construed either as matter or as spirit or as something else that is "naturally" both: "subject to the hazards of becoming yet capable of being fully understood."[68] Modern science cleaves closest to the first and the third approaches, though the second does recur, in combination with the others or alone.[69] The concept of *becoming* suggests that of emergence, of mind and consciousness evolving together and continuing to do so. For those who accept such an idea, the process of evolution can be seen in two ways, depending upon how radical we think it has been. Martindale calls these contrasting views *intellectualistic* and *holistic* in turn. An intellectualist appeals to the "gradual accumulation of knowledge . . . [and] the principle of psychic unity . . . [the idea] that all human minds are always and everywhere the same."[70] Consciousness passes over time from more primitive modes that construct explanations in terms of supernatural forces to a contemporary, naturalistic, and scientific one. Ignorance gradually dissipates as more is known and civilization comes to prevail. Holists assume that "across the course of history consciousness itself has changes or evolved . . . that there are differences not merely in amount of knowledge [though this has increased too] but more fundamental differences in mode of reasoning, perception, conceptualization, emotion, and so on."[71] "Primitives" are psychically *not* the same as contemporary "modern" adults. They emerge from a subjectivist, myth-infested morass, where the natural universe to which they belong is immediately perceived (or rather experienced) as continuous with themselves, into the hard light of the present day with its distinctions and its analytic hierarchies, its abstract concepts, and its objectivist ideas.

The most recent version of the second approach attributes the change to a change in the balance between the brain's cerebral hemispheres. One might well wonder how such a hypothesis ever occurred, and the story is indeed a fascinating one, though I can only allude to it here. In an attempt to control epileptic seizures in chronically afflicted patients, some American surgeons attempted a radical operation—they severed the main connecting link between the left and right halves of the neocortex of those so affected. Having done this and subsequent research, they were able to suggest ways of refining results from earlier studies of individuals whose brains had been injured or damaged in some way, results that suggested that there is a division of labor within the brain itself.[72] The dominant hemisphere (usually the left) seems to be the more verbal, vigilant, conceptual, and analytical one that mediates our complex motor functions and may directly provide us with conscious experience.[73] The nondominant side is much less verbal. It is also, however, more musical and more proficient in creative-associative thought, more pictorial and pattern sensing, and better at spatial integration. This side may also work largely subconsciously as far as the individual is concerned. Later work with people not subjected to such surgical treatment has confirmed these conclusions. There are tasks that both sides perform, like simple motor functions, "basic patterns of learning . . . the capacity to process information, . . . the ability to hold information in perceptual stores," and the capacity for rational thought itself. To this extent the brain is a *duplicate* mechanism and not a *differentiated* one.[74] Each side does have specialities, however, and, though complementary in effect, they are distinctive and discrete:

> . . . [T]he human cerebral hemispheres exist in a symbiotic relationship. . . . [E]ach side . . . is able to perform and chooses to perform a certain set of cognitive tasks which the other side finds difficult or distasteful or both. . . . The right hemisphere synthesises over space. The left hemisphere analyzes over time. The right hemisphere notes visual similarities to the exclusion of conceptual similarities. The left hemisphere does the opposite. The right hemisphere perceives form, the left hemisphere, detail. The right hemisphere codes sensory input in terms of images, the left hemisphere in terms of linguistic descriptions. The right hemisphere lacks a phonological analyser; the left hemisphere lacks a Gestalt synthesiser.[75]

There is even evidence for a difference in emotional response, the right hemisphere seeming to view the world as more unpleasant and horrific than the left, which suggests that the right is the more paranoid and pessimistic and potentially depressive of the two and that its cerebral companion is more optimistically inclined.[76] The most "dramatic dichotomy," however, remains that between *language* and *manipulospatiality*.[77]

A division of labor of this sort would seem to confer evolutionary advantages. Why else, we may well ask, would it have occurred (by accident?) It provides for various combinations of capacities, for different sorts of specialists and generalists in the human population, and, more important perhaps, for a flexible decision-making system within the brain itself that allows of efficient function overall.[78] We must be careful not to go too much beyond the evidence at hand, and, indeed, the relative differences are often less apparent or certain than my summary above suggests. This has not, however, prevented current commentators from going so far as to conclude that

> there are multiple mental systems in the brain, each with the capacity to produce behavior, and each with its own impulses for action. . . . The mind is not a psychological entity but a sociological entity . . . [and] the uniqueness of man, in this regard, is his [sic] ability to

verbalize and, in so doing, create a personal sense of conscious reality . . . the verbal system's role in creating our sense of conscious reality is crucial. . . . In attributing cause to behavioral and psychological states, an attitudinal view of the world involving beliefs and values is constructed, and this view becomes a dominant theme in our own self-image.[79]

To the extent that the subordinate hemisphere provides another persona in the mind, we open the way to a quite literal interpretation of that idea. Sperry has said that "modern society discriminates against the right hemisphere."[80] He seems to suggest, in other words, that our capacity for language has become so important that it has somehow crowded out less striking mental attributes, relegating them to an inferior status and place. This was not always so, perhaps, and may have occurred comparatively recently in evolutionary terms—a notion that has proved sufficiently suggestive for Jaynes, for example, to give it central play.[81] He begins with the concept of consciousness, asking that if this is an emergent property of the living brain, as Sperry (and others before him) have maintained, then at what evolutionary point does it emerge? Once we have language (which is an "organ of perception" he says, and not simply one of "communication"), it becomes possible to ambush reality with metaphors, to develop a feeling of familiarity about what is unknown and hence some understanding of it. This is the beginning, but it is only the beginning. Iliadic man, for example, as Jaynes terms the ancient Greeks, had speech, but he (she, they) "did not have subjectivity as do we; he had no awareness of his awareness of the world . . . the earliest writing of men in a language that we can really comprehend . . . reveals a very different mentality from our own." In particular, ". . . human nature was split in two, an executive part called a god, and a follower part called a man. Neither part was conscious."[82] The split corresponded, he maintains, to the left hemisphere/right hemisphere functioning described above, though under conditions of stress the right hemisphere was wont to "speak" in the head (and occasionally "appear"), and was "heard" (and "seen") by the left, as a divine mentor in what we would now call a hallucinatory way: "the speech of the gods was directly organized in what corresponds to Wernicke's area on the right hemisphere and 'spoken' or 'heard' over the anterior commissures to or by the auditory areas of the left temporal lobe" (the hallucinations were usually auditory "because that is the most efficient method of getting complicated cortical processing from one side of the brain to the other").[83]

What evidence exists for this extraordinary claim? Jaynes himself cites the sort of studies done above to establish the fact that there are two autonomous hemispheres possessed of independent properties, the left in most people commanding language (though both right and left can in fact comprehend it) and the right demonstrating "vestigial godlike functions" like the capacity to "organize action according to an ongoing . . . purpose . . . sorting out the experiences of a civilization and fitting them together into a pattern that could 'tell' the individual what to do. . . ." The right hemisphere, like any good god, "sees parts as having a meaning only within a context; it looks at wholes."[84] He refers further to Penfield and Perot's work to suggest that stimulation of the relevant area on the nondominant side generates hallucinations of a sort that three thousand years ago would have been attributed to an admonitory deity.[85] Environmental changes in learning and culture have since suppressed them, changes that represent new modes of social control and new modes of material production (the transition, that is, from hunting and gathering to agriculture).

Now if, as Jaynes says, human language evolved comparatively recently; if Ice Age climactic changes did prompt, as he suggests, the use of auditory signalling of a sort that led in turn to ever more complex linguistic constructions, ever more complex perceptions and "attentions," and concomitant changes in culture; if this did provide the capacity for internally monitored hallucinations that conferred divine guidance and could be organized to hierarchic social effect; what happened then? Basically, Jaynes argues, writing, trade, and increased cultural contact—each of these helped to objectify such seemingly supernatural directives and made it possible on a popular scale to drive a wedge—consciousness itself—between god and man.[86] Thus it is with the ancient Greeks that we get the first flowering of general subjective awareness.

The transition was a fraught one and loss of the "other" was never total and complete.[87] Should there not, therefore, be some evidence of "bicamerality" still among preliterate, relatively isolated, "primitives" of more recent times and the present day? The findings are diverse and unclear, but tribes that have lived largely outside contemporary world society for the last few thousand years or so, like those of Melanesia, Australasia, or the Kalahari, for example, do *not* seem, on contact, to report the "head" voices they ought to have if Jayne's speculations are to be confirmed.

This has not stopped others, however, from putting the more modest point that the differences in the logical processes of "traditional" as opposed to "modern" modes of cognition may be due, not to any psychic inequality on the part of the former, but to the sort of cerebral specialization that is possible there. Thus Paredes and Hepburn suggest that the cultural change from a more primitive to a more modern milieu, however this occurs, means a shift in emphasis from the right hemisphere to the left with the cerebral refocus this now implies.[88] Accordingly, adult members of a tribe from the interior of Malaita with only the most tenuous awareness of the outside world have the same brains as board members of IBM, but, as a result of differences in culture, they have come to use them differently. Should they be introduced subsequently to the urban environment of their country's capital, with its quantities and complexities and more cosmopolitan ways, they might be expected to lose some of their earlier (right hemispherical) expertise, or perhaps keep it on in a schizophrenic way as left-cognition becomes more relevant and hence more dominant in shaping behavioral response. (The other alternative would be to refuse to adapt outright.) This does not *exclude* the possibility that a cultural tradition may, to some extent, so shape the developing and learning brain as to produce the specific pattern of neuronal pathways appropriate to such a cognitive outcome, though should this be the case one would expect that it would be more difficult to effect a later change. It rather favors the view of the brain as a more or less given parcel of components that different cultures can exploit in different ways, each culture then activating the mental functions it prefers. And this means that, except for those who make the transition, who keep both modes of cognition alive, the brain will be using less than its whole potential. Or would using our ''whole potential'' in this respect ask too much of what the brain has evolved to withstand?[89]

It is easy to make far too much out of what has been established so far, which is really only a little, remarkable though that little may be. The parallels posited are suggestive, but, given the very tentative nature of any honest conclusion on brain research in this area, and the equally tentative character of attempts to categorize the differences between whole human cultures, to assert things in the way of casual significance would seem presumptuous at best.[90] Indeed, some[91] have characterized all such arguments as an elaborate appeal to the ''mythology'' of polar oppositions, to the seductive yet misleading power of analytically intuited dichotomies. Other evidence here, on abstract and conceptual thinking, for example, would seem to implicate *both* hemispheres, and hence at least the possibility that *front* and *back* as well as *left* and *right* divisions are relevant too.[92] Furthermore, when (as Jaynes does) we appeal to written works to assess how historical societies and those who lived in them actually thought, we need to remain alert to the differences that exist between the history of visual and verbal forms and the evolution of consciousness as such. Human artifacts like literature and art represent the ideas and emotions of their authors, and of the social environments they have lived in. These correspondences are suggestive, but they may also mislead, particularly when, as they do in the West, such modes of expression become ever more individualistic.

COGNITION AND POLITICS

What political implications can be drawn from the above? Government in general has lost its access to divine sanction. Over millenia it has become less the extension of a transcendent domain and progressively more a matter of possessing and administering secular power. The historical prevalence of sacred kings, priestly elites, and other suitably inspired leaders went with another sort of consciousness that is now clearly on the wane. However the transformation occurred, the advent of a modernizing outlook and its mental insights has been to bring the business of politics, of socioeconomic assertion and submission, back to earth. It seems rather fanciful to link this to the competence of one particular cerebral hemisphere, and even if there *is* something in the idea, there seems no way yet to establish to what extent this has been consequence or cause. Culture and cognition chase each other's tails, and there seems plenty of scope still for the extravagance of our less verbal selves, (there was certainly a good deal of ecstatic expression of the mythological sort under the Third Reich, for example, suitably exploited by those who saw its unifying fervor as the ultimate instrument with which to satisfy their transcendent and individual desires.)

Whatever changes in human consciousness have occurred then, they have not been reflected always and everywhere in political systems that foster individual awareness. A fair number of earth's people are now exhorted to bend their best efforts to realize the good of god-surrogates—the nation, for example, the Party, conspicuous consumption or their collective and collectivized selves. The concept of private self-interest, which is one consequence of being self-aware, seems to work its way through regardless, however, and we are back once more to debates about the evolution of altruism versus that of individual aggrandizement. At one end stands those historical materialists who mostly consider conscious-ness a product of modes of production and who find the whole idea of positing a human nature apart from society and socioeconomic place and time antipathetic. At the other we have the sociobiologists who are much less shy on the whole of positing a "natural" component to mental change: "A hundred generations—about 3000 years—is held to be sufficient to support at least some non-negligible degree of selection for behavioral traits, or any traits for that matter. In this context, Jaynes' contention that there may have been . . . selection pressures in favor of left-dominance (or differentiated consciousness) over the last several millenia is not unreasonable."[93]

Whatever the case, the most potent evidence still supports the concept of human plasticity. An average inclination toward left-dominance could be bred out as quickly as it was bred in, and it is increasingly apparent to researchers in this field just how flexible and adaptable an organ the brain can be. While findings suggest that the lopsided development of the speech centers actually begins before birth and that there really is a physiological division of labor, with perhaps some more generalized outcome, if we handicap the process of specialization, it takes place in other ways to no notable behavioral effect on the individual's final performance. This physiological flexibility is matched by cultures that encourage self-analysis and the voluntaristic assumption that something can always be done.

While the mystic sanctions for values have been worn away, whether this reflects a shift of some physiological sort or whether that shift has followed innovations in human belief, the end result has helped to reveal the very human strata upon which all values ultimately rest. There may well be grooves that direct the flow of our thoughts, feelings, and actions down which they most readily run. But an important human capacity is our ability to score new grooves across what we inherit; to make other runnels than those that are biologically defined. It costs to intervene in order to achieve what we want or believe, but it may cost less than letting some subterranean logic take what seems its natural course. Unfortunately, all we really know at the moment is that if we get it wrong we will cease to survive. The awareness of awareness is at once a wonderful and a terrible trait.

NOTES

1. G. H. von Wright, *The Varieties of Goodness* (London: Routledge and Kegan Paul, 1963), p. 86. For an identity theorist who sees these concepts as the same, see N. Bradburn, *The Structure of Psychological Well-Being* (Chicago: Aldine, 1969).
2. B. Moore, "On the Unity of Misery and the Diversity of Happiness," in *Reflections on the Causes of Human Misery* (London: Allen Lane, 1972), pp. 1–2, 11.
3. M. Kalin, *The Utopian Flight from Unhappiness*: Freud against Marx on Social Progress (Chicago: Nelson-Hall, 1974), p. X.
4. Ibid., pp. 108, 199.
5. Ibid., p. 160.
6. Clearly contrasted by S. Lukes, "Alienation and Anomie," in P. Laslett and W. Runciman, eds., *Philosophy, Politics and Society* (Oxford: Basil Blackwell, 1967).
7. J. Passmore, *The Perfectibility of Man* (London: Duckworth, 1970), p. 281. Passmore also notes the need not to

> sentimentalize the past. Unremitting toil is also dehumanizing; in some cases at least, technological advances have freed men [sic] from toil and left them time and energy for human relationships. Men's complaints about the dehumanizing character of modern social relationships are in large part a product of ideals that we have only come, since the Enlightenment, to take for granted: neither the medieval serf nor the brutalized eighteenth— or nineteenth—century workman was commonly regarded as a human being" except, one might add, by him or herself. "What we have always to watch is that, however admirable our intentions, we do not, in trying to abolish a particular form of dehumanization, substitute others even worse and more widespread. [P. 281]

8. R. Lane, "Cognition, Consciousness and Depression: Effects of the Market and the Democratic State" (Paper presented at the 11th World Congress of the International Political Science Association, Moscow, August 1979), p. 5, 6.
9. Ibid., p. 17. Also pp. 19, 30:

> The irony of history is that the market, true to its innovative role, has prepared the ground for a change in the conception of the mature person and has created in a portion of the population the cognitive skills which make that conception a realizable possibility. Without so intending, the market created the alternatives that both disembedded the population from tradition and required reflective choice among the alternatives. It was a stimulus to cognitive complexity. It freed the human spirit from sexual guilt and licensed self interest, depriving the superego of its tyranny and permitting forbidden knowledge of the self into the realm of a wider consciousness . . . it released what seems to be a biologically given drive, curiosity, now employed to explore what religion, custom,

family and state had once proscribed as dangerous and sinful. The market has supported institutions of higher learning whose students, with the tools and incentives given to them, have turned, with mixed success, to the "inner frontier." In these and other ways, the market has prepared the way for the democratic state, in its own good time, to discharge its welfare responsibilities by extending its concern for mental illness to that version of mental health that includes "knowledge of the self."

10. Ibid., p. 54.
11. Distinctions that can be traced back at least to Aristotle, *Ethica Nichomachea* (Oxford: Clarendon Press, 1925), Book 6, parts 3, 4, 5.
12. J. Plamenatz, *Man and Society*, vol. 2 (London: Longmans, 1962), Ch. 7, "The Belief in Progress."
13. Ibid., p. 411.
14. Ibid., pp. 411–12.
15. Ibid., p. 444.
16. von Wright, *Varieties of Goodness*, pp. 92–94. There are other meanings of the word, like "lucky" or "fortunate," for example, that do not apply here. See also N. Bradburn and D. Caplovitz, *Reports on Happiness* (Chicago: Aldine, 1965). It is interesting to note in the light of an earlier chapter that the predisposing factors are sometimes seen as sex-linked: "men are doers, and hold that to be happy you must achieve something. Women are be-people and maintain that to achieve something you must be happy" (p. 70, G. Taylor, *Rethink* [London: Secker and Warburg, 1972].) The crudeness of such an assertion ought to be self-evident by now.
17. W. Tatarkiewicz, *Analysis of Happiness* (The Hague: Mortimer Nijhoff, 1976), p. 8. I would disagree with this author on his use of an "objective" sense of happiness. One can describe those objective conditions that seem to predispose the subjective feeling we call felicity, but happiness is not those objective conditions. It is the individual or collective response to them. Only where "happy" is defined as "fortunate" does his argument apply. See also T. Smith, "Happiness: Time Trends, Seasonal Variations, Intersurvey Differences, and Other Mysteries," *Social Psychology* 42, no. 1 (1979): 18–30.
18. R. Yensen, "On the Measurement of Happiness and its Implications for Welfare," in L. Levi, ed., *Emotions—Their Parameters and Measurement* (New York: Raven Press, 1975), p. 633: "It is suggested that the overall happiness of the individual is made up of the sum of the feelings of happiness that he [sic] experiences in each important life area, when these feelings of happiness are suitably weighted in accordance with the relative salience of each area."
19. For the seminal statement, see Aristotle, *Ethica Nichomachea,* Book 10, para. 8. Also, para. 7: "That which is proper to each thing is by nature best and most pleasant for each thing; for man, therefore, the life according to reason more than anything else *is* man. This life is also the happiest."

    Or, as paraphrased by J. Barnes: "A man is 'happy' if and only if, over some considerable period of time [pleasure or ecstasy being by contrast short-lived] he performs with some success the most perfect of typically human tasks" (*The Ethics of Aristotle* [London: Penguin, rev. ed., 1978], p. 36).
20. H. Jones, *The Pursuit of Happiness* (New York: Cornell University Press, 1966), pp. 67–68. Also U. von Eckardt, *The Pursuit of Happiness in the Democratic Creed* (N.Y.: Praeger, 1959).
21. I. Berlin, "John Stuart Mill and the Ends of Life," in *Four Essays on Liberty* (Oxford: Oxford University Press, 1969), pp. 176–177.
22. H. Jones, *Pursuit of Happiness*, pp. 146–147.
23. These notions themselves cover enormous ground. See, e.g., D. Perry, *The Concept of Pleasure* (The Hague: Mouton and Co., 1967) on "enjoyment" as opposed to "being pleased about"; also Passmore, *Perfectibility of Man*.

24. J. Bentham, *An Introduction to the Principles of Morals and Legislation* (London: University of London, 1970), Ch. 4: "Value of a Lot of Pleasure or Pain, How to be Measured."

25. Ibid., p. 12.

26. J. S. Mill, *Utilitarianism* (London: J. H. Dent, 1962), p. 6.

27. Bentham, *Introduction to the Principles*, pp. 11, 13.

28. Mill, *Utilitarianism*, p. 36.

29. H. J. Campbell, *The Pleasure Areas* (London: Eyre Methuen, 1973), p. 11.

30. Ibid., p. 61.

31. Ibid., p. 32.

32. Mill does discuss this sort of criticism, acknowledging, for example, a distinction between "will" and "desire." "Will," however, "is the child of desire," he says, "and passes out of the dominion of its parent only to come under that of habit" *Utilitarianism*, p. 38.

33. Plamenatz, *Man and Society*, pp. 14, 15.

34. See fn. 76, Ch. 1.

35. Cf. J. Cowan, *Pleasure and Pain* (London: Macmillan, 1968); J. Gosling, *Pleasure and Desire* (Oxford: Clarendon Press, 1969).

36. Stephen observes at this point that

> the application of Mr. Mill's test about the different kinds of happiness is impossible. Where are we to find people who are qualified by experience to say which is happier . . . a very stupid prosperous farmer who dies of old age after a life of perfect health, or an accomplished delicate woman of passionate sensibility and brilliant genius, who dies worn out before her youth is passed, after an alternation of rapturous happiness with agonies of distress. . . . [It is] like asking the distance from one o'clock to London Bridge. [J. Stephen, *Liberty, Equality, Fraternity* (Cambridge: Cambridge University Press, 1967), p. 230]

This is to parody Mill's rather more sensible appeal, but the point is so well put that I cannot forego citing it.

37. Mill, *Utilitarianism*, p. 12.

38. W. Stace, *The Concept of Morals* (N.Y.: Macmillan, 1962).

39. Mill, *Utilitarianism*, p. 13.

40. See B. Russell, *The Conquest of Happiness* (London: George Allen and Unwin, 1930).

41. L. Tiger, *Optimism*: The Biology of Hope (New York: Simon and Schuster, 1979), p. 21. See also M. Maklin and D. Stang, *The Pollyanna Principle:* Selectivity in Language, Memory and Thought (Cambridge, Mass.: Schenkman Publishing Co., 1978).

42. Ibid., p. 160.

43. Ibid., p. 24.

44. S. Diamond, *In Search of the Primitive*: A Critique of Civilisation (New Brunswick: Transaction Books, 1974), pp. 159–160, 164–165, 168–171:

> If the fulfillment and delineation of the human person within a social, natural and supernatural (transcendent) setting is a universally valid measure for the evaluation of culture, primitive societies are our primitive superiors. . . . We talk about values or morality . . . at the moment that the sacred character of human experience becomes problematic, and, when compelled by our social structure, we segregate values from the general flow of our experience. As soon as we become capable of analyzing values they have become . . . commodities, detached from ourselves . . . demystified as a transcendent linguistic idea somehow reflecting either an ultimate creation of the demi-urge—a final category, or an immanent genetic entity. . . . Among primitives [however] . . . Morality *is* behavior, values are not detached, not substantives; the good, the true, the beautiful or rather, the idea of these things, do not exist.

Primitive societies provide, in Diamond's opinion, superior nurturance, superior personal relationships, superior opportunities for institutionalized deviancy, relief from social and existential anxieties (through ritual), engagement with nature, with natural physiological functions, and with culture, and superior socioeconomic support (in the sense of more equitable distribution).

45. See also R. Heath, "Pleasure Response of Human Subjects to Direct Stimulation of the Brain: Physiologic and Psychodynamic Considerations," in R. Heath, ed., *The Role of Pleasure in Behavior* (N.Y.: Harper and Row, 1964); C. Sen-Jacobsen and O. Styri, "Manipulation of Emotion: Electrophysiological and Surgical Methods," in Levi, ed., *Emotions.*
46. E. McMullin, "What Difference Does Mind Make?" in A. Karczmar and J. Eccles, ed., *Brain and Human Behavior* (Heidelberg: Springer-Verlag, 1972), p. 444.
47. D. Holvey, ed., *The Merck Manual of Diagnosis and Therapy*, 12th ed. (Rahway, N.J.: Merck and Co., 1972), p. 1606. Also D. Rioch, "Psychological and Pharmacological Manipulations," in Levi, *Emotions*; S. Kety, "Norepinephrine in the Central Nervous System and its Correlations with Behavior," in Karczmar and Eccles, *Brain and Human Behavior.*
48. For a review of this problem see Ch. 7, "Biopolitics: The Human Brain," in my *Human Behaviour and World Politics* (London: Macmillan, 1975). To paraphrase John Glashan, "we have traced the fault to the shoddy condition of your mediocre mind."
49. Kety, *Norepinephrine*, p. 120.
50. D. Hamburg et al., "Anger and Depression in Perspective of Behavioral Biology," in Levi, ed., *Emotions*, p. 237:

> In the case of emotions experienced as rewarding, the action associated with the emotions have been linked with survival. This linkage may have occurred in the history of the species and be encoded in the genes or may have occurred in the history of the individual and be encoded in the brain through learning or both. In either case, the occurrence of the emotional response . . . says, in effect, "This is important . . . in a good and desirable way; it should be done again in the future." In the case of emotions experienced as distressing, the associated actions have also been linked with survival, phylogenetically or outogenetically or both. . . . They have a signal function which warns the organism . . . that something is wrong, attention must be paid, learning capacities utilized [and] resources mobilized to correct the situation. [P. 239]

51. R. Lazarus, "The Self-Regulation of Emotion," in Levi, ed., *Emotions*, p. 50. "In *primary* appraisal the issue to be judged is whether or not a danger (threat) has been signalled . . . *secondary* appraisal involves evaluation by the person of the kind of adoptive action called for. . . ." As far as *coping* is concerned, Lazarus distinguishes this as an "integral, biological part of emotion" from the "attempt to extricate oneself from a situation of jeopardy or harm" (pp. 47–48).
52. Hamburg et al., "Anger and Depression," p. 268.
53. P. Pancheri, "Measurement of Emotion: Transcultural Aspects," in Levi, ed., *Emotions.*
54. G. Steiner, "Has truth a future?" *The Listener*, Jan. 12, 1978, p. 43.
55. H. Elliott, *The Shape of Intelligence*: The Evolution of the Human Brain (London: George Allen and Unwin, 1970), p. 6.
56. J. Lewis, *Ecstatic Religion* (Harmondsworth: Penguin, 1971), pp. 34–35.
57. A. Mandell, "Neurobiological Barriers to Euphoria," *American Scientist* 61 (Sept.–Oct. 1973): 572.
58. Ibid., p. 572.
59. C. Naranjo and R. Ornstein, *On the Psychology of Meditation* (N.Y.: Viking Press, 1971), p. 6.
60. S. Grof, *Realms of the Human Unconscious:* Observations from LSD Research (N.Y.: E. P. Dutton, 1976), p. 30.
61. "The liberated have continually stressed that words are only *about* truth, not truth itself. Truth

cannot be known except through direct experience, through 'enlightenment.' And often language is a barrier . . . because there is a confusion between beams of non-verbal intuition and that learned arbitrary framework'' (p. ix, J. White, ed., *The Highest State of Consciousness* [N.Y.: Doubleday, 1972]). To which one might reply: while the *sounds* are arbitrary, need the *meanings* be so?

62. A. Huxley, *The Doors of Perception* (N.Y.: Harper and Bros., 1954), p. 23.
63. C. Tart, *States of Consciousness* (N.Y.: E. P. Dutton, 1975), p. 3.
64. A Deikman, ''Deautomatization of the Mystic Experience,'' in C. Tart, ed., *Altered States of Consciousness* (N.Y.: Wiley, 1969), p. 30:

> A mystic experience is the production of an unusual state of consciousness. This state is brought about by a deautomatization of hierarchically ordered structures that ordinarily conserve attentional energy for maximum efficiency in achieving the basic goals of the individual: biological survival as an organism and psychological survival as a personality. Under special conditions . . . the pragmatic systems of automatic selection are set aside or break down in favor of alternate modes of consciousness whose stimulus processing may be less efficient from a biological point of view but whose very inefficiency may permit the experience of aspects of the real world formerly excluded or ignored.[Pp. 42–3]

65. Ibid., p. 42.
66. Ibid., p. 43.
67. '' 'Illumination' may be derived from an actual sensory experience occurring when in the cognitive act of unification, a liberation of energy takes place, or when a resolution of unconscious conflict occurs. . . . Liberated energy experienced as light may be the core sensory experience of mysticism'' (ibid., p. 38).
68. McMullin, ''What Difference,'' in Karczmar and Eccles, *Brain and Human Behavior*, p. 426. Also L. Whyte, *The Unconscious Before Freud* (N.Y.: Basic Books, 1960), Ch. 4.
69. See, e.g., W. Penfield, *The Mystery of the Mind* (Princeton, N.J.: Princeton University Press, 1975).
70. C. Martindale, ''Theories of the Evolution of Consciousness,'' *Journal of Altered States of Consciousness* 3, no. 3 (1977–8): 263.
71. Ibid., p. 265.
72. Though it has been found that ''right dominant people have only a minimal degree of lateralisation and . . . only somewhat less than two-thirds of left dominant people have maximal lateralisation (J. Levy, ''Psychobiological Implications of Bilateral Asymmetry,'' in S. Dimond and J. Beaumont, eds., *Hemisphere Function in the Human Brain* (London: Paul Elek, 1974), p. 168.
73. J. Eccles, ''Cerebral Activity and Consciousness,'' in F. Ayala and T. Dobzhansky, eds., *Studies in the Philosophy of Biology* (Berkeley: University of California, 1974). The question of locating consciousness, it hardly needs repeating, is a vexed one. Whether one sees the emergent whole as more ''significant'' than the action of the component parts, even as integrated in the ordinary individual and not surgically sectioned, seems at present a question of philosophic preference more than scientific result. See also W. TenHouten, ''More on Split-Brain Research, Culture, and Cognition,'' *Current Anthropology* 7, no. 3 (September 1976): 504; S. Dimond, ''Brain Circuits for Consciousness,'' *Brain, Behavior and Evolution* 13 (1976): 376–395, who would locate consciousness in the corpus callosum, the hemispherical systems spanned and united by it, plus the parietal lobes. It is an extraordinary fact that the removal of a whole cerebral hemisphere will not actually destroy consciousness, though; O. Zangwill, ''Consciousness and the Cerebral Hemispheres,'' in Dimond and Beaumont, eds., *Hemisphere Function*, says ''both the separated left and the right hemispheres may be conscious simultaneously in different and even conflicting mental experiences that run along in

parallel. From its non-verbal responses we infer that the minor hemisphere senses, perceives, thinks and feels all at a characteristically human level . . .'' (p. 213); R. Sperry, ''Lateral Specialization of Cerebral Function in the Surgically Separated Hemispheres,'' in F. McGuigan and R. Schoonover, eds., *The Psychophysiology of Thinking* (N.Y.: Academic Press, 1973).

74. S. Dimond and J. Beaumont, ''Experimental Studies of Hemisphere Function in the Human Brain,'' in Dimond and Beaumont, eds., *Hemisphere Function*, p. 83.

75. Levy, p. 167. ''Psychobiological Implications,'' in ibid.

76. S. Dimond et al., ''Differing Emotional Responses from Right and Left Hemispheres,'' *Nature* 26 (1976): 690–2:

> How far the right hemisphere enters into the everyday emotional appraisal of the environment is a matter open for debate. With regard to the question of the ultimate unity of emotional judgement our results suggest that the left takes precedence over the right. . . . There could be a parallel to ideas of unconscious determination of conduct in the view that the right hemisphere provides a source for unconscious motivation within the brain. The right hemisphere does not seem to be denied access to consciousness, but instead contributes an alternative voice to mental action at the conscious level. See fn. 72 above.

77. M. Gazzaniga and J. LeDoux, *The Integrated Mind* (New York: Plenum Press, 1978), p. 63. This has been borne out by subsequent electroencephalographic studies on untreated individuals, e.g., P. Dumas and A. Morgan, ''EEG Asymmetry as a Function of Occupation, Task, and Task Difference,'' *Neuropsychologia* 13 (1975): 219–228. They conclude that

> when a person has a dominant cognitive style, he [sic] does not necessarily use one hemisphere for the tasks appropriate to the other hemisphere, but rather has differential aptitudes in lateralized functions and perhaps seeks out environments in which the more developed mode is utilized more. . . . [Furthermore], right and left hemisphere functions represent equally sophisticated and ''high level'' functioning rather than the right hemisphere representing basal functions and the left hemisphere the more sophisticated processes involved in ''consciousness.'' [P. 227]

78. M. Gazzaniga, ''Cerebral Dominance Viewed as a Decision System,'' in Dimond and Beaumont, eds., *Hemisphere Function*. Also F. Nottebohm, ''Origins and Mechanisms in the Establishment of Cerebral Dominance,'' in M. Gazzaniga, ed., *Neuropsychology*, in *Handbook of Behavioral Neurobiology*, vol. 2 (New York: Plenum Press, 1979), pp. 336–7: ''The analytic idiosyncrasies of the left hemisphere, particularly those involving fine temporal judgements, may be an indispensable part of an executive network.'' Furthermore, the hemispheres may actually pass dominance from one side to another as different capacities are employed.

79. Gazzaniga and LeDoux, *Integrated Mind*, pp. 150–1, 155. Also p. 72: ''lateralized functions do not reflect the genetically specified cognitive styles of the hemispheres but instead represent specific, localized differences in cerebral organization that are closely tied to the inter- and intra-hemispheric localization of linguistic mechanisms''.

80. Sperry, ''Lateral Specialization,'' in McGuigan and Schoonover, *Psychophysiology of Thinking*, p. 209.

81. J. Jaynes, *The Origin of Consciousness in the Breakdown of the Bicameral Mind* (Boston: Houghton Miflin, 1976).

82. Ibid., pp. 75, 82, 83.

83. Ibid., p. 105.

84. Ibid., p. 119.

85. W. Penfield and P. Perot, ''The Brain's Record of Auditory and Visual Experience: A Final Summary and Discussion,'' *Brain* 86 (1963): 595–702. Note in this context their observation,

contradicting Jaynes, that, "although there is a strong sense of immediacy in these experiences, none of the patients has ever confused the hallucination with reality except perhaps for a moment" (p. 679). It may have been always like this, though the *interpretation* of the mental event may now differ as cultures have come to teach greater subjective self-awareness and the principles of empirical and experimental science. The "interpretive cortex" Penfield tested apparently provides for the recall of previous perceptions, their comparison with present experience, and the latter's ultimate "interpretation." The "signals" used in this process have culturally acquired meanings, and it is this point Jaynes is able to exploit.

86. Whyte, *The Unconscious Before Freud,* cites here the fact that English and German only acquire words that denote awareness and self-awareness in the 17th century. In French the pertinent expressions appear even later.

87. See further Ch. 1, "Culture and Consciousness," of my *State and Class: A Sociology of International Affairs* (London: Croom Helm, 1979). Also Whyte, *The Unconscious Before Freud*; Jaynes, *Origin of Consciousness*:

> In spite of all that rationalist materialist science has implied since the Scientific Revolution, mankind as a whole has not, does not, and perhaps cannot relinquish his fascination with some human type of relationship to a greater and wholly other . . . something that for modern religious people communicates in truths of feeling, rather than in what can be verbalized . . . bicameral absolutes . . . an external hierarchy reaching through a cloud of miracle and infallibility to an archaic authorization in an extended heaven. . . . While the universal characteristics of the new consciousness, such as self-reference, mind-space, and narratization, can develop swiftly on the heels of new language construction . . . [t]he matter and technic of earlier ages of civilizations survive into the new eras uneroded, dragging with them the older outworn forms in which the new mentality must live. . . . But living also . . . is a fervent search. . . . Why are the gods no longer heard and seen? . . . more assurances are needed than the relics of history or the paid insistences of priests . . . that behind all this hesitant subjective groping about for signs of certainty, there is a certainty to be had. [Pp. 318–19, 320]

Whyte sees the "European and Western ideal of the self-aware individual confronting destiny with his [sic] own indomitable will and skeptical reason" as "perhaps the noblest aim which has yet been accepted by any community" (p. 8). Whether one agrees or not, and whatever the influence of this ideal—which has, in fact, been enormous—Whyte himself considers it a "moral mistake" and an "intellectual error" because it radically overestimates the significance of individual awareness. This became clear only once the "unconscious" had been identified as such, and clearer still, perhaps, now we know of the bicameral brain. "If there is a God" Whyte argues, writing fifteen years or more before Jaynes,

> he must speak there; if there is a healing power, it must operate there; if there is a principle of ordering in the organic realm, its most powerful manifestation must be found there . . . the conscious mind will enjoy no peace until it can rejoice in a fuller understanding of its own unconscious sources. . . . [p. 10] [S]elf-awareness is not itself an independent organ. It is one differentiated aspect only of the total . . . mind, important for the identification and ordering of contrasts, yet never the ultimate determinant of any ordering process, in thought or behavior. The decisive factors, the primary decisions, are unconscious. [P. 37]

Cf. Dimond, who finds "nothing inherently difficult about the idea that much of what the brain accomplishes is not available to consciousness" ("Brain Circuits," *Brain, Behavior and Evolution,* p. 390). Studies of bicameralism (or of the tri-unity posited by Paul Maclean are primarily, however, attempts to describe more precisely the biological organization, the unified and coordinated structure and process of the brain, that *precedes* any reliable and comprehensive theory of mind.

88. J. Paredes and M. Hepburn, "The Split Brain and the Culture-and-Cognition Paradox," *Current Anthropology* 17, no. 1 (March 1976): 124. See also Dumas and Morgan's conclusion, fn. 79 above.

89. E. Armstrong, "On Split-Brain Research and the Culture-and-Cognition Paradox," *Current Anthropology* 17, no. 2 (June 1976): 318.

90. J. Chisholm, "On Split-Brain Research and the Culture-and-Cognition Paradox," *Current Anthropology* 17, no. 2 (June 1976): 318.

91. Ibid., p. 320.

92. TenHouten, "More on Split-Brain Research," p. 505.

93. Martindale, "Theories," p. 275; Jaynes, *Origin of Consciousness*, p. 205: "In the bicameral era, the bicameral mind *was* the social control, not fear or repression or even law. There were no private ambitions, no private grudges, no private frustrations, no private anything, since bicameral man had no internal 'space' in which to be private, and no analog 'I' to be private with. All initiative was in the voices of gods." What was it that "heard" such all-pervasive admonitions, however, if not some nascent "self" not totally continuous with divine command? One suspects Jaynes here of fast skating on some rather thin conceptual ice.

6

Science, Society
(and Can They Survive)

However we wish to define it, politics remains a very human affair. Whether we fasten upon the institutional manifestations of political behavior, and the power-seeking and power-broking processes large human societies display, or choose rather to emphasize the actual business of governmental bargaining and the wheedling, the bludgeoning, and the obedience, we confront very diverse aspects of human being. As a matter of intellectual convenience, we might mark off particular social systems, particular issues, or particular human undertakings as typically *political* in some way, and find empirical justification for doing so in our common sense analyses of the world. There are, after all, important dimensions of our experience to which the word "nonpolitical" does apply. But governments and governing are so expressive of societies or the self, they have such immediate and such pervasive effects, that it has always proved problematic deciding just what bits of being or belief we might safely exclude from the discussion of political affairs.

BIOPOLITICS

It is no accident then that as knowledge of ourselves has grown—and nowhere in more spectacular fashion than the life sciences—the question has arisen as to what this all means for political theory and practice. Hence the advent of "biopolitics" as a "useful piece of shorthand" to suggest our "political efforts to reconcile biological facts and popular values—notably ethical values—in the formulation of public policies."[1] And hence the sort of investigations I have made above.

Those who pursue such a transdisciplinary enterprise, who struggle to win professional recognition for their methodological and substantive concerns, are usually fairly modest about the importance of what they do. Often enough such modesty is well-founded. There have been sufficient attempts to apply biological analogies and insights to the political realm that are either patently marginal or misconstrued for us to find sentiments such as these well warranted. But this is not all the story. When we think again about what it is the biopolitical project involves, we can, I believe, conclude that diffidence is inappropriate. Beyond its more specific interests—in the biochemical manipulation of public mood, for example, or voice-stress analysis, or the nutritional aspects of global misdevelopment—biopolitics affords one particular approach to the whole issue of the relationship between society and science.[2] It poses, in fact, the most profound philosophic puzzles known to humankind, puzzles intrinsic to any understanding of how society and science interact. I can think of no more important intellectual domain.

Whether biopoliticians pursue mundane or more ambitious concerns, or whether they merely seek to include in explanations of civic and international events biological factors that traditional scholars either neglect altogether or treat in only a cursory way, they are very far from behaving as reductionists.[3] Big questions flow from what, biologically, we have come to or are coming to know, and human values may have to be reassessed radically as a result. Which gives the lie to the satirical definition of "man" as an animal "so lost in rapturous contemplation of what he thinks he is as to overlook what he undubitably ought to be." ("His chief occupation," Bierce adds, "is extermination of other animals and his own species, which, however, multiplies with such insistent rapidity as to infest the whole habitable earth and Canada.")[4] The process of reassessment carries important implications for social ordering and control, and it is an ongoing one; it continues to this day.[5]

INTENTIONS AND CONSEQUENCES

How in general are such reassessments made? What shape are the basic debates? Perhaps it will help to remind ourselves that when we confront any human act and call for its justification, when we seek to sustain what we think we ought to be, the reasons advanced will fall into one of two categories or both. We find *either* an appeal to some overarching beneficial *intention* in the form of a firm ideal or principle of some sort that we think should be realized regardless (plus perhaps the general desire to do good or at least, as one sees it, not harm) *or* a description of the *consequences* that being what we "ought to be" portends or has actually produced, resting our case on an assessment thereof. Such a distinction is only an analytic one since our intentions—the principles and ideals and the desire to do good that our imagination allows us to entertain—can derive from and are certainly influenced by contemplation of past and possible consequences. Morality always depends to some degree at least upon a personal understanding of the link between the two. Similarly, consequences can be judged in different ways, depending upon our understanding of the motives of those involved. (The question of intent is a complex one both philosophically[6] and psychologically.[7] Intention can be subliminal as well as deliberate, and the more subliminal it is the more likely it is that we are dealing with behavior that is not willed and hence principled in this way.) The distinction can still assist us, however, in sorting out the way biology has been brought to bear upon society in general and upon the making of public policy in particular, and for this purpose alone it is worth keeping to it here.

What, to take the first, do biologists *intend?* Their singular aim, like that of scientists at large, has been to produce as objective an account of the natural universe as possible, including in that account one of ourselves. This guiding grail enjoins us "to know" and, if necessary, "to be damned."[8] And the consequences have been profound. They include, most obviously in this context, specific improvements in death control and now, perhaps, of the very evolutionary process itself. Yet the most important effects have flowed from the Darwinian doctrine at large, and the radical influence this has had upon Western thought and upon those, now globally dispersed, who subscribe to the ideas and beliefs that European moral and natural philosophy define.

Despite the ample scope for pessimism that recent discoveries provide, there seems nothing certain (yet) that would suggest that after our fashion we cannot actually cope with them, or that given the appropriate individual and social choices even flourish. By the same token one cannot say we actually *will* cope or flourish, and much of what has been learned in the last century or so confirms traditional intimations of just how radically mixed and compromised we really are; how human values emerge from the struggle to contain the less civilized side of ourselves;[9] and how it would be facile to expect the species to survive and the life-lot of the human population to improve of its own accord.[10]

Explaining the advent of humanity, as Darwin did, in naturalistic terms has made it much easier to appreciate the continuities that exist between ourselves and the rest of Creation. It has made it easier to imagine that sociopolitical organizing principles and moral judgments occurred in our species even before we had words and concepts like these with which to isolate and analyze them (which has led to the search for homologous behavior among our collateral relatives in the nonhuman realm).[11] It has made the notion of Creation itself redundant, at least in the literal Christian sense, and the idea of human values as divinely inspired also increasingly difficult to sustain. And it has occasioned fresh emphasis upon the particular qualities with which our species, by seemingly fortuitous means, has been endowed—more espeically the considerable extent to which it has become "human nature to change itself."[12] Understandably enough, there have been confusions while at the same time there has been the pragmatic promotion of a certain presumptive pride. Hubris and humility have flourished by halves.

Once Darwin had established his central concepts and these had become generally know, the connection commonly drawn (most notably by Herbert Spencer)[13] between *biological evolution* and *social change* seemed more plausible. Connections of this sort were eventually used to excuse all sorts of nonsense about comparative national and racial superiority. Strictly construed they were only ever suggestive, however. The fact that cultural evolution transmits so quickly what we learn (that in essence it is a Lamarckian device) means that biological parallels will remain limited ones.[14] They continue to be employed to place contemporary discussions of human socialization, innovation, selection, and progress in an evolutionary context,[15] and the last concept in particular has had the most far-reaching influence. Its scientific status, however, remains tenuous at best.

J. Huxley argued that ". . . while to the evolutionist ethics can no longer be regarded as having any absolute value, yet their relativity is neither chaotic nor meaningless: ethics are relative to a process which is both meaningful and of indefinitely long duration—that of evolutionary progress";[16] a view that stands in marked contradiction to that of Huxley's grandfather (and, indeed, Darwin himself) who said that: "once more we have a misapplication of the stoical injunction to follow nature . . . the cosmic process has no sort of relation to moral ends. . . ."[17] Both morality *and* immorality receive "natural sanction,"[18] the elder Huxley thought, and hence evolution could never provide a way of discriminating between the two. His grandson disagreed. Progress is given substance, he averred, in terms of the biological penchant for genetic variety and for new possibilities.[19] And as an ethical precept this must mean prime respect for human individuality and for societies that are organized under the cardinal concern for the person per se. (One thing Huxley, the younger, did not consider was that even if evolution did provide moral lessons for humankind that might prove benign in sociocultural practice, the individuality so prized could be developed in different ways, and in choosing between these ways *variety* as such offers no help at all. This has prompted others to talk in terms of human *survival* as the ultimate value and to measure the political process in terms of how badly or well it secures what we need physically to persist.[20] The problems *this* has posed I have discussed elsewhere and will return to briefly in due course.)

Does evolution really mean that "some truths can be known only from the point of view of a responsible moral agent,"[21] and, if so, what does this make of science and of objective judgment? Where there is no transcendant test of validity, one may argue, "there is no truth of falsity. There is only the bare fact of belief . . . the passion for science then appears as an odd preference . . . for a certain kind of activity." And this is "precisely," it seems, the "situation in which Darwin found himself. . . . He was sure that he had been right in devoting his life to science, but he could not say why.''[22] Fixing the human figure to its biological background leads, he sensed, to moral pessimism, to nihilism. It does not fit well with the "optimistic anticipation of secular salvation" that has been so much a part of the scientific milieu.[23] No wonder that feelings of anxiety and doubt abound.

Thus those who came after Darwin were not always so sure that the devotion to science that he evinced was a warranted one. There were others, however, who thought it was, and, what is more, sought to make a virtue out of it, resolving any possible anguish by establishing the capacity for choice as ontologically sufficient and as morally supreme. Jacques Monod,[24] for example, noting that the ethical principles people appeal to have always been suprahuman ones ("how essential to Man it always has appeared . . . to discover in Nature his [sic] own 'meaning' and in himself the 'meaning' of Nature"),[25] declares the destructive effects science has had upon moral certainty and the "community of purpose" to be "the greatest revolution that [has] ever occurred in human culture.''[26] He accepts a distinction between values and facts, between true knowledge and ethical beliefs, but sees no reason why we should not, however arbitrary the choice, assert the singular value of "objective knowledge itself and for its own sake.''[27] Humankind, divorced from the universe, can turn this divorce to positive account. A "new humanism" should be designed to foster free, well-fed educated human beings, who alone but undaunted find certainty in their own selves and sufficient cause there to lead good lives, develop "culture and creativity,'' and combat "any form of alienation.''[28]

Note how Monod makes the move he says himself is inadmissible. He reads what we ought to do from what actually is; inferring moral prescriptions from what science ostensibly only describes. The fact that we can get comparatively objective knowledge about how the cosmos works does not in itself mean that knowledge of this sort is good, or that it is good to further the garnering and winnowing process.[29] It may, by other criteria, be bad, though likewise this alone is not reason for us to eschew it.

What, furthermore, if the scientific enterprise proves to be the actual *source* of the alienation that Monod explicitly deplores? Do we, as he would probably suggest, push on, prescribing more of the same? Or do we reaffirm the mystic links that science obscures or destroys? Or do we resist either option, merely accepting Darwin's dilemma as something we must live with: ''. . . an adequate ethical theory . . . cannot [in other words] distort moral experience in order to make it fit the conceptual forms of factual science, nor can it set up morality as transcendent and exalted from human lives. It must express in its evaluation the living integrity of personal character, and it must also undertake to see morality in its cosmic perspective.''[30] Or, as another concerned rationalist has it, ''Of course we cannot logically deduce value from fact, but why split logic from life?''[31]

FACT vs. VALUE AGAIN

The original assertion of the fact/value dichotomy helped the scientific enterprise get a foot in the door. By largely excluding spiritual, ideological, and parochial bias; by erecting a discernible '' 'prejudice' against prejudice'';[32] it was possible to win very broad agreement on the criteria that could be used to establish *scientific* truth. As we know now, however, having got a foot in the door, scientists went on to take the whole thing off at the hinges. The scientific demand for evidence led, in the social realm, to the systematic scrutiny of how values are actually made and used. Greater appreciation of their diversity seemed to reduce the special standing of any one clutch of them, and, in the end, values began to fade altogether before the earnest gaze of the intruders—those who could see in human behavior only "valuations,"[33] and the wide variety of what humankind actually seemed to want. All of this made it that much more difficult to say just what one *should* want and what is most valuable in feeling and fact.

When it seems as natural as anything else for human values to differ, as our languages differ and as our cultures do in general, then the idea of deriving them from attributes of a species-specific kind is an *un*natural act. The idea of ultimate values joins that of physical motion as something relative to agent and observer alike. This does provide the opportunity for human beings to consider, if they have a mind to, whether they are well served or not by the values they have been taught to espouse, and to consider what a morality based upon the human enterprise without appeal to transcendental sanctions might contain. It also allows us to exorcise all those "transcendental ghosts,"[6] to forget all those "pure minds intuiting ethical essences."[34] In this sense, therefore, the scientific outlook is a particularly penetrating one, the "essence of a culture which has not yet been established— a *culture-studying* culture. . . ." In this sense, too: "The moral attitudes contained in the scientific outlook have a different genesis from those contained in ordinary 'unconscious' cultures. They are the result of a 'freer' choice, because they involve a deeper insight into the consequences of . . . choice" itself.[35] New insights allow enlarged value perspectives and new knowledge about "why we as cultures do what we do," and frees us, or so rationalists assume, to do "something else. . . ."[36] Relativism and materialism allow of no transcendental authorities. Yet equally they do not exclude the possibility of discovering "invariants."

At the present time we look to a species-specific ethic based on the notion of *needs*. Are we likely to get one? Would it exhaust the moral sense? Probably not.

Indeed, "most Westerners today would surely be reluctant to accept the concept of 'end' as on a level with the concept of 'need' . . . [as] neither more or less built into the structure of the universe, neither more nor less a matter of our convenience."[37] And if this does not obtain in the West, then we are hardly likely to find it elsewhere. So where do we go from here?

Science, it has been said, consists of the "accumulation and explanation of evidence about the past with all that that implies for our knowledge of the future." The theory of values, on the other hand, consists in the "formulation and justification of arguments about the future," with all that that implies for our attitude toward the past.[38] For the *social* scientist this means, in part, assembling those facts that demonstrate the consequences particular values imply, thus making our choice of values and our choice of the appropriate means for realizing them better informed ones. For the social *reformer,* there is the prospect of finally bringing past and future together in the present; when we finally "know what we want and want what we know."[39] Here fact and value would coalesce.

In practice fact and value also converge whenever we seek to justify values in debate. They come together too in the minds of scientists themselves, as they confront the influence of society at large. Thus moral arguments, however forward-looking in form and however abstract, will always appeal at some point to what are considered good reasons, and here science, as we have seen, has much to say.[40] Furthermore, what scientists seek to prove and explain will always be determined to some extent by what the enveloping society or those who lead it decide they want, be it better health or bigger bombs. Both phenomena blur the line between the "intellectual demands of good science and the ethical demands of the good life."[41]

An objectivist outlook provides deep points of correspondence. Knowing and believing, seen in this light, are both *elaborative* processes.

Valuing bears to . . . raw feeling rather the relationship that knowing bears to untrained seeing; science starts from the fact that we have some knowledge . . . and goes on to determine as best it can what we really know and do not know. Naive conation, in a similar way, comes to naive conclusions about action; the theory of value starts from the fact that we have some desires [needs], even if they are clumsy, and goes on to determine as best it can what we really want and do not want.[42]

The final point of appeal is a valuation nonetheless. Scientists have flourished because they have generated extraordinary results. Their positivistic creed is premised, however, on something not demonstrable in terms of that creed: "The obligation" that is "to tell the truth . . . [the] social axiom . . . that *we OUGHT to act in such a way that what IS true can be verified to be so*."[43] Their facts are ultimately artifacts, observations, dynamic interpretations that are only relevant in the contexts we construct for them, conditioned at every point by the preadaptations we make as a result of our evolutionary descent.[44] Moralists can always argue, moreover, that society would be impossible without primary values (a shared commitment to divine will, for example, enlightened self-interest, happiness, survival, self-fulfillment, whatever can be given rational universal credence, or the pursuit of cosmic peace). And that commitments like these can only be made after due consideration of the whole human predicament, "which includes what is scientifically established and much that is not."[45] Our societies rely upon their cohesive qualities, and without society and its resources—the educational and material ones in particular—there would be no science at all.

Yet this does not mean that we must resort to transcendental obscurantism once again. If we want to accept the objectivists' claims, then we can always see the significant distinction as the one between

> description and evaluation . . . between secular efforts of description and evaluation and those exercises of description and evaluation which employ supernatural premises. . . . The basic fact of cultural polarization has been misinterpreted so as to put knowledge (conceived as deriving from descriptive judgements) on the one side of the picture, and value (conceived as deriving from normative judgements) on the other side; whereas the real problem is that of distinguishing true knowledge from false knowledge, and true values from false values.[46]

Scientific concepts, as Toulmin observes, lie along a spectrum from the comparatively value-free to the irretrievably value-laden.[47] At one extreme we have the picture of people industriously mining data and manipulating the environment, wholly oblivious to human welfare. At the other we have the opposite image of those acutely concerned for the good of the species, both its place in the environment and its capacity to carry on. In reality, while science *can* be pursued to wholly esoteric and academic ends there is never a guarantee these ends will remain so pure, even if social authorities wanted them to or allowed them to. Value-free science could only be done outside society in fact, in a value vacuum: presumably on "some application-proof project . . . conducted by a friendless and stateless bachelor of independent means"[48] in a place without an industrial mode of production or those who seek or assert political power.

THE SOCIAL DETERMINATION OF SCIENCE

The social determination of science is much more pervasive than many suspect. The industrialization and the bureaucratization of it, themselves made possible on a global scale by the findings that scientific research has produced, work back on the original principles to direct effect.[49] Science is a tender plant and the standards that allow of scientific truth seeking are easily perverted. Securing room for independent maneuver for individual practitioners, and intellectual tolerance and respect for empirical endeavor, is not easy. The dedicated defend what they do by declaring its intrinsic worth and the way it enriches the human estate. Group tolerance and permissive environments that allow of personal creativity, the values implicit here that make science possible; these, they say, have social applications too. "Science" has "humanized our values, and men have asked for freedom, justice and respect," they maintain, "precisely as the scientific spirit has spread among them. . . . Our conduct as states clings to a code of self-interest which science, like humanity, has long left behind."[50] Science has proved compatible, however, with the most repressive of regimes, and many analysts are more pessimistic as a result. They decry what all this free thinking has done and despair of humanity's ever managing either to stuff such a malevolent genie back into its bottle or, failing that, to control its awesome powers. They resist any desire to see the scientifically attestable as politically expedient or ethically pure and point up humanity's record for truculence and ill-will.[51]

The genie is out regardless, and, as humanity's power for seemingly constructive intervention has increased, as intimations of dire effects have become more acute, and as the awareness of values as human artifacts—and indeterminate ones at that—has spread, so our choices have become more tentative and more decisive at once. The dilemmas abound: whether we abandon posterity and future options in favor of more immediate concerns; whether, given what we can now do, we actually know what those options should be; whether modernizing cultures can survive a spiritual onslaught of the sort hapless folk have had to sustain throughout history—the effects of an ideology, that is, "which claims to be scientific and is in fact a new version of nihilism in its denial of values, purpose and meaning . . .";[52] whether the prospects of the global poor can be improved without rendering gains illusory because of their alienating effects; whether we can put sufficient social purpose into the scientific enterpries without sacrificing its productive methodology or its canons of assessment; whether, that is, the "competing claims" of "autonomy and responsibility" can be reconciled;[53] whether social expectation of the benefits research brings will continue to outweigh public apprehensions of harm; whether the freedom to "find out" (wherever that leads) can survive the routinization of inquiry under the mass conditions of the modernizing world, or the sort of "ethical imperialism" that finds a moral issue, "real or imagined, at every turn!";[54] whether between a "value-free science" and "science-free values" we can find somewhere convivial for the human race to live.[55]

One may well be wary of the ability of scientists themselves to respond to these issues with the degree of prudence and the sense of occasion required. The research enterprise, even when it is set up to serve a specific industrial or medical or military purpose, is to some extent a retreat, a place of active contemplation where the scientist can go and feed his or her personal sense of significance in communion with truth; a place that intrigues and distracts the practitioner with problems that are not, in their scientific form at least, *in* the world as a social and political realm. Scientists have generally shied away from social and political involvement, while harboring the feeling that, should need arise, they can be relied upon to sort out their communal surrounds in a decisive way. As their common enterprise has expanded, both policies "for science," and "science policy," have become more important.[56] This has not produced, however, overmuch evidence of the sort of independence of mind that the ethos of objectivity would lead one to expect. Indeed, though hardly alone in this respect, "scientific leadership has tended, almost without exception, to acquiesce in any fundamental confrontation with the state, especially when opposition . . . [is] likely to evoke serious sanctions. . . . Lacking the anchor of ultimate commitment, the scientific community has shown a marked predisposition to fill this hiatus by emphasising instrumentalism. . . . Science has become power incarnate."[57]

As big research has burgeoned then, pure work (if there really is such a thing) and the issue of the public possession and use of it have become ever more closely intertwined, and questions of the social accountability of science have grown more acute—which does not make them any easier to assess. Should researchers deliberately forego experimentation, for example, that might, if particular potential outcomes prove to be real, result in extensive if not wholesale human devastation?[58] A key committee of American scientists once thought as much, and in doing so started up a long-running sociopolitical hare. With the advent of new techniques for rearranging the genetic structure of viruses, for introducing them into bacterial hosts and thence into living organisms, and for shuffling our own genetic pack, biologists now face not only the promise of new knowledge of a fundamental theoretical kind, but the chance that in making such advances they might manufacture new compounds with unpredictable and perhaps catastrophic properties. The above group called for voluntary deferral of certain sorts of experiments in this field and the formation, in the United States at least, of a supervisory body to evaluate the risks of accidental infection involved and to work out safeguards and guidelines to protect the scientists in their laboratories and the public outside.

Scientists as a profession prefer to decide such matters by domestic means rather than having to defer to what outsiders decree.[59] One might suspect a certain amount of pre-emptive defense, and given the vested interests involved this is hardly surprising. Expert status does, however, breed the more general assumption that, where the experts *agree*, this should be reason enough for accepting what they decide. That such a ready assumption is not in fact sufficient nowadays to allay public fears is one measure of how far science has become a social concern, how much has been moved into the domain of human choice, and how necessary it is to ask: what are we to choose? And what is all this actually *for*?

GENETIC ENGINEERING

The sense of alarm the above techniques inspired has waned somewhat as more has become known and early fears have proved, if not baseless, then less dramatic than was originally believed. Fundamental questions persist, however. When the hazards might have to be borne by the whole human population or large, undeserving parts of it, or the threats are particularly significant ones, or there prove to be important evasions or errors in the relevant research reports, then that is hardly surprising. When human knowledge includes the capacity for directly engineering,[60] the "inherent capacity for choice" and control of the physical universe extends to the human substance itself, when the evolutionary process itself comes under human sway, then biologists put upon us dangers and opportunities of a kind that only physicists have so far imposed.[61]

Intervention of this sort, like the detonation of nuclear devices in highly populated areas, can have irreversible results. Some skills, like that of transplanting vital organs or manipulating electrical potentials in the brain, have comparatively individualized applications. Others like birth control, or the use of chemicals to alter mental moods or repress anxiety and aggression or enhance mental powers and the sense of delight, allow of much wider use. The most portentous, however, are those that promise eugenetic improvement (both *negative*— as in the treatment of inherited disease syndromes,[62] and *positive*—as in the attempt to manage, to some extraneous purpose the composition of particular eddies in local gene pools or that of the species at large)[63] and here it is the capacity to replicate individual genetic templates by cloning them,[64] the capacity to program the genetic complement of the clones, and the capacity to join together the most unlikely organic entities in some sort of viable union that are most often remarked upon. Such experiments raise very important doubts about individual rights as against social ones.[65] They also prompt us to ask what human integrity might mean (particularly given the impending possibility of man-beast hybrids). What is human excellence (whom should we seek to replicate in this way: political power-brokers? the intellectually skilled? the artistic? the fair?). What does the idea of human worth involve? What human characteristics are most healthy? More generally, we might ask what is right and just about how such techniques should be applied and for whom, to do what, for how long?

To some extent, such questions distract from real-world issues about who loses out under present-day circumstances and why. The more sociologically sophisticated biologists castigate those in rich countries preoccupied with the problems of genetic control, while enormous numbers of individuals because of the sociopolitical conditions under which they live, are prevented from enjoying the relatively normal genetic complements they already possess.[66] As we have seen in chapter 4, these critics have good cause;[67] likewise, those who argue the prior need for checking the possible genetic effects of the myriad pollutants industrial societies pour into the biosphere at large.

Concerns of this sort do not exclude, however, a legitimate interest in the welfare of those, wherever they are born, who inherit one of the 1,600 or so forms of illness that result from genetic defects.[68] Nor does it meet the need to measure the consequences of scientific acts already extant, and the complex equations that have to be done—if one eschews absolutes—to weigh up the potential goods and bads they entail. "Our species," it has been said, "stands at the edge of a remarkable evolutionary precipice, from which we could either fall or learn flight, . . ."[69] and if this is anywhere near the contemporary case we do well to follow these events with special care. Michael Polanyi feared the advent of scientific directorates, issuing certificates of social usefulness to those scientists deemed worthy to receive them.[70] Control need not extend so far, and indeed probably could not since it would likely prove impossible in the end to regulate basic research on a world scale in this way. If we did try, then it could well be at considerable cost to other values and to the acquisition of beneficial information and techniques that we do need. It would seem not unreasonable, nonetheless, to find some way to hold scientists to social account. While one must not exaggerate the implications of the research cited above since very few of the evolutionary novelties contrived in laboratories would likely survive beyond the artificial environments in which they were made, and blanket measures against every activity that could have dire results would severely inhibit a much wider range of work as well as other quite nonscientific undertakings,[71] it would be foolish not to be actively concerned when the social and ethical implications are so immediate. The value-dimension means that the arguments involved will be endless. And they will also have very general empirical referents.[72]

What sort of regulation does ultimately prove most appropriate will depend upon the area of research involved and the particular applications it might have. Many such domains allow of relatively straightforward legislation, and they very clearly deserve, where they do not already receive, social attention of this sort[73] (Graham includes here what he terms "destructive," "slippery slope," and "economically exploitative technologies" plus "human subjects" research, "expensive science," and "accidents"). Other domains involve more complex issues (these he calls "subversive knowledge," "inevitable technology," "prejudicial science," and "ways of knowing." For the latter group the choices are harder to make, for it is here that human ingenuity could most easily be stifled.)

Regulation is a tough issue. In general, we may say that science is valuable in terms of what it contributes to the larger community, both local and global, to which those who practice and apply it belong. If nonscientists alone could decide how to define what "valuable" means, and what basic work is legitimate or not, then science would be in deep trouble. Equally significant, however, researchers and technologists ought not decide for everyone else what the moral, mental, and spiritual consequences of what they are doing might be and whether those consequences are supportable.[74] We strive to strike some kind of balance and hope that, with constant adjustment, this will continue to fall on firm ground.

INDIVIDUALISM vs. COLLECTIVISM AGAIN

The talk above of "community" betrays something of the bias implicit in discussions of this sort toward collectivist concerns over and above individualistic ones. Whether this bias must always prevail is not clear, but the tensions between individualism and collectivism raise once again questions discussed in chapter 2. Survivalist ethics that ostensibly serve either the species as a whole or local populations within it can prove personally tyrannical in practice. And we do well as a result to resist "normative biologism"[75] and the notion that what seems natural is therefore good. Once again we must remind ourselves of the distinction between what *will* happen, what usually *does* happen, and what *might* happen if circumstances were different or we wanted them to be so.[76]

AN ETHICS OF CHANGE

The fact that some things *will* happen suggests a pre-emptive process of some sort. Thus Darwin found in our physical constitution the deep impress of our evolutionary descent,[77] and the brain too, we might surmise, bears within it the marks of its inheritance. (Some take this further still, contending that the organic "even in its lowest forms prefigures mind . . . [as] mind even on its highest reaches, remains part of the organic.")[78] To the extent that consciousness transcends determination, however, there remains the capacity for change.[79] And here it is the *cultural* prejudgments are are important.[80]

Because such assumptions *are* cultural we can allow for them if we are sufficiently aware of how they are applied. Which is not to advocate environmental determinism, of which society sees quite enough, but an ethics of change. While human values have been predicated in the past upon conceptions of humankind and the human condition as ever-endowed in some way, we know this today to be at best a partial view. How we come to terms with it is another matter again, particularly when the knowing erodes *a priori* certainties and the sense even of meaning and purpose itself. We ourselves as part of Nature must frame intention *in* Nature of a kind our own understanding of it has called into question.

Need we be tentative in doing so? While some see only the prospect of despair, others find it all quite fascinating. Carl Jung, for example, glimpsed in growing awareness a sustaining myth of a most comprehensive sort. Humankind, he said, completes creation. Human consciousness makes objective meaning possible, and, having happened in the world, is sufficient in fact to invest the whole cosmic process with objective being. In a similar vein, Hans Jonas speaks of Giordono Bruno, who, "lonely among men, welcomed cosmic infinitude as the revelations of a divine superabundance of reality and something kindred to himself."[81]

This is all very well, but how does such a general celebration apply in any specific instance? What is it that humankind, as their power to direct the evolutionary process grows, actually want to be?[82] We may well possess cosmic significance; we may well command the most potent of biological controls; but these mean very little to more than a few. The Jungs and Brunos may bask in their sense of some humanistic whole, but controls in particular are always to a purpose, even if it is only the satisfaction of individual or social self-esteem. Survival is one aim, and science can help to establish what we should avoid if we want to persist (though other, perhaps superior, values may be denied in the process).[83] Science for its own sake is another such ideal. The "disinterested pursuit of abstract truth"[84] in its extreme form is a denial of the world however; a "passionate autism" defiant of social feelings and common sense. Replete with its own "morality of fact," it would harness every ultimate human aspiration to haul its own. Can it be held to account in its current form? We do not know, since human curiosity, once aroused, is seemingly insatiable. And new knowledge feeds back into our self-image in self-denying *and* self-substantiating ways that, despite all the manifest dangers, we find difficult to resist. Exercising the mind in this way offers tangible material rewards as well, the "leap of the tensed intellect across the laziness of illusion"[85] allowing the most brilliant displays of practical competence. Whether "truth," human survival, and human conviviality can lie together in this light remains to be seen, and though it is humankind that puts the point, this could prove small comfort to those who might have to live with consequences that are spiritually or physically insupportable. Science, we must remind ourselves, is neither necessary to human persistence, nor sufficient to effect every social end.

Human nature, however firmly fastened to its foundations, is open to the sky. If we are talking of social change, that is the main thing we need know.[86] It is not everything, as biopolitical scientists have now demonstrated, but it is the main thing. It has not, for example, yet been proven that we have to harm each other "and hence it cannot be said that we are born corrupt." On the other hand constraints on malevolent behavior are never absolute, "and hence it cannot be said that we are born perfect."[87] Perhaps nonetheless we are *perfectible*, though I doubt it. That depends anyway upon what we think perfection is and which biopotentials we value most and will seek to augment, or which we disvalue and would rather deny.

"The fact is," the poet says, "I'm
    turning to gold, turning to gold,
It's a long process, they say,
it happens in stages.
This is to inform you that I've already turned
    to clay."[88]

NOTES

1. L. Caldwell, "Biopolitics: Science, Ethics and Public Policy," *The Yale Review* 54, no. 1 (October 1964): 3.
2. Ibid.
3. The possibilities may be summarized thus:
    1. Man [sic] shares some attributes with *all* living things.
    2. Man shares some additional attributes with certain other forms of life, but not with all.
    3. Man has still other attributes which he does not share with any other form of life. [G. Lenski, *Human Societies* (N.Y.: McGraw-Hill, 1970), p. 11]
4. A. Bierce, *The Devil's Dictionary* (N.Y.: Dover, 1958), p. 85.
5. See, for example, H. Cravens, *The Triumph of Evolution:* American Scientists and the Heredity-Environment Controversy 1900–1941 (Philadelphia: University of Pennsylvania Press, 1978), p. 274.
6. J. Findlay, *Values and Intentions* (London: George Allen and Unwin, 1961).
7. T. Ryan, *Intentional Behavior* (New York: Ronald Press, 1970).
8. E. Gellner characterizes the syndrome of progressive post-Enlightenment preoccupations as follows:
    anti-clericalism and hostility to religion; rejection of supernatural or "spiritual" explanations of phenomena; an insistence or preference for explanations of phenomena in terms of the structure and activity of matter; a positive expectation that everything in nature and man can be explained in natural intramundane terms; determinism; empiricism in epistemology; hedonism and/or egoism in psychology; belief in reason as the guide and arbiter of life, and utilitarianism and/or democracy in politics; pragmatism with regard to the theory of truth; relativism; and belief in the power of education and of government and in the possibility of deliberate improvement of human life. [*The Devil in Modern Philosophy* (London: Routledge and Kegan Paul, 1974), p. 113]
    See also F. Jacob, *The Logic of Living Systems* (London: Allen Lane, 1974).
9. A point made, among others, by S. Freud, *Civilization and its Discontents* (London: Hogarth Press, 1930); see also T. Tuxley in T. H. Huxley and J. Huxley, *Evolution and Ethics* (London: The Pilot Press, 1947).
10. A point satirized by Kurt Vonnegut in *The Sirens of Titan* (N.Y.: Dell, 1959), p. 5: "Every passing hour brings the Solar System forty-three thousand miles closer to Globular Cluster M13 in Hercules—and still there are some . . . who insist that there is no such thing as progress."
11. For example, see F. Wilhoite, "Primates and Political Authority: A Biobehavioral Perspective," *American Political Science Review* 70 (December 1976): 1110–1126.
12. W. Hocking, *Human Nature and Its Remaking* (New Haven: Yale University Press, 1923), p. 17.
13. See *The Principles of Sociology* (London: Williams and Norgate, 1882–96). Thus, ". . . nine years before Darwin's *Origin of Species* appeared, Herbert Spencer made population pressure,

struggle for existence and survival of the fittest the key concepts in a theory of social evolution" (J. Greene, *Darwin and the Modern World View* [Baton Rouge: Louisiana State University Press, 1961], p. 93). Also R. Tsanoff, *The Moral Ideals of Our Civilization* (London: George Allen and Unwin, 1942), Ch. 32, "Ethics and the Theory of Evolution."

14. L. Wispé and J. Thompson, "The War Between the Words: Biological Versus Social Evolution and Some Related Issues," *American Psychologist* 31 (May 1976): 342, which is a reply to the Campbell piece referred to in Ch. 1, fn. 65. By "Lamarckian" I mean the inheritance of acquired characteristics.

15. Lenski, *Human Societies*, pp. 60–85.

16. Huxley and Huxley, *Evolution and Ethics*, p. 235.

17. Ibid., p. 82.

18. Ibid., p. 80

19. Ibid., p. 124: ". . . modern genetics . . . stresses the *fact* of man's [sic] immense genetic variability, and also the *value* of that fact, both for biological reasons and for its own sake. Ethics must include a respect for human difference . . ." (p. 27). Among these differences will be, Huxley argues, inherited ones in "moral temperament." He does not say where we are to draw the line on the "natural" scale here, except (p. 28) that "there will be a considerable number of people who are "sub-normal" . . . and . . . [p]er contra, there will always be a certain proportion of ultra-normal people, whose ethical zeal outruns society's needs . . ." (whatever *they* might be).

20. For example, P. Corning, "Toward a Survival Oriented Political Science," in A. Somit, ed., *Biology and Politics* (Paris: Mouton, 1976).

21. Greene, *Darwin*, p. 127.

22. Ibid., pp. 127–8.

23. Gellner, *Devil in Modern Philosophy*, p. 122.

24. J. Monod, "On Values in the Age of Science," in A. Tiselius and S. Nilsson, eds., *The Place of Value in a World of Facts* (Stockholm: Almsqvist and Wiksell, 1970); "On the Logical Relationship between Knowledge and Values," in W. Fuller, ed., *The Social Impact of Modern Biology* (London: Routledge and Kegan Paul, 1971). See also G. Simpson, *The Meaning of Evolution* (New Haven: Yale University Press, 1949); R. Cattell, *A New Morality from Science: Beyondism* (Elmsford, N.Y.: Pergamon Press, 1972), who considers the current dilemma as not one of "bringing morality into science" but of developing morality *out* of it (p. xiii).

25. Monod, "On Values," in Tiselius and Nilsson, *Place of Value*, p. 22.

26. Monod, "On the Logical Relationship," in Fuller, *Social Impact*, p. 14.

27. Ibid., p. 15.

28. Ibid.

29. See further, F. Oppenheim, *Moral Principles in Political Philosophy* (N.Y.: Random House, 1968), "Naturalism as a Political Philosophy."

30. Tsanoff, *Moral Ideals*, p. 601. Also: "It is possible that values derive their meaning and their sanction not only from tribal deities, and not merely from parochial beliefs, but—at least in considerable part—from the human adventure itself, from the quest for knowledge . . . from the never-ending struggle to harness forces of nature to human use . . . from the life process of mankind?" (C. Ayres, *Toward a Reasonable Society*: The Values of Industrial Civilization [Austin: University of Texas Press, 1961], pp. 6, 15).

31. E. Becker, *The Structure of Evil* (New York: George Braziller, 1968), p. 385.

32. S. Hayakawa, "Foreword," in A. Rapoport, *Science and the Goals of Man* (N.Y.: Harper and Bros., 1950), p. ix.

33. E. Kamenka's address on "Empiricism and Ethics" (Canberra: Australian National University, 1967), p. 5.

34. A. Edel, *Ethical Judgement:* The Use of Science in Ethics (Glencoe, Ill.: The Free Press, 1955), p. 123.
35. Rapoport, *Science and the Goals of Man*, p. 233.
36. Ibid., p. 243. The problem remains, as C. Brinton observes, that "in real life . . . basic drives or urges or what you will emerge into actual human conduct only through a long process which involves sentiments, emotions, symbols, 'ideas,' some of them 'abstract,' like the idea that abstract ideas have no activating part in human conduct" (*A History of Western Morals* [London: Weidenfeld and Nicolson, 1959], p. 15). This makes "needs" very difficult, some would say impossible, to define for all, which does not of course deter those who would rather legislate them anyway.
37. Ibid., p. 11.
38. P. Caws, *Science and the Theory of Value* (New York: Random House, 1967), p. 65; also pp. 68–74: "Facts as Values, Values as Facts," "Facts as Inadequate to Values," "Values as Outreaching Facts."
39. Brinton, *History of Western Morals*, p. 478.
40. And "if anyone asks . . . *why* they are 'good reasons,' I can only reply by asking in return 'what better kinds of reason could you want?' " (S. Toulmin, *Reason in Ethics* [Cambridge: Cambridge University Press, 1961], p. 224).
41. S. Toulmin, "Can Science and Ethics be Reconciled?" *The Hastings Center Report* 9, no. 3 (June 1979): 27.
42. Caws, *Science and the Theory of Value*, p. 67.
43. J. Bronowski, *Science and Human Values* (London: Hutchinson, 1961), p. 66.
44. J. Bruner, "Reason, Prejudice and Intuition," in A. Tiselius and S. Nilsson, eds., *Place of Value*, p. 117: ". . . in the nature of things, man [sic], like other animals is highly prejudiced in his acquisition of knowledge, is specialized in imposing highly selective forms on a world of stimulation. . . . In the nervous system, intention precedes information gain."
45. J. Butler, *Modern Biology and its Human Implications* (London: Hodder and Stoughton, 1976), p. 105.
46. Ayres, *Toward a Reasonable Society*, p. 50.
47. Toulmin, "Can Science and Ethics," p. 28.
48. Ibid., p. 33.
49. See J. Ravetz, *Scientific Knowledge and its Social Problems* (Oxford: Clarendon Press, 1971).
50. Bronowski, *Science and Human Values*, p. 80.
51. H. Morgenthau, *Scientific Man vs. Power Politics* (London: Latimer House Ltd., 1947): "To know with despair that the political act is inevitably evil, and to act nevertheless, is moral courage. To choose among several expedient actions the least evil one is moral judgement" (p. 173).
52. A. Koestler, "Rebellion in a Vacuum," in Tiselius and Nilsson, eds., *Place of Value*, p. 228.
53. K. Ryan, "Ethics and Pragmatism in Scientific Affairs," *Bio Science* 29, no. 1 (January 1979): 35.
54. Ibid., p. 37.
55. L. Graham, "The Multiple Connections between Science and Ethics," *The Hastings Center Report* 9, no. 3 (June 1979): 39.
56. J. Haberer, *Politics and the Community of Science* (New York: Van Nostrand Reinhold, 1969), p. 302.
57. Ibid., p. 303, 306.
58. For the pivotal epistle, see P. Berg et al., "Potential Biohazards of Recombinant DNA Molecules," *Science* 185, no. 4148 (July 26, 1974): 303.
59. See here the distinction Imre Lakatos has made between the three schools of thought that characterize, as he sees it, the normative problem of appraising scientific theories: "skepti-

cism'' (which regards scientific theories as "just one family of beliefs which rank equal, epistemologically, with the thousands of other families of beliefs''); "demarcationism" (which reconstructs "*universal* criteria which explain the appraisals which great scientists have made of *particular* theories or research programmes" and is quite happy to "overrule the apologetic efforts of degenerating programmes"); and "elitism" (which argues that science "can only be judged by case law, and the only judges are the scientists themselves") ("Understanding Toulmin," *Minerva* 14, no. 1 [Spring 1976]: 127, 128, 129).

60. For a discussion of the difference between biological and commercial engineering, and the extent to which this qualifies such an analogy given what we usually understand by the word, see H. Jonas, *Philosophical Essays* (Englewood Cliffs, N.J.: Prentice-Hall, 1974) pp. 142–146.

61. L. Kass, "The New Biology: What Price Relieving Man's Estate?" *Science* 174, no. 4011 (November 19, 1971): 779. "There are certain risks that one may not take," Möbius declares in one of Dürrenmatt's plays, "the destruction of humanity is one." "Our knowledge has become a frightening burden." "Our researches are perilous, our discoveries are lethal. For us physicists there is nothing left but to surrender to reality. . . . We have to take back our knowledge and I have taken it back" (see F. Dürrenmatt *The Physicists* [London: Johnathan Cape, 1973], pp. 57, 58).

62. However, "zealots need to be reminded of the consequences should each geneticist be allowed an equal assault on his [sic] favorite genetic disorder, given that each human being is a carrier for some four to eight such recessive, lethal genetic diseases" (Kass, *New Biology*, p. 781).

63. Note here Darwin's conclusion that humankind "might by selection do something not only for the bodily constitution and frame of his [sic] offspring, but for their intellectual and moral qualities. Both sexes ought to refrain from marriage if they are in any marked degree inferior in body or mind; but such hopes are Utopian and will never be even practically realised until the laws of inheritance are thoroughly known" (C. Darwin, *The Descent of Man, and Selection in Relation to Sex* [London: John Murray, 1883], pp. 617–8).

64. A capacity that would allow us, theoretically at least, to do quite decisive experiments on the extent to which genes influence human behavior. The ability to make multiple replicas of specifically selected human genotypes and then to raise the results in appropriately diverse environments would be an important contribution to this debate. Monozygotic twin studies are the closest we have come so far (see Ch. 3, fn. 68). The ethical issues involved would probably preclude the experiment, however, at least in societies that have more than a nominal respect for human rights (a human clone would be, after all, human), particularly if we acknowledge the *consequentialists'* as opposed to the *a priorists'* point that rights are "nothing but a formal recognition by society of certain human needs" (needs that a truly *human* clone would presumably share) (R. Fletcher, "Ethical Aspects of Genetic Controls," in *Genetic Engineering*: Evolution of a Technological Issue, Supplemental Report I (Washington, D.C.: U.S. Government Printing Office, 1974), p. 170.

65. R. Blank, "Human Genetic Technology: Some Political Implications," *The Social Science Journal* 16, no. 3 (October 1979): 1–19.

66. C. Birch, "Genetic and Moral Responsibility," in C. Birch and P. Abrecht, eds., *Genetics and the Quality of Life* (Elmsford, N.Y.: Pergamon Press, 1975); also R. Lewontin, "Science and Ethics," *Bio Science* 21 (August 1971): 799. Note the manifesto of the Ann Arbor Science for the People Editorial Collective: ". . . human potentialities are boundless . . . the question is not what we can do, but what we will do. . . ." This is so, they say, since our possibilities are limited not by our biological makeup but by the social, economic, and political institutions of society, of which science is one of the most important ". . . [c]ontrary to the ideology of biological determinism . . . humanity can be free" (*Biology as a Social Weapon* [Minneapolis: Burgess Publishing Co., 1977], pp. 4–5); also Lewontin's essay "Biological Determinism as a

Social Weapon,'' where he characterizes sociobiology in general as "basically a political science whose results may be used, eventually, as the scientific tools of correct social organisation.'' The "world to be made," he concludes, however, "will be pretty much the aggressive, domination-ridden society we live in now" (p. 16).

67. R. Lewontin, "Science and Ethics," "The chief and overwhelming ethical and moral issue facing us is that the organisation of our political economy guarantees that a large fraction of human beings will be the victims of the omissions and commissions of science because they lack the material wealth and the social power to control their own lives. . . ."

68. Birch, "Genetic and Moral Responsibility," in Birch and Abrecht, *Genetics,* p. 10. See also R. Blank, "Human Genetic Technology," p. 15, who cites the "one out of every 15 babies" who will suffer one or more of the "2,000 known genetic abnormalities."

69. M. Roger, *Biohazard* (N.Y.: Alfred A. Knopf, 1977), pp. 207–8. Also R. Sinsheimer, "Two Lectures on Recombinant DNA Research," in D. Jackson and S. Stich, eds., *The Recombinant DNA Debate* (Englewood Cliffs: Prentice-Hall, 1979). The genetic combinations possible are quite bizarre. As one biologist points out, should we choose to do so, we could now mix the genetic complements of entities as naturally diverse as a duck and an orange. We would not get "oranges with wings" or ducks with seeds or even "duck a l'orange." We could get information from such an experiment of some scientific interest. See D. Jackson, "Principles and Applications of Recombinant DNA Methodology," in Jackson and Stich, eds., *Recombinant DNA Debate.*

70. M. Polanyi, *The Logic of Liberty* (London: Routledge and Kegan Paul, 1951), p. 83.

71. S. Stich, "The Recombinant DNA Debate: Some Philosophical Considerations," in Jackson and Stich, eds., *Recombinant DNA Debate.*

72. S. Hampshire, *Thought and Action* (London: Chatto and Windus, 1959), p. 272, who cites three reasons for "interminability," namely, the contrast between
    1. the variety of life and the units of language,
    2. the individual's knowledge of his or her situation, and capacity to understand and change it, and
    3. universal principles and their particular cultural and socially specific applications.

73. L. Graham, "Concerns about Science and Attempts to Regulate Inquiry," *Daedalus* 107 (1978): 1–21, who distinguishes categories of concern over a very broad area indeed.

74. Ibid., pp. 19, 20.

75. D. Campbell, "Comments on the Sociobiology of Ethics and Moralizing," *Behavioral Sciences* 24 (1979): 39.

76. Since the survival of mankind is the precondition of every other good and even of the sighs and grunts of the emotivists, annihilation appears to be the ultimate evil. Yet it is some measure of our madness that the question can be asked at all, and that a leading philosophical school can say no more about it than "I like survival and I wish you would too"—especially when that same school can find no reason *not* to say: "I don't like survival and I wish you wouldn't either." [B. Dunham, *Ethics Dead and Alive* (N.Y.: Alfred A. Knopf, 1971), p. 9]

77. Darwin, *Descent of Man*, p. 619.

78. H. Jonas, *The Phenomenon of Life* (N.Y.: Harper and Row, 1966), p. 1.

79. Again Darwin (p. 318): "For the moral qualities are advanced, either directly or indirectly, much more through the effects of habit, the reasoning powers, instruction, religion, etc. than through natural selection; though to this latter agency may be safely attributed the social instincts, which afforded the basis for the development of the moral sense."

80. M. Capek, *The Philosophical Impact of Contemporary Physics* (N.Y.: D. Van Nostrand, 1961), pp. 384–5. In Western thought there is the "perennial illusion," for example, that

"becoming can be reduced to being, process to substance, time to the timeless, and *events to things.*"

81. H. Jonas, *Philosophical Essays*, p. 58. Also Hocking, *Human Nature*, p. 439: "Absence of belief that the world as a whole has an active individual concern for the creatures it has produced need neither destroy happiness nor the morality of compassion. Life would always be worth living and worth living well, so long as free from the major torments . . . it is only the martyrs that have played the fool; only to saints and sages the world has lied."

82. Hence:

> If man were "just an animal" he [sic] would never have found that fact out. If he were "just a machine" he could never have invented machines. If his existence were in fact purposeless, he might have survived without having a conscious purpose of his own; but he would never have been concerned with his own further development; and he would not have found it impossible to fulfill his animal needs without finding a place for them in some wider plan of life which transforms biological need into social ritual and social ritual into significant forms of communal and personal drama. [L. Mumford, *The Conduct of Life* (London: Secker and Warburg, 1952), pp. 4–5]

83. "*Principia Ethica*, we might remember," was published in the same year as Jack London's *People of the Abyss* . . . it has one paragraph about property, it has none about poverty" (Dunham, *Ethics Dead and Alive*, p. 31).

84. G. Steiner, "Has Truth a Future?" *The Listener,* Jan. 12, 1978, p. 42.

85. Ibid., p. 45.

86. On the whole, I suppose, the aloof do mankind less harm but also less good than the committed, the skeptics than the convinced. Nevertheless, morality requires commitment, and asks us to have some confidence in our moral knowledge. But perhaps, even so, it will be well if skepticism, creeping back, softens from time to time our commitment with hesitation and our knowledge with doubt. [Dunham, *Ethics Dead or Alive*, p. 93]

87. Ibid., p. 101.

88. L. Cohen, *The Spice-Box of Earth* (N.Y.: Viking, 1965), p. 43.

Conclusion

Those who have turned to the back of this book to find out what it is about are referred to the front. The Preface provides a short rationale of the project as a whole and a brief summary of the major chapters where I describe what each contains in turn.

As far as the *biological* debates go, there is no conclusion. There is the continuing attempt to approximate material truths; there is the pottering dialogue with the unknown, as Bernard once called it; there are the staging posts that have been reached along the way; and that is all. That is also quite a lot. An essay of this sort is necessarily unfinished, however, and it would be presumptuous to do more than indicate that fact plus the need to follow the debates as closely as we can with an eye to new clues.

As far as the *philosophic* arguments are concerned, we are forever finding more fuel to feed upon. And should "science" ever manage to establish particular human *differences* as being beyond reasonable doubt, room will always remain for disagreement as to the justifiable bases for individual and social *discrimination*. The political theorist or practitioner is justified in feeling that he or she still has a place.

There is a continual tension, a continual to-ing and fro-ing, between what we value and what we know for a fact. As long as we hold an open mind (an important proviso), "facts" will continue to influence our "values", while our values, wherever we get them from, will always affect what we research and learn. No one has proved yet that we are slaves to our "passions" or are more than moderately servile in this regard. Yet passions have their place. How important a place that is will depend. They can serve both constructive and destructive purposes (these in turn being open to divergent definition) and we will therefore be able, contingent in part upon the circumstances, to make a case both for and against allowing passions to prevail. "Reason" in the form of particular biopolitical research findings has provided many significant insights. How we apply such insights remains problematic though. It is not clear, for example, whether we ought to make such applications at all if they do not denote "reasonable" policies of a life-affirming, species-supportive, personally satisfactory kind—whatever *these* concepts might mean. Perhaps it is a wonder we

174

come up with coherent propositions of *any* sort when we confront complexities so daunting and so profound.

What *is* the truth of the matter and what *is* illusion, and how can we be sure when "science," which is probably our sharpest instrument for cutting through the latter, conjures up more of the same (perhaps not the same, but something elusive still, and even harder to transcend because so powerfully placed)?[1] In our pursuit of knowledge and meaning the possibility of an infinite regress is always immanent, reaching forward seemingly forever. However unsatisfactory it may sound, here is at least an honest note on which to end. I would only cite Geertz[2] and his engaging account of this, the ultimate human dilemma:

> There is an Indian story—at least I heard it is an Indian story—about an Englishman who, having been told that the world rested on a platform which rested on the back of an elephant which rested in turn on the back of a turtle, asked (perhaps he was an ethnographer; it is the way they behave), what did the turtle rest on? Another turtle? "Ah Sahib, after that it is turtles all the way down."

NOTES

1. The conceit of Homo sapiens is that the evolution of our brain produced a greater capacity for rational, technical and logically formal thought rather than confusion, oceanic moods, private inefficiencies and public selfishness. Yet, in effect, a direct consequence of adding cortical tissue to the brain—*and of the continuing evolution of the lower centers of the brain as well*—was an enhanced capacity for producing illusionary notions. [L. Tiger, *Optimism: the Biology of Hope* (New York: Simon and Schuster, 1979), p. 46]

2. C. Geertz, *The Interpretation of Cultures* (London: Hutchinson, 1975), pp. 28–29.

INDEX

Crusoe, R., 38
culture, 9, 32 n. 61
  culture-studying, 159
  scientific-industrial, 7, 37, 84
  urban, 11
  world, 11

Darwin, C., 18, 22, 43, 52, 131, 156,
    157, 158, 166
Declaration of the Rights of Man and
    Citizen, French, 13
Democritus, 125
depression, 134-135, 136
desire, 148, n. 32
despair, 126, 130
determinism, 15
  and human needs, 23-28
  biological, 171, n. 66
  environmental, 166
De Tocqueville, Alexis, 40, 57
development, 5
Diamond, S., 134
Dobzhansky, T., 77, 80
DNA, recombinant, see *recombinant*
    DNA
Durkheim, E., 14

economy, world, 6, 11, 13
  world, capitalist, 111
ecstasy, 138
egoism, 43, 49, 119, n. 2
  coupled, 46
emotions, as evolutionary mechanism,
    149, n. 50
  biochemistry of, 135
  definition of, 136
empathy, 49
equality, x, 12, 13, 19, 36, 52, 58-63, 81,
    85
  and fraternity, 63
  and individuality, 57-58
  and liberty, 65-66
  fear of, 58
  legal, 61-62
  liberal, 66
  of human worth, 90-91

of opportunity, 58, 64, 66, 87
political, 61-62
religious, 61
sexual, 85
socialist, 66
support for, 58-61
essence, human, 40
eternity, 53
ethics, 36
  American, 40
  and evolution, 19-20
  collectivist, x, 7, 43, 69, 74
  individualistic, x, 40, 43, 68, 74, 90
  naturalistic, 19
  of change, 166-168
  of consequences, 155-156
  of intentions, 155-156
  solidarist, 113
  Soviet, 40
  survivalist, 166
eudemonism, 130
eugenetics, 164
euphoria, 138
evil, 65
evolution, 117, 157
  biological, 157
  cultural, 15, 34, n. 85, 157
  genetic, 34, n. 85
  human, 15, 17-20, 44
  theory of, 18
existentialism, 112
exploitation, 12
Eysenck, H., 73, 74, 144

fact-value dichotomy, 28, 158, 159,
    160-161, 174
fairness, 62
faith, pharmacology of, 137
  physiology of, x
family, 36, 91, n. 7, 119, n. 2
fatalism, 108
Feinberg, J., 106
felicity, x, 13, 27, 125, 129, 131
fraternity, x, 13, 52
  semantics of, 35-36
freedom, 9, 12, 19, 37, 51-52, 65, 114

About the Author

Ralph Pettman is currently visiting as an Associate Professor in the Department of Politics of Princeton University, Princeton, New Jersey. Prior to this appointment, he was a Senior Research Fellow for the Institute of Advanced Studies at the Australia National University, Canberra. His publications include: *State and Class: a sociology of international affairs; Moral Claims in World Affairs* (an edited collection); and *Human Behavior and World Politics: a transdisciplinary introduction.*